CHALLENGING
THE
PERFORMANCE
MOVEMENT

CHALLENGING THE PERFORMANCE MOVEMENT

Accountability, Complexity, and Democratic Values

Beryl A. Radin

Georgetown University Press
WASHINGTON, D.C.

10 9 8 7 6 5 4 3 2 1   2006

This book is printed on acid-free paper meeting
the requirements of the American National Standard
for Permanence in Paper for Printed Library Materials.

As of January 1, 2007, 13-digit ISBN numbers will replace the current 10-digit system.
Paperback: 978-1-58901-091-8

Portions of chapter 6 are reprinted from the author's article "The Government
Performance and Results Act (GPRA) and the Tradition of Federal Management
Reform: Square Pegs in Round Holes?" in *Journal of Public Administration Research and
Theory* (January 2000). Portions of chapter 7 are reprinted from the author's article
"Intergovernmental Relationships and the Federal Performance Movement," in *Publius:
The Journal of Federalism* (winter 2000: 143–58). Both are reprinted with permission.

Library of Congress Cataloging-in-Publication Data
Radin, Beryl.
   Challenging the performance movement : accountability, complexity, and democratic
values / Beryl A. Radin.
        p.   cm. -- (Public management and change series)
   Includes bibliographical references and index.
   ISBN- 13: 978-1-58901-091-8 (pbk. : alk. paper)
   ISBN- 10: 1-58901-091-4 (pbk. : alk. paper)
   1. Organizational effectiveness—Measurement. 2. Administrative agencies—
Management—Evaluation. 3. Performance. 4. Performance technology—Political
aspects—United States. I. Title. II. Public management and change.
   HD58.9.R33 2006
      658.4'013—dc22   2005027246

contents

LiST OF TaBLes

preface

I was introduced to the formal world of performance measurement when I spent several years in the Office of the Assistant Secretary for Management and Budget in the U.S. Department of Health and Human Services (HHS). Although I had been involved with earlier efforts to encourage program and policy evaluation, this new set of activities was different. My time in HHS coincided with the early days of implementing the Government Performance and Results Act (GPRA)—the first formal set of performance requirements issued government-wide. While I certainly supported the urge to find ways to make federal programs more effective than they had been in the past, the closer I came to the GPRA process, the more skeptical I became about the means that were put in place to carry out its goals. Too frequently, the agency officials who had the most difficulty complying with GPRA requirements were the very people who were most concerned about achieving effective programs.

As the years passed and performance measurement activities became more pervasive, my skepticism increased. Wherever I looked I encountered the same paradox I had found in HHS. The performance requirements that were formalized to carry out commendable goals tended to be insensitive to the differences between program structures and often bypassed the judgments of professional staff members who were essential to program implementation success. In addition, I found that the performance requirements rarely acknowledged the complex goals of public action and, instead, focused only on efficiency outcomes.

All of this led me to examine the world of performance. I've published several articles on aspects of this world that served as the backdrop to this book. Some of my observations about performance have been welcomed by individuals both inside and outside organizations who have found the requirements onerous and unproductive. Others have viewed my perspective as heretical and the work of an apologist for the status quo. I assume that similar reactions will be elicited by this volume. But it is my hope that the pages that follow will stimulate a discussion about both the opportunities and the limitations of the performance movement.

I am indebted to the advice and skill of Gail Grella at Georgetown University Press, whose perspective helped to make this a more balanced book. In addition, I would like to thank Burt Barnow, Carroll Seron, John Callahan, Valerie Richardson, Norma Riccucci, George Frederickson, and others who have offered useful comments along the way.

1 THE UBIQUITOUS NATURE OF PERFORMANCE

Concern about the performance of organizations has become a pervasive element in the world we live in. Increasingly, citizens both within the United States and across the globe are unwilling to blindly accept the level of work of a range of institutions within their societies. These include not only government institutions but also foundations and organizations in the health sector, education, and other areas. Yet it is not always clear why this occurs. There is an array of possible explanations for this set of concerns. Some citizens worry about the expenditure of funds—largely public sector funds—and are skeptical about the way that limited fiscal resources are allocated. Other citizens are dissatisfied with the results of the decisions made by various organizations and seek to modify or even eliminate those programs and projects that make up organization agendas. Still others believe that organizations are not responsive to those who are the beneficiaries of their work and, instead, have devised processes that insulate staff of those organizations from those who are supposed to be served by them. And yet others simply want to make sure that institutions are able to adapt to the changing circumstances of the twenty-first century.

All of this creates a somewhat paradoxical situation. Dissatisfaction with a range of institutions—both public and private—is widespread and is often expressed in strong and critical rhetoric. Yet the reasons for these views are complex, and thus they are difficult to translate into concrete action. Despite this, however, many performance measurement efforts have been put in place that have established formal processes for determining whether program goals have been achieved and problems with performance have been avoided. Assessments of performance are expected to feed into decisions about program effectiveness and become a major factor in determining how to make budget decisions.

The formal processes that have been developed are also enveloped by another paradoxical situation. The rhetoric of performance that has become commonplace usually focuses on the achievement of program outcomes. Outcome assessment is proposed as an alternative to other ways of examining program performance. Traditionally, organizations tended to describe their work in terms of the resources that they used (often called inputs), the processes that they put in place to produce the work, or the specific activities that emerged from the organization (often called outputs). Occasionally, organizations describe their work in terms of the quality of the effort that emerged. A focus on outcomes, however, jumped over these elements and asked the organization to focus instead on the impact of their activities.

While the emphasis on outcomes is appealing, it is difficult to put into operation. This is particularly true in the public sector, where the complexity of public action frequently involves a range of actors with different agendas and conflicting values operating within a fragmented decision process. And the decisions that emerge from the public sector do not always create a situation that makes it possible to determine what program outcomes are anticipated. Yet performance measurement efforts set up requirements in which programs and policies are expected to report their progress in terms of specific outcome assessments.

Yet another paradox also surrounds the performance activity. At the same time that citizens are exasperated by the behavior of officials and professionals charged with implementing programs and policies, they also acknowledge that action by officials and professionals is required to actually achieve the desired goals. In a world that is increasingly characterized by specialized and technical knowledge, there does not seem to be a way to avoid reliance on those who have been trained as professionals in a field. It is difficult to criticize these specialists and yet rely on them to deliver a service or implement a policy.

These three paradoxes—ambiguous rhetoric turned into formal processes, an emphasis on unmeasurable outcomes, and a critical stance on officials and professionals but ultimately relying on them—produce a set of tensions that make the achievement of performance measurement much more complex and difficult than is communicated by the language surrounding the field. Despite the legitimate concerns that have motivated advocates of performance measurement, the process of putting these motivations into practice has generated consequences that often create problems within a variety of institutions and at times inhibit the achievement of performance. The misfit between expectations and practice in a range of institutions is what constitutes the core of this book.

The Genesis of My Argument

For many years I have been writing about a range of federal management reform efforts. These include the development of the Planning, Program, Budgeting System (PPBS) in the 1960s and later related techniques such as Management by Objectives (MBO) and Zero-Based Budgeting (ZBB). These analytical approaches became a part of the evolution of the policy analysis field.[1] I also examined the effort through the National Performance Review during the Clinton administration.[2] Over the past decade, I have spent time analyzing the federal government's performance management activities, namely the Government Performance and Results Act (GPRA) and the more recent Program Assessment Rating Tool (PART).

I have emphasized a number of themes in dealing with these initiatives, including the conflict between analytical approaches and political approaches (particularly attention to different agendas that are attached to advocacy of the initiatives), the emphasis on achieving efficiency values without attention to other values, a reliance on government-wide strategies and centralized top-down approaches, a tendency to adopt one-size-fits-all initiatives, and a separation of management activities from program substance. These are themes that have also emerged from the work of others who have examined management reform activities.[3]

There are at least three agendas at play that are difficult to disentangle. Some advocates seek to eliminate programs and find it helpful to blame bureaucrats and program officials for problems. Others simply want to find a way to modify programs and argue that what worked in the past does not always make sense in a current or future environment. And still others believe that performance information will allow them to make a case for their programs and respond effectively with that data to those to whom they are accountable. As will be discussed, the existing analytical approaches to performance do not allow a disentangling of these three agendas.

While these themes are also present in the performance measurement activity, they are rarely acknowledged. Perhaps this is because performance activities have moved beyond narrow or traditional management agendas and have taken on a life of their own.

It is hard to find any aspect of the American society today that does not focus on issues related to performance. Pick up any daily newspaper and one is likely to find some discussion and consideration about the way that one or several of the institutions of our society are able to perform according to expectations. The daily press is especially concerned about performance in the public sector and provides a rich picture of these issues. This concern focuses on all levels of government (federal, state, or local) and cuts across many policy sectors. The most frequent treatment of performance in the press focuses on education and public expectations that children in public schools will perform more effectively than they had in the past. But this anxiety moves beyond education; it includes health, environment, welfare, foreign policy, national security, and a range of other public sector areas. It also is found in the for-profit private sector as well as the nonprofit sector. Performance measurement has become one of the main tenets of the global movement called New Public Management, an attempt to apply market-based and private-sector concepts to the public sector. It is not an exaggeration to characterize the concern about performance as ubiquitous.

Because the concern about performance is so pervasive, it takes on the form of a movement. It moves beyond specific initiatives in a few areas to reflect a general consideration in the society at large. It has become part of the language, and words such as "outcomes" and "performance measurement" and "achievement" roll off the tongues of a wide range of citizens. It may not be an overstatement to say that "performance" has joined motherhood and apple pie as one of the truisms of the contemporary American culture. Who would want to say that they are against performance assessment?

Why This Book?

The extant literature dealing with performance issues is heavily weighted towards work that makes a case for performance measurement. Much of the literature is of the "how to do it" variety, providing advice to organizations and individuals who believe that it is important to describe work in outcome terms. Very little of the literature communicates a cautionary tone, suggesting that performance measurement may not always produce the types of results anticipated or may not be appropriate in all situations.

This book seeks to address what I view as an imbalance in the literature and to suggest instead that there are other ways to look at the issues raised by the performance advocates, beyond an approach that relies on the use of language rather than action and beyond a one-size-fits-all strategy. For some, the process of raising alternative approaches seems heretical, and I would expect these individuals to be critical of my slant and methodology.

This is not a book that argues for the status quo. Rather, it draws on a range of examples from various institutions to show how the approach that has taken root in the contemporary American society does not always lead to productive change. Whether it is a parent dealing with the education sector, a doctor or teacher, a public sector official, or a leader in the private sector, all are currently facing what appear to be unanticipated consequences of the performance movement. The volume seeks to explicate the dimensions of this problem and to suggest alternative approaches to the legitimate concern about improving the accountability and effectiveness of our public and private institutions.

This book, thus, is an attempt to discuss performance measurement within a broader context. It seeks to place these developments within a framework that deals with complexity, multiple values and meanings, and pragmatism. I am not arguing against performance measurement per se. Rather, I hope that people will understand that it is not the panacea that some of its proponents have presented.

It is useful to review the reasons why the performance movement has taken form. Joseph Wholey has written, "Throughout the world, both in government and in the not-for-profit sector, leaders and managers are grappling with closely related problems that include tight restrictions on resources, increasing demand for effective services, low levels of public trust, and increasing demand for accountability."[4] Gormley and Balla have noted that "[i]n the 1990s the concept of **performance** came to rival accountability as a standard for evaluating executive branch agencies. On its own merits, performance is important in democratic institutions, as the public is well served by government organizations that operate effectively and produce generally acceptable results."[5]

Few would argue against the goal of performance activities. But there is a growing negative response to the way that the goal has been defined and implemented. Various aspects of this argument have been raised in different settings. For example, within the public management community Allen Schick has focused on the use of performance measures. He has commented that arguments over performance "often make it appear as if performance measurement were an end in itself, as if measuring performance has no utility other than to generate measures."[6] Further, he noted, "when performance measurement becomes a beauty contest through score-cards and rankings, what the process gains in popularity it surrenders in rigor and soundness."[7] Schick reports the findings of the Congressional Research Service that twice as many laws enacted in the 105th Congress (1997–98) included provisions pertaining to performance as those enacted by the previous Congress. However, he notes, performance reports are effective only if they have an audience.

In an interesting essay titled "Weak States and the Black Hole of Public Administration," Francis Fukuyama has written that "formal systems of monitoring and accountability . . . either entail very high transaction costs or are simply impossible because of the lack of specificity of the underlying activity."[8] Further, he concludes that "[t]he effort to be more 'scientific' than the underlying subject matter permits carries a real cost in blinding us to the real complexities of public administration as it is practiced in different societies."[9]

The issues that are raised by Schick and Fukuyama resonate with my concerns about previous management reform efforts. They too worry about efforts that minimize the importance of political and social variables in the management and policy process and highlight inattention to the difficult experience of implementing the performance requirements.

The Nature of the Problem

During the past decade, the concern about performance has taken many different forms. It is the basis for a federal law, the Government Performance and Results Act (GPRA), enacted in 1993 and implemented several years later with interest by both the Congress and the executive branch. It is the basis for a process undertaken in 2001 in the federal Office of Management and Budget (OMB) called the Program Assessment Rating Tool (PART), which attempts to link executive branch budget recommendations to the performance of specific federal programs. Governors' offices and state-level agencies (particularly in the education sector) have adopted report cards that seek to rate the performance of specific program areas against other state, local, or federal agencies.[10] When Governor Arnold Schwarzenegger took office in California, one of his first efforts was to commission a report of the California Performance Review that emphasized measuring performance in its recommendations.[11] In a 1998 study, 47 out of 50 states had adopted some form of performance budgeting.[12] Quarterly reports of profit levels by corporations are actually required as a form of performance, accountability, and transparency. Through the World Bank and other international bodies, countries have been encouraged to devise methods of assessing performance of public sector activities. And even some foundations have adopted processes of assessing requests for funds against formal and quantitative performance metrics.

The momentum to continue along this path is very strong. Yet there are counterindications that the focus on performance is limited and can be misleading. Much of what has been devised in the name of accountability actually interferes with the responsibilities that individuals in organizations have to carry out work and to accomplish what they have been asked to do. The processes that have been put in place often illustrate some of the problems that were experienced with previous management reform efforts—relying on formal analytical approaches without attention to the political context in which they occur, jumping to measure outcomes without attention to decision processes, highlighting efficiency goals without including a focus on equity questions, a reliance on a one-size-fits-all approach, difficulty finding decision processes that will use the information developed, and separating management activities from substantive program concerns.

The book that follows explores these issues. It is designed to raise a series of questions that should be asked before one plunges into a performance measurement effort. Some of the chapters may be of interest to some readers and not to others. But collectively they represent my attempt to step back from specific performance measurement activities and ask broader questions about these efforts than those that are usually asked. While most of the examples and discussion in the book center on performance management in government, I have attempted to include examples from other sectors that illustrate similar issues.

There are a number of themes that structure the argument that follows. There is an attempt to emphasize both the content and the context of the performance activity. Consideration is given to the variety of program and policy structures that face performance demands and the multiple values and expectations that are built into program goals. This creates a complexity that makes it difficult to develop information sources and to focus on program outcomes. The perceptions of those faced with performance requirements are emphasized, and each substantive chapter begins with a vignette about a person who has to deal with the requirements. These vignettes are based on real situations but written in a fictional style. Each chapter also draws on theoretical literature as well as topical examples to illustrate the relevant topics.

The Organization of the Book

Chapter 2, *The Performance Mindset,* contrasts what I have called the "classic approach to performance measurement" with an alternative set of assumptions about the nature of intelligence, about the complex nature of the world, about numbers, and about the appropriate strategies that should be used to make change. The vignette that is used to illustrate the issues in this chapter presents a dilemma for someone who does not share the assumptions that are found in the performance mindset.

Chapter 3, *One Size Fits All,* discusses the tendency of past management reform efforts to minimize the uniqueness of programs or organizations and explores some alternative approaches to deal with differences that occur between types of organizations, as well as different approaches to the study of organizations. It gives attention to the problems faced by those who are confronted with "one-size-fits-all" requirements that don't fit their organizational realities.

Chapter 4, *Demeaning Professionals: Throwing Out the Baby with the Bathwater?* draws on a sociological literature dealing with professionalism and indicates how the drive to hold professionals accountable to a particular set of standards can lead to ineffective and inappropriate behaviors. The chapter includes examples from the world of public school teaching, the practice of medicine, scientific research, and methods of allocating resources to university faculty.

Chapter 5, *Competing Values: Can the Performance Movement Deal with Equity?* attempts to draw on the classic value conflict between efficiency and equity and focus on efforts to include equity concerns in the performance movement. It discusses the struggles involved in the process of defining equity, the resistance to including equity questions in the measurement of performance, and difficulties involved in including equity measurements in the performance process.

Chapter 6, *The Reality of Fragmentation: Power and Authority in the U.S. Political System,* focuses on the most recent federal performance efforts—the Government Performance and Results Act (GPRA) and the Program Assessment Rating Tool (PART). It draws on the experience of the U.S. Department of Health and Human Services to illustrate the problems faced in implementing these programs within a system characterized by fragmented institutional structures, multiple functions, and political realities.

Chapter 7, *Intergovernmental Relationships: Power and Authority in the U.S. Political System,* reviews the impact of performance activity on intergovernmental relationships in the United States. Framed in the constant debate over the appropriate role of the federal government, the chapter discusses the conflict between efforts to hold federal government agencies accountable and the effort to provide state and local governments and third parties with discretion. It reviews various efforts to balance the elements in this conflict

Chapter 8, *Information, Interests, and Ideology,* discusses the assumptions that have been made within the performance movement about information and provides contemporary examples of problems involved in measuring performance. Many of the problems that are confronted by players in the performance effort revolve around difficulties involving information—its availability, types of information, ability to measure outcomes, and the appropriateness of measuring and quantifying all organizational behavior.

Chapter 9, *Competing Values in a Global Context: Performance Activities in the World Bank,* provides a case study of efforts within the World Bank to balance public management reform efforts with what has been called "social accountability." The latter draws on equity concerns and involvement of the nongovernmental sector. This is a case that illustrates problems in finding ways to utilize different approaches to performance information in a complex organization that values market-based economic reasoning.

Finally, chapter 10, *Conflicting Patterns of Assumptions: Where Do We Go from Here?* provides a conclusion and lessons for those who seek to embark on performance measurement activities. It compares the classic assumptions about performance measurement with alternative approaches, suggesting that there are other ways to look at the issues raised by the performance advocates beyond the rhetorical approach and beyond a one-size-fits-all strategy.

It is my hope that this volume will lead to a new discussion about performance management that integrates the issues of complexity into the consideration of these efforts. Without such consideration, individuals who raise questions about the effectiveness of the multiple aspects of the performance movement are assumed to oppose all performance measurement activities. That is not my intention. Rather, this book seeks to find ways to devise activities that are appropriate and effective.

Notes

1. See Beryl A. Radin, *Beyond Machiavelli: Policy Analysis Comes of Age* (Washington, D.C.: Georgetown University Press, 2000).
2. See, for example, Beryl A. Radin, "Varieties of Reinvention: Six NPR 'Success' Stories," in Donald F. Kettl and John J. DiIulio, Jr., eds., *Inside the Reinvention Machine: Appraising Government Reform* (Washington, D.C.: Brookings Institution, 1995).

3. Paul Light's *The Tides of Reform: Making Government Work, 1945–95* (New Haven, Conn.:Yale University Press, 1997) provides a rich account of different approaches to management reform efforts.

4. Joseph S. Wholey, "Performance-Based Management: Responding to the Challenges," *Public Productivity and Management Review* 22, no. 3 (March 1999): 288.

5. William T. Gormley, Jr., and Steven J. Balla, *Bureaucracy and Democracy: Accountability and Performance* (Washington, D.C.: CQ Press, 2004), 14.

6. Allen Schick, "Getting Performance Measures to Measure Up," in Dall W. Forsythe, ed., *Quicker, Better Cheaper: Managing Performance in American Government* (Albany, N.Y.: Rockefeller Institute Press, 2001), 40.

7. Gormley and Balla, *Bureaucracy and Democracy*, 41.

8. Francis Fukuyama, *State Building: Governance and World Order in the 21st Century* (Ithaca, N.Y.: Cornell University Press), 51.

9. Fukuyama, *State Building*, 91.

10. William T. Gormley, Jr., "Using Organizational Report Cards" (paper presented at the National Public Management Research Conference, Washington, D.C., Georgetown University, October 11, 2003).

11. See The California Performance Review, *A Government for the People for a Change*, vol. 1, *Prescription for Change*, http://cpr.ca.gov/report/.

12. Julia E. Melkers and Katharine G. Willoughby, "The State of the States: Performance-Based Budgeting Requirements in 47 out of 50 States," *Public Administration Review* 58, no. 1 (1998): 66–73.

2 THE Performance minDset

Professor Francine Fisher was approaching a foundation for support of an innovative lecture series that focused on current issues in bioethics. The series was planned as an interdisciplinary effort that involved the medical school and the departments of biology, philosophy, political science, anthropology, and sociology. While she knew that the issues were topical, it was hard for her to estimate the number of individuals who would be interested in the series.

Her topic seemed to match the substantive interests of a foundation that was known to fund somewhat similar efforts on other issues. She asked the foundation for their guidelines for submitting a proposal, anticipating that this organization (like many others) would call for a general proposal that would serve as the basis for further discussion.

She was very surprised when she received the guidelines. The foundation described itself as an organization that was directed toward change and that used the business investment model to assess proposals. Prospective grantees were expected to present their proposed activity in a way that produces results using quantitative methods. The guidance that she received included examples of several quantitative measures of efficiency and cost-effectiveness. She was expected to show how her activity would leverage other funds, define the per lecture cost and expected audience, and identify specific outcomes or outputs of the lecture series (such as publications).

While Professor Fisher hoped that the lecture series would generate interest and multidisciplinary discussions that could eventually result in future research, she found it daunting to attempt to present her idea in the format that the foundation required. Part of her agenda was to broaden the interest in the bioethics topic beyond the traditional players. Thus it was particularly difficult to predict their response to the lecture series and to quantify the outcomes. She realized that she approached this work with a very different mindset than did the foundation.

A sizeable portion of this book discusses, there are many traps that can be confronted by those who take the performance assessment journey. Some stem from technical questions and others from questions of values. Still others are enmeshed in the structure and construct of the institution in which they operate. But undergirding these traps are very different assumptions about the nature of the world.

Much of the advocacy for performance activity rests on what I have called the "classic" approach to performance measurement. Yet there is an alternative set of assumptions that provides a different way of thinking about this process. A significant number of the problems faced by those involved with performance measurement stem from the assumptions that they have made about the nature of intelligence, the nature of the world, and the appropriate strategies that should be used to make change. I have termed this set of assumptions "the performance mindset" and argue that there are alternative ways to think about these issues.

The Classic Approach to Performance Measurement

Although there is a wide range of examples of performance measurement in both the public and private sectors in various jurisdictional levels, most of the efforts have been constructed around a basic planning process. That process usually begins with the specification of long-term or mid-term goals and highlights desired outcomes related to these goals. These goals can be defined at an organizational level or at a programmatic level and often involve the translating of general, long-term strategic goals to more specific goals and objectives. Following this, the process involves the development of performance measures that give one a quantifiable set of expectations that are defined as reasonable levels for expected performance. These measures are usually annual or short-term in duration. The third step involves collecting, verifying, and analyzing data that allow one to assess the level of accomplishment of the stated goals.[1]

Others have embellished this basic process and emphasize specific steps within it. For example, Harry Hatry of the Urban Institute established a sample performance measurement system development schedule of thirty months that involved the following steps:

> Step 1: Set overall scope, get top-level support, and establish working group
> Step 2: Identify mission and customers
> Steps 3 to 5: Identify what is to be measured
> Step 6: Identify data sources and data collection procedures
> Steps 7 to 9: Determine data breakouts, comparisons, and analysis plan
> Steps 10 to 12: Prepare for pilot test
> Step 13: Pilot test; make revisions
> Steps 14 to 15: Plan for implementation.[2]

Others have focused on what they call a "managing-for-results culture" and recommend that four steps should be followed in the process: Start with a personal commitment, be clear in what you're trying to do, create a supply of performance information, and create a demand for performance information.[3]

Both Hatry and the "managing-for-results" advocates suggest that planners and those involved with change can be successful if they follow a rational and detailed process. Good organization, commitment, and analysis should lead to success.

With confidence in the rational process, the proponents of performance measurement believe that it is possible for performance analysts to emphasize the *outcomes* of organizational activity, not the inputs or outputs of the processes. Much of the classic performance activity is constructed on a differentiation between various stages of the decision process.[4] This differentiation rests on a belief that most organizations lose sight of the ultimate outcomes produced by their activity, which are believed to be the reason for their existence. The classic definition of the terms used in this process differentiates between inputs, outputs, outcomes, and indicators:

Input: Resources (expenditures or employee time) used to produce outputs and outcomes. Performance advocates often argue that organizations emphasize the importance of inputs to the exclusion of other elements and, as a result, equate the availability of these resources with success.

Output: Products and services delivered. Outputs are completed products of internal activity: the amount of work done within the organization or by its contractors (such as miles of road repaired or number of calls answered). A focus on outputs is criticized as a way for organizations to continue to do the work they have always done without determining whether that work actually leads to desired outcomes.

Outcome: An event, occurrence, or condition that is outside the activity or program itself and is of direct importance to program customers or the public. We also include indicators of service quality, those of importance to customers, under this category.[5] While the definition of outcomes may emerge from organizational goals, the organization may not have the authority or resources available that allow it to actually reach for the goal.

Intermediate outcome: An outcome that is expected to lead to a desired end but is not an end in itself (such as service response time, which is of concern to the customer making a call or requesting a service but does not indicate anything directly about the success of the call or request). A program may have multiple intermediate outcomes.

End outcome: The end result that is sought (such as the community having cleaner air or reduced incidence of disease). A program may have more than one end outcome.[6]

Outcome indicator: A numerical measure of the amount or frequency of a particular outcome.

Performance indicator: A specific numerical measurement for one
   aspect of performance (for example, output or outcome)
   under consideration.[7]

While the language of performance measurement has its own
stylized vocabulary, it actually shares many attributes with the classic scientific method. It emphasizes the rigor of following a logical
process, it focuses on ultimate outcomes, and it relies on the collection and interpretation of data.

It's Not So Easy

The constantly growing literature on performance measurement has increasingly acknowledged a range of problems that have
been encountered by those who have tried to use the classic process. This acknowledgement spans a number of different explanations but begins to provide a picture of the limitations of the classic approach and indicates that achieving the goals of performance
measurement is not so easy.

In one article, Christopher Hood and Guy Peters returned to
the work of some earlier social scientists to explain what they call
"the middle aging" of New Public Management (NPM).[8] Since
performance measurement is one of the processes integral to NPM,
this analysis is relevant to this discussion. One of the themes of the
Hood–Peters article was the presence of what sociologist Robert
Merton called the "unintended consequences of purposive social
action." Nearly seventy years ago, Merton noted that the subject
of unanticipated consequences was "treated by virtually every substantial contributor to the long history of social thought."[9] Merton
cited the work of Machiavelli, Adam Smith, Marx, Engels, Pareto,
Max Weber, and others as a part of this array of theorists.

Others followed Merton, pursuing the themes of "limited information, various forms of erroneous assumptions or tunnel vision,
and self-defeating prophecies."[10] In the early 1980s, Sam Sieber applied these themes to the experience of the past decades, particularly the government activity that followed the War on Poverty and
the activism of the federal government in the Great Society era.
Sieber began his book, *Fatal Remedies: The Ironies of Social Intervention,* with the observation that "few institutions, programs or leaders

are immune to the vexatious experience of worsening the condition that they set out so nobly to alleviate."[11] At the same time, he noted that there has been little effort by contemporary social scientists to examine this behavior. He commented that social scientists have not attempted (like the performance measurement advocates) to draw out the negative implications of their approach.

Both Sieber and Hood and Peters suggest that advocates of change have been so enamored of their prescriptions that they ignore or play down the likelihood of unanticipated side effects. Hood and Peters have suggested that the advocates of NPM exhibited "overconfidence in the general efficacy of the remedies they advocated." The result, they argue, is that the activity generated a paradox and that NPM became "a set of politically driven reforms that tended to distract middle- and upper-level officials, create massive paperwork, and produce major unintended effects."[12] Their assessment of the NPM developments shares many aspects of the experience of performance activity.

Because the mainstream of American society highlights what seems to be a very positive face of these efforts to improve performance, the voices that have pointed to unanticipated consequences—or, as some argue, perverse consequences—of the performance measurement activities have tended to be peripheral to the conversation. Yet some have specifically raised concerns about the activity. Some of the critiques come from inside the public management field, while others emerge from the public policy field.

Within the public management community, Peter Smith of the University of York has focused on the unintended consequences of publishing performance data in the public sector. He writes, "While not challenging the desirability of publishing performance data . . . the performance indicator philosophy is based on inadequate models of production and control."[13]

Gloria Grizzle commented on the unintended consequences of the pervasive practice of performance measurement. She notes, "We expect that measuring efficiency leads to greater efficiency and measuring outcomes leads to better outcomes, but we don't always get the results we expect."[14] She points to unintended consequences in test scores, crime reports, corporate earnings, and the practice of "creaming" clients or customers.

Sandra van Thiel and Frans L. Leeuw have written about the unintended consequences of the international interest in performance measurement. They comment on an increase in monitoring costs as a result of an emphasis on regulation and auditing and effects such as lack of innovation that limit the effectiveness of policy implementation. Further, they note that in some cases monitoring has led to symbolic behavior: it appears to be in place but is actually not occurring.[15]

Still another Dutch academic commented on what he called "[t]he perverse effects of performance measurement." Hans de Bruijn wrote about the form of strategic behavior called "gaming the numbers." He also commented on the tendency of performance measurement to block innovation and ambition, to veil actual performance, to kill the professional attitude, and to lead to punishment of performance.[16]

Three of the four public management academics just cited are European, suggesting that there may be more attention to these negative effects in Europe than in the United States. These cautionary comments begin to mirror other skeptical analyses of earlier organizational change efforts.

Others have written about unanticipated consequences from the perspective of specific program areas. These comments emerge from individuals who are a part of the public policy community. Blalock and Barnow's evaluation work on the Job Training Partnership Act and its successor led them to conclude that "the 'performance management movement' that has swept the post-industrial world in the late 1980s and early 1990s, and has redirected information collection and analysis toward a focus on social program *results* (outcomes), may lead to misinformed judgments of the value of social programs." They note:

> This potential problem could result in misguided social remedies if those designing and directing performance management systems, and the users of information flowing from such systems, are not careful about distinguishing between 1) results that can be attributed relatively exclusively to the unique interventions of these programs—that is, to net impacts or cause-effect relations, and 2) results that are

due to a variety of influences both within and *outside* these programs, or are occurring simply by *chance*.[17]

Clotfelter and Ladd have focused on performance-based incentive programs in education. They note that "to be effective, recognition and reward systems must change behavior in ways that encourage learning." They observe that "[d]espite the potential of school-based incentive programs—especially in the context of a school system where significant power has been decentralized to the school level—a number of concerns remain. These include 'teaching to the test,' program manipulation and outright cheating, and effects of the program on teacher morale."[18]

These two critiques approach performance measurement from a concern about the substance of policy—one in job training and the other in education. They focus on the specific effects of performance programs on the achievement of program goals embedded in program design. Yet some of their concerns overlap with those of analysts from the public management field.

Holding On to the Traditional Assumptions

While commentators often point to problems faced in the implementation of the performance activity, many of them continue to use the basic logic of that process and seek to modify that approach in order to deal with these problems. They continue to hold on to the assumptions that are intrinsic to the traditional approach. These are:

Goals can be defined clearly and set firmly as the basis for the performance measurement process.

Goals are specific and the responsibility of definable actors.

Outcomes can be specified independently of inputs, processes, and outputs.

Outcomes can be quantified and measured.

Outcomes are controllable and susceptible to external timing.

Data are available, clear, and accurate.

Results of the performance measurement can be delivered to an actor with authority to respond to the results.

Thus there are three possible approaches to the "performance mindset." One approach emphasizes the positive impact that can emerge from a reliance on clarity, information, and the logic of the scientific method. The second approach is more modest about the possible impact of the classic process but continues to believe that in the future it will be possible to achieve clarity of goals, quantify information, and find actors who will use that information. The third approach, however, suggests a much more skeptical approach to this process. It suggests that there may be alternative ways to approach this task that include multiple approaches to intelligence, the demands of complexity, and assumptions related to quantification.

Is There a Single Type of Intelligence?

Since ancient times, there has been a debate about the way that people organize the world that they see. Drawing on the phrase of the eighth-century B.C. Greek poet Archilochus—"The fox knows many things; the hedgehog knows one big thing"—philosophers and more contemporary psychologists have noted that some people view the world with a clear, central vision and others see it as a fragmented, multicomponent system. Philosopher Isaiah Berlin is well known for his characterization of these two visions of the world:

> For there exists a great chasm between those, on one side, who relate everything to a single central vision, one system less or more coherent or articulate, in terms of which they understand, think and feel—a single, universal organizing principle in terms of which alone all they are and say has significance—and, on the other side, those who pursue many ends, often unrelated and even contradictory, connected, if at all, only in some *de facto* way, for some psychological or physiological cause, related by no moral or aesthetic principle; these last lead lives, perform acts, and entertain ideas that are centrifugal rather than centripetal, their thought is scattered or diffused, moving on many levels, seizing upon the essence of a vast variety of experiences and objects for what they are in themselves, without, consciously or unconsciously, seeking to fit them into, or

exclude them from, any one unchanging, all-embracing, sometimes self-contradictory and incomplete, at times fanatical, unitary inner vision.[19]

Psychologist Howard Gardner has noted that this dichotomy has been used to determine whether individuals are more or less "smart," "bright," "clever," or "intelligent."[20] Gardner writes that there is a tradition that glorifies the distinct functions or parts of the mind. "In Classical times, it was common to differentiate between reason, will, and feeling. Medieval thinkers had their trivium of grammar, logic, and rhetoric, and their quadrivium of mathematics, geometry, astronomy, and music."[21]

Gardner uses this intellectual tradition to argue that several relatively autonomous competences exist; he calls these human intelligences, and they become the basis for his view that these are the "frames of mind." [22] His quest to understand how knowledge is attained stems from his effort to classify human intellectual competences because

> [t]here is much recent evidence emerging from scientific research, cross-cultural observations, and educational study which stands in need of review and organization; and perhaps above all, because it seems within our grasp to come up with a list of intellectual strengths which will prove useful for a wide range of researchers and practitioners. . . . In other words, the synthesis that we seek can never be all things for all people, but it holds promise of providing some things for many interested parties. [23]

According to Gardner, the prerequisites of an intelligence involve a set "of skills of problem solving—enabling the individual to *resolve genuine problems or difficulties* that he or she encounters and, when appropriate, to create an effective product—and must also entail the potential for *finding or creating problems*—thereby laying the groundwork for the acquisition of new knowledge.[24]

Gardner establishes both positive and negative criteria for the identification of intelligences. They are not equivalent to sensory systems; they should be thought of as entities at a level of generality;

they should not be defined in evaluative terms; they should be thought of as separate from particular programs of action; and they should differentiate between know-how (knowledge of how to execute something) and know-that (knowledge about the procedures involved in execution).[25]

Gardner's theory includes six different types of intelligence: linguistic intelligence, musical intelligence, logical-mathematical intelligence, spatial intelligence, bodily-kinesthetic intelligence, and what he calls the personal intelligences.[26] In his discussion of the application of intelligences, he suggests that individuals "cast the net widely" and look beyond traditional methods of determining whether goals have been achieved. He argues: "For every goal currently being pursued, there is presumably a set of intelligences which could readily be mobilized for its realization, as well as a set of intelligences whose mobilization would pose a greater challenge."[27]

Others have built on Gardner's work. Daniel Goleman, in *Emotional Intelligence*, reports an interview with Gardner.

> The time has come . . . to broaden our notion of the spectrum of talents. The single most important contribution education can make to a child's development is to help him toward a field where his talents best suit him, where he will be satisfied and competent. We've completely lost sight of that. Instead we subject everyone to an education where, if you succeed, you will be best suited to be a college professor. And we evaluate everyone along the way according to whether they meet that narrow standard of success. We should spend less time ranking children and more time helping them to identify their natural competencies and gifts, and cultivate those. There are hundreds and hundreds of ways to succeed, and many, many different abilities that will help you get there."[28]

Goleman argues that a high IQ "is no guarantee of prosperity, prestige, or happiness in life," but "our schools and our culture fixate on academic abilities, ignoring *emotional* intelligence, a set of traits—some might call it character—that also matters immensely for our personal destiny. Emotional life is a domain that, as surely as math or reading, can be handled with greater or lesser skill, and requires a unique set of competencies."[29] According to Goleman, emotion includes anger, sadness, fear, enjoyment, love, surprise, disgust, and shame.[30]

Why is the discussion of intelligence relevant to those who are involved in the performance movement? As one reviews the types of performance measures that have been devised across a range of institutions, it appears that there is a single definition of success, based on just one of the types of intelligence. The performance movement is dominated by lateral thinkers, or what we normally associate with the scientific approach. These individuals think in a way that moves from one piece of data to another, along a linear path. Thus a leads to b leads to c, etc. Often these individuals focus on the literal meanings of words and information. Others, by contrast, think in symbolic forms, dealing with multiple meanings and often reasoning by analogy. For example, Murray Edelman reminded us that the administrative system is "symbol and ritual" and should be acknowledged as such.[31]

The language that is used to define the classic approach to performance measurement does not provide the space for individuals with concerns about multiple goals and qualitative impacts to report their assessment of performance. For example, individuals who are engaged in scientific research often believe that negative findings may be more useful to the research enterprise than findings that report success. Yet the classic process does not easily give them the ability to report these findings.

How Do We Deal with Complexity?

While Gardner and others have emphasized the ways that individuals comprehend and deal with the world, others have focused on the changes that have taken place in that world and how those changes demand different approaches to it. Dietrich Dorner has argued that problems have emerged because of the "seeming failure of our capacity to think. . . . Some analysts complain that all our difficulties stem from the fact that we have been turned loose in the industrial age equipped with the brain of prehistoric times."[32]

Using a range of examples as the basis for his perspective, he argues that we have a tendency to rely on established measures and cannot think in terms of nonlinear networks of causation. The problems that exist in the world relate to the reality of complexity—the presence of many interdependent variables in a system.

> The more variables and the greater their interdependence, the greater that system's complexity. Great complexity places high demands on a planner's capacity to gather information, integrate findings, and design effective actions. The links between the variables oblige us to attend to a great many features simultaneously, and that, concomitantly, makes it impossible for us to undertake only one action in a complex system.

Dorner notes that "it is difficult to arrive at a satisfactory measure of complexity because the measurement should take into account not only the links themselves but also their nature." Further, he writes that "complexity is not an objective factor but a subjective one."[33]

Dorner highlights the limitations of information. "Planners and decision makers may have no direct access, or indeed no access at all, to information about the situation they must address. They have to look, as it were, through frosted glass." He believes that

> If we want to operate within a complex and dynamic system, we have to know not only what its current status is but what its status will be or could be in the future, and we have to know how certain actions we take will influence the situation. For this, we need "structural knowledge," knowledge of how the variables in the system are related and how they influence one another.[34]

Further, he notes that it is important to acknowledge the dimensions of the environment in which one is working. The system that he describes is not a set of unrelated systems, but we often approach it as such to simplify our analysis. "It is the method that guarantees neglect of side effects and repercussions and therefore guarantees failure."[35]

Goal setting, he writes, is an important aspect of problem solving; however, there are pitfalls and difficulties that interfere with successful goal setting. He finds that goals come in many forms. Some are positive and some are negative. Some are general and some are specific, and some are clear and some are unclear. They are simple or multiple and implicit or explicit. This multiplicity of goals means that "we have to attend to many factors and satisfy several criteria at once when we act." And in complex situations, "we cannot do only one thing."[36] He notes that the unclarity that is inherent in these complex situations requires us to "deconstruct" them. The classic approach to performance measurement rests on an assumption that programs and policies have goals that can be clarified and analyzed separately.

> We have to take them apart and isolate what we mean *in detail* when we talk about comfort, favorability to labor, and so forth. That brings clarity. It also brings difficulties, for we will often note after we have analyzed a complex concept this way that it has no single "center" but involves many different things in different places at different times.[37]

Failing to acknowledge the interrelationship between goals leads to difficulties. "Not only do we then almost inevitably end up concentrating on the wrong problems but we neglect long-term considerations, especially when partial or interim goals capture our attention and displace primary goals. Realizing we are attacking the wrong problems only makes us more uncertain."[38]

Dorner advises decision makers to begin by thinking of problems within a system analysis framework. He also recommends that individuals think by analogy, moving away from the concrete situation to an abstract stance.[39] This is the framework that he uses to conceptualize his view of planning. He sees planning as a way to "think through the consequences of certain actions and see whether those actions will bring us closer to our desired goal."[40] Dorner is skeptical about the ability of people to undertake the structure of planning (lay out a sequence of actions, combine forward and reverse planning, and move toward the goal).

Dorner provides a number of maxims about the planning process. Among them are: "In very complex and quickly changing situations the most reasonable strategy is to plan only in rough out-line" and "The more uncertain we are, the greater our tendency to overplan."[41] This approach provides flexibility to deal with uncertainties in the future and to deal with policies and programs that contain multiple and often conflicting goals. In many ways, it is the antithesis of the classic approach to performance measurement.

He reports on work that has been done by researchers to identify characteristics of good problem solvers. One such study is from Thomas Roth, who studied the problem-solving language that good and bad participants used while engaged in a simulation game. Roth found that the bad problem solvers tended to use unqualified expressions: *constantly, every time, all, without exception, absolutely, entirely, completely, totally, unequivocally, undeniably, without question, certainly, solely, nothing, nothing further, only, neither . . . nor, must,* and *have to.* The good problem solvers, on the other hand, tended more toward qualified expressions: *now and then, in general, sometimes, ordinarily, often, a bit, in particular, somewhat, specifically, especially, to some degree, perhaps, conceivable, questionable, among other things, on the other hand, also, moreover, may, can,* and *be in a position to.*[42]

Dorner suggests that we should "meditate on Kant's warning: 'Making plans is often the occupation of an opulent and boastful mind, which thus obtains the reputation of a creative genius by demanding what it cannot itself supply, by censuring what it cannot improve, and by proposing what it knows not where to find.'"[43]

Among the recommendations that Dorner provides in the conclusion of his book are the following:

> We can learn that we cannot always realize all our goals at once, because different goals may contradict one another. We must often compromise between different goals.
> We can learn that we have to establish priorities but that we cannot cling to the same priorities forever. We may have to change them. . . .
> We can learn how to adapt information gathering to the needs of the task at hand, neither going into excessive detail nor stopping too short. . . .
> We can learn the consequences of hastily ascribing all events in a certain field to one central cause. . . .

We can learn when to continue gathering information and
   when to stop. . . .
We can learn that we sometimes act simply because we want
   to prove to ourselves we *can* act. . . .
We can learn that it is essential to analyze our errors and draw
   conclusions from them for reorganizing our thinking and
   behavior.[44]

Assumptions about Numbers

There is perhaps no element within the performance measurement process that is more important than the reliance on numbers
and quantitative presentation of accomplishments. In this sense, the
movement owes much to the contribution of Jeremy Bentham, the
English philosopher who is viewed as the individual who started
"the numbering of the modern world" and heralded the arrival
of the number crunchers. Bentham's utilitarianism was followed
by John Stuart Mill, who was able to "humanize the utilitarian
gospel."

According to David Boyle, "[a]fter Mill came a long tradition
of counting pioneers who unleashed the flood of statistics on
the modern world, and then had serious doubts."[45] But today, he
writes:

> The trouble is brandishing numbers doesn't work any-
> more. They mean little and they have plunged us into a
> world packed full of figures, where almost every aspect
> of our lives is measured—from our purchases to our in-
> surance risk—and transformed into numerical half truths.
> This obsessive calculation of things that can't be measured
> is one of the most extraordinary features of the modern
> world, yet it comes in for remarkably little debate. We sim-
> ply accept it.[46]

Boyle finds that the obsession with numbers is related to other
problems. He argues: "The collapse of politics and ideology into
numbers is probably more responsible than anything for the intense
dullness of politics these days, as fewer people are prepared to take

part in the political process."[47] He identifies a series of paradoxes; for example, he argues that "numbers replace trust but make measuring even more untrustworthy. . . . Numbers are democratic. We use them to peer into the mysterious worlds of professionals, to take back some kind of control. They are the tools of opposition to arrogant rulers. Yet in another sense they are not democratic at all. Politicians simply like to pretend that numbers take the decisions out of their hands."

Another paradox is what Boyle describes as "when numbers fail, we get more numbers. . . . If the targets fail, you get more targets. . . . Because counting and measuring are seen as the antidote to distrust, any auditing failure must need more auditing."[48] Boyle acknowledges that numbers "are an absolutely vital tool for human progress . . . [but] they are not objective, nor the final answer, and they dull our good sense and intuition."[49]

Boyle argues:

> The whole of Western culture is geared to measuring. All around us, we can hear the noise of the modern world applying sports-style league tables to complex political or business problems. Or searching for the single, measurable gene that causes complex human attributes like love or learning or intelligence. . . . You can hear us all shifting the power from one kind of professional to another, in the name of democracy—from teachers and doctors to accountants, auditors, and academics. . . .
>
> Yet if you don't put figures to what's really important, then you also know your competitors will do it for you, the regulators and politicians will impose some fancy numerical code on you, and the pressure groups will demand what they call "accountability." Without putting numbers to your business case, your report, or your argument, you risk sounding woolly, or not completely serious. [50]

Joel Best described the problem similarly as he focused on the use of standardized tests in education:

The problem with such bureaucratic measures is that we lose sight of their limitations. We begin by telling ourselves that we need some way of measuring teaching quality and that this method—whatever its flaws—is better than nothing. Even if some resist adopting the measure at first, over time inertia sets in, and people come to accept its use. Before long, the measure is taken for granted, and its flaws tend to be forgotten.[51]

It is difficult to draw a line that allows one to collect appropriate information without moving into the traps that are described by Boyle and Best. Information does tend to have a life of its own, and the caveats that may be in place at the point of data collection may indeed be forgotten as the information continues to be collected over time. (Many other issues dealing with information are also discussed in chapter 8.)

Conclusion

This chapter has discussed three topics—multiple intelligence, complexity, and approaches to numbers—to support the argument that the assumptions embedded in the "classic" approach to performance measurement are not the only way to think about these issues. Concern about performance measurement and resistance to its requirements could be viewed as unwillingness to be accountable. But this discussion has shown that there are alternative ways to approach the accountability demands. One might step back from the conflict over specific performance requirements and, instead, acknowledge that individuals operate in multiple ways in a world beset by complexity and ambiguity about numbers and data.

This book does not argue that all performance measurement activities are inappropriate. Rather, it calls on those who deal with these issues to recognize that there are many ways to approach these demands. Certainty about performance measurement is particularly inappropriate in volatile and rapidly changing issues where goals are complex and multiple.

The vignette that begins this chapter—the problem faced by Professor Francine Fisher—illustrates a situation where traditional performance measurement approaches drawn from the private sector are inappropriate. The dilemma for Professor Fisher is that she needs the funding from the foundation to develop a lecture series that promises to be creative and quite innovative. She may try to convince the foundation to allow her to present her proposal in a different way or she may try to force her proposal into their very narrow structure. If she does the latter, she may find herself moving in a direction that she knows is not likely to yield the sort of results she desires. It's not clear what she should do. Should she play the game? Or should she search for another source of funding? Should she give up or try harder?

Notes

1. See U.S. Government Accountability Office, *The Government Performance and Results Act: Government-Wide Implementation Will Be Uneven* (Washington, D.C.: U.S. Government Printing Office, June 1997).
2. Harry P. Hatry, *Performance Measurement: Getting Results* (Washington, D.C.: The Urban Institute Press, 1999), 32.
3. John M. Kamensky and Albert Morales, eds., *Managing for Results* (Lanham, Md.: Rowman & Littlefield Publishers, Inc., 2005), 10.
4. These stages are based on a systems model of decision making.
5. While service quality is included in this definition, it is not always measured in a performance assessment.
6. Some individuals define the achievement of an organization's ultimate objectives as impacts rather than outcomes.
7. Harry P. Hatry, Elaine Morley, Shelli B. Rossman, and Joseph S. Wholey, "How Federal Programs Use Outcome Information: Opportunities for Federal Managers," in Kamensky and Morales, *Managing for Results*, 199.
8. Christopher Hood and Guy Peters, "The Middle Aging of New Public Management: Into the Age of Paradox," *Journal of Public Administration Research and Theory* 14, no. 3 (2004): 267–82.
9. Ibid., 894.
10. Ibid., 269.
11. Sam D. Sieber, *Fatal Remedies: The Ironies of Social Intervention* (New York: Plenum Press, 1981), 3.

12. Hood and Peters, "Middle Aging," 277–78.

13. Peter Smith, "On the Unintended Consequences of Publishing Performance Data in the Public Sector," *International Journal of Public Administration* 18, nos. 2 & 3 (1995): 277.

14. Gloria A. Grizzle, "Performance Measurement and Dysfunction: The Dark Side of Quantifying Work," *Public Performance and Management Review* 25, no. 4 (June 2002): 363.

15. Sandra van Thiel and Frans L. Leeuw, "The Performance Paradox in the Public Sector," *Public Performance and Management Review* 25, no. 3 (March 2002): 270.

16. Hans de Bruijn, *Managing Performance in the Public Sector* (London: Routledge, 2002), 21, 23–32.

17. Ann B. Blalock and Burt S. Barnow, "Is the New Obsession with Performance Management Masking the Truth about Social Programs?" in Dall W. Forsythe, ed., *Quicker, Better Cheaper, Managing Performance in American Government* (Albany, N.Y.: Rockefeller Institute Press, 2001), 485.

18. Charles Clotfelter and Helen Ladd, "Recognizing and Rewarding Success," in Helen F. Ladd, ed., *Holding Schools Accountable: Performance-Based Reform in Education* (Washington, D.C.: The Brookings Institution, 1996), 43.

19. Sir Isaiah Berlin, *The Hedgehog and the Fox* (New York: Simon and Schuster, 1953).

20. Howard Gardner, *Frames of Mind: The Theory of Multiple Intelligences* (New York: Basic Books, 1983), 7–8, 20.

21. Ibid., 20.

22. Ibid., 8.

23. Ibid., 60.

24. Ibid., 60–61.

25. Ibid., 68.

26. Ibid., part II.

27. Ibid., 384.

28. Quoted in Daniel Goleman, *Emotional Intelligence* (New York: Bantam Books, 1997), 37. From Daniel Goleman, "Rethinking the Value of Intelligence Tests," in *New York Times Education Supplement*, Nov. 3, 1986.

29. Ibid., 36.

30. Ibid., 289–90.

31. See Murray Edelman, *The Symbolic Uses of Politics* (Urbana, Ill.: University of Illinois Press, 1964), 68.

32. Dietrich Dorner, *The Logic of Failure: Recognizing and Avoiding Error in Complex Situations* (New York: Perseus Books, 1996), 6.

33. Ibid., 38–39.

34. Ibid., 41.

35. Ibid., 88.

36. Ibid., 51–52.

37. Ibid., 54.

38. Ibid., 63.

39. Ibid., 77.

40. Ibid., 153–54.

41. Ibid., 161, 163.

42. Ibid., 175.

43. Ibid., 176–77.

44. Ibid., 197–98.

45. David Boyle, *The Sum of Our Discontent: Why Numbers Make Us Irrational* (New York: Texere, 2001), 15, 27.

46. Ibid., xii.

47. Ibid., 35.

48. Ibid., 38–39.

49. Ibid., 45.

50. Ibid., 45–46.

51. Joel Best, *More Damned Lies and Statistics: How Numbers Confuse Public Issues* (Berkeley: University of California Press, 2004), 25.

3 one size FiTS ALL

Raymond Wilson was appointed secretary of the U.S. Department of Health and Human Services (DHHS) less than three years ago. His experience in the California Department of Health and in the private sector had given him some sense of the breadth of DHHS. But he was very surprised to realize that issues related to the health program were only one part of the portfolio of this department. He prepared for his confirmation hearings in the Senate with a crash course on the multiple accountability demands to which he was required to respond. He learned that he was responsible for many programs that covered a range of issues and policy approaches. Indeed, there are more than three hundred programs in his department.

Since his appointment, his experience in the budget process involving both OMB and the congressional appropriations committees and subcommittees made him realize how difficult it is to think of the department as a single unit that is responsible to a single source of performance expectations. Each of the program areas within the department is surrounded by a set of interest groups and constituencies that is specialized and focused on that specific policy area. And each of the program areas has a number of members of Congress who pay particular attention to the details of the area that interests them. The partisan nature of congressional activity means that many of the programs have two sets of congressional and interest group players. One set supports the program, while the other is skeptical about its approach

or goals. So when he thought about describing the performance of the department's programs, he realized how difficult it would be to please all the players in the system.

While a few of the programs within DHHS are actually administered by federal officials, most of the programs
are implemented by others—state or local governments or
private for-profit or nonprofit organizations. As a result,
efforts to hold federal administrators accountable for programs over which they have limited control are difficult.

Raymond Wilson learned about the requirements of
the Government Performance and Results Act (GPRA)
early in his tenure as secretary. He found it somewhat ludicrous that this huge department was expected to write
a five-year strategic plan that established goals and objectives covering all of the programs within the department
when these programs are based on conditions that change
rapidly. The document he inherited was written at a level
of generality that attempted to avoid conflict. As a result,
it often seemed to him to be an exercise simply to com-
ply with the Act's requirements. But he was required to
sign off on such a document and submit it both to OMB
and to the Congress along with yearly performance plans
and performance reports. It does not seem to him that
this process actually contributes to effective performance
assessment for many of the programs in his department.
Yet in order to advocate for what he views as an adequate
budget for the department within OMB he has to satisfy
the GPRA document requirements.

Managers and officials who face performance measurement
demands often find that these requirements come from those who
seem to ignore the special requirements of programs or organizations. As Raymond Wilson was appreciating the diversity of the
programs within his department, others were expecting him to fit
those programs into a format that was devised as a government-
wide effort. As I have written elsewhere, one could call this a situation where square pegs are expected to fit into round holes.[1]

Conflict occurs because so much of management reform tends to move toward a "one-size-fits-all" strategy, generating tension between what seems to make sense for an individual program and what satisfies those who seek a uniform approach to change. These are issues that have been classic subjects of the field of organization theory as scholars have sought to devise typologies that either accentuate generic approaches to organizations or emphasize differences among organizations.

Organizational Theory: The Backdrop to Performance Measurement

Performance measurement activities, whether they are found in the public, private, or nonprofit sectors, confront a set of assumptions about the organizations that are the object of their attention. However, this literature does not have a clear view on how to approach these organizations. A one-size-fits-all emphasis emerges in some of the literature, while other aspects of the literature emphasize differences. Still other literatures fall into a mixed approach to the generic-uniqueness dichotomy. Frederickson and Smith have catalogued nine conceptual frameworks that can be seen to fall into these three categories:[2]

Theories that support the "one-size-fits all" approach:
   Bureaucratic or administrative behavior.
   Managerialism or new public management
   Privatization, contracting out, and nonprofit organizations
   Institutionalist theory focused on political economies and
      rational choice perspectives

Theories that support mixed approaches:
   Structural theories
   Performance, outcomes, program evaluation and results

Theories that support the uniqueness approach:
   Organizational design theories
   Democratic control of bureaucracy
   Politics of bureaucracy

The frameworks related to the one-size-fits-all method tend to be generic approaches to organizations, spanning both public and private sectors. These generic approaches tend to focus on a series of decision and control processes that appear to be relevant to both types of organizations. In that sense, they are similar to the functional elements that were identified by Luther Gulick in his classic "Notes on the Theory of Organization." Gulick identified seven functions that he named POSDCORB.

> Planning, that is working out in broad outline the things that need to be done and the methods for doing them to accomplish the purpose set for the enterprise;
>
> Organizing, that is the establishment of the formal structure of authority through which work subdivisions are arranged, defined and coordinated for the defined objective;
>
> Staffing, that is the whole personnel function of bringing in and training the staff and maintaining favorable conditions of work;
>
> Directing, that is the continuous task of making decisions and embodying them in specific and general orders and instructions and serving as the leader of the enterprise;
>
> Coordinating, that is the all-important duty of interrelating the various parts of the work;
>
> Reporting, that is keeping those to whom the executive is responsible informed as to what is going on, which thus includes keeping himself and his subordinates informed through records, research, and inspection;
>
> Budgeting, with all that goes with budgeting in the form of fiscal planning, accounting, and control.[3]

Gulick and others who have followed him have searched for a science of organizations—an approach that attempts to develop rules and approaches that are appropriate for all organizations. This enterprise looks inside the organizations and emphasizes the processes that emerge from these functions without attention to the external elements that surround the organization. The Gulick et al. emphasis appears to lead to a national macro, aggregate, optimizing approach to management reform. It attempts to craft reforms that are government-wide and emphasizes the institutions that speak to this perspective. Such institutions include the executive branch central management agencies and the legislative committees and organizations such as the governmental operations committees. Much of the management reform that has occurred within the past has emerged from these entities; it emphasizes commonalities rather than differences among governmental organizations and usually discusses reform in abstract and general terms. It tends to fall into the "one-size-fits-all" approach and rarely focuses on the substantive policy or program results of action.

Concentrating on the internal processes allows analysts to ignore what have come to be acknowledged as two elements that differentiate public from private organizations. The first element relates directly to performance measurement. The private sector can use the bottom line of profit to determine whether an organization is effective; there is no comparable measure for the public sector. The second element involves the relationship between organizational control and the institutions of a democracy that tend to move away from internal control mechanisms. This second aspect brings one to another literature dealing with public organizations, specifically with how these organizations operate within an environment characterized by multiple perspectives, shared powers, and suspicion of concentrated power.

Judith Gruber, whose work has focused on this relationship, has identified five broad approaches: "(1) control through participation, (2) control through clientele relations, (3) control through pursuit of the public interest, (4) control through accountability, and (5) self-control."[4] She highlights the conflicts that are found in the U.S. system between control and democracy and, especially, the structural limitations of control mechanisms that are imposed by the complexity of the system. In addition, Gruber accentuates the costs of control on bureaucrats. Reform, she notes, has costs as well as benefits. She also emphasizes the need to create control mechanisms that are appropriate for different settings, moving quite far away from the "one-size-fits-all" advice found in other commentators.

The elements in a democracy lead one to acknowledge that much of public action carries multiple and often conflicting goals. As a result, unlike the private sector where profit becomes the ultimate measure of success, it is difficult to establish a standard against which to measure outcomes. Thus process, not outcomes, becomes

essential. Gruber argues that "procedure, not substance, is the focus of the accountability approach. . . . The emphasis on procedure
derives from the diagnosis that bureaucracies threaten democracy
when they abuse their power by acting corruptly, inefficiently, or
unfairly. Procedural safeguards, or limits, are therefore advocated to
ensure that such abuses do not take place."[5]

Fesler and Kettl have also commented on the attributes of a
democracy that make it very challenging to establish a surrogate for
the profit outcome of the private sector. They emphasize the complexity of most organizational systems and note that "the complexity of any large-scale organization seems not to be one of the kinds
of puzzles that a single key will unlock." Further, "a single reality-
based model is unavailable because most writers on organization
happen to have sought not to describe a particular organization
but to describe organizations in general—that is organization in
the abstract." And "organizational theorists do not agree on a single
theory or model."[6]

Yet the most recent attempt to define the world of the public
manager borrows directly from the private sector. That approach,
called the New Public Management (or what some call the new
managerialism), borrows heavily from the private sector's business
management approach and emphasizes contracting out, competi-
tion, outcomes, deregulation, and risk taking.[7]

It is difficult to find attention within this approach to the types
of issues that have concerned Gruber, Fesler and Kettl, and others.
In many ways, New Public Management avoids dealing with politics and does move into a managerial approach. As March and Olson
have written, there are two types of rhetoric that have been used in
the world of administrative reform: what they call "administrative"
rhetoric on one hand and "realpolitik" rhetoric on the other.[8] The
"administrative" approach is specific and technical while the "realpolitik" rhetoric is general and broad based. Much of what has been
written about performance measurement is in the rhetorical style
of the administrative language and does not move into the specifics
and details that are required to make a policy come alive.

Those who focus on the parameters of organizations as they
operate within a democracy highlight issues of diffuse and multiple
accountability relationships and the reality of politics. Fesler and

Kettl have argued that five issues continually resurface in attempts
to ensure the accomplishment of particular outcomes:

> The uncertainty that surrounds programs.
>
> The resources to get the job done.
>
> Organizational features that determine how bureaucracies
>   react to problems.
>
> Leadership that guides bureaucracies through difficult issues.
>
> Growing interdependence among levels of government, and
>   between government and the private and nonprofit
>   sectors.[9]

This short summary of some aspects of the debate in organizational theory indicates that it is difficult to sort out the aspects
of organizations that set the framework for performance measurement. The generic perspective (minimizing differences between
public and private sectors) tends to emphasize the way that the
organization actually functions in terms of organizational processes.
It also attempts to substitute the concept of "outcomes" for private
sector profits. In addition, the generic perspective tends to emphasize issues related to control; as a result, despite the belief in a market, it often tends to emphasize centralized control, following the
structure of a hierarchy.

Management Reform and the Generic Approach

As has been suggested, much of management reform flows from
the generic approach to management. In part this occurs because
the public sector continually models itself on what has been done
in the world of private sector management. It is a prime example of
the difficulty of dealing with federal management as a government-
wide strategy and set of generic activities and requirements.

This tendency to minimize the special attributes of public
programs and organizations is not new. Much of the inheritance of
management reform in the United States has emphasized a set of institutions and processes that do not really touch the core of the nation's
decision-making processes. They operate largely as entities based on
language and oratory without the ability to influence substantive

Table 3.1 Differences between Generic and Unique Program Approaches to Government Reform

Area of Difference	Generic Approach	Program Approach
Techniques	Analytical	Political bargaining
	Best practice	Bottom up
	Top down	
Value debates	Efficiency	Multiple values
	Effectiveness (defined nationally)	Individual program trade-offs
	Coordination	
Institutions	OMB, OPM	Multiple players in both Congress and the executive branch
	Government operations committees	Authorizing and appropriations committees
		Program agencies
Goals	Government-wide compliance	Tied to specific programs
	Management as separate activities	Management as means to program ends

Modified from Beryl A. Radin, "Balancing Policy and Administrative Change," in Yong Hyo Cho and H. George Frederickson, eds., *The White House and the Blue House: Government Reform in the United States and Korea* (Lanham, Md.: University Press of America, 1997), 13

policy and budgetary processes. The rhetoric has emerged from the executive branch through those concerned about management in the Office of Management and Budget (OMB), from the legislative branch through the government operations and affairs committees of the two houses of Congress, and from organizations such as the National Academy of Public Administration. The conflict between the generic approach and the unique program approach includes differences between techniques used, value debates, institutions involved, and goals. Table 3.1 summarizes the conflict that has been found between these two approaches in past management reform efforts.[10] They differ dramatically in all of the elements analyzed.

Others have written about the limits of the generic approach. Downs and Larkey have noted that past attempts to reform government have achieved "only modest success." They write that "[t]hose who seek to reform government must realize both that some otherwise commendable schemes enjoy only a miniscule chance of successful implementation and that simple-minded solutions to complex problems are capable of doing as much harm as good."[11] Their observations resonate with my analysis.

A Recent One-Size-Fits-All Example: The National Performance Review

The National Performance Review (NPR), developed in the first term of the Clinton administration, is one of the more recent management reform efforts that illustrates the limitations of strategies borrowed from the private sector and a generic approach. While much of what the NPR included was found in earlier administrative reform efforts over the twentieth century, by the 1980s a force emerged on the scene in the United States (and around the world) that reinforced the emphasis on private sector values. Models for change came from the private sector, and the antibureaucracy mood that emerged from this made it difficult to even justify the existence of the public sector.[12]

Osborne and Gaebler's book *Reinventing Government*, published in 1992, served as the handbook for this reinvention activity. It emphasized the ways in which analogies can be drawn between the public sector and the private sector, particularly in the discussion of markets. The authors praise contracting out of government services, draw on the concept of citizens as "customers," and call for the development of an "entrepreneurial spirit" within the public administration sector.[13] This was particularly attractive to President Clinton, who was taken with private sector approaches to management change and the political benefits that could be accomplished as a result of the reinvention concept. In addition, these approaches gave him a way to deal with the budget deficit without invoking a blame-the-bureaucrat rhetoric of past presidents.[14]

The instructions for implementing the NPR agenda came directly from the office of the vice president and clearly illustrated the private sector mindset. Federal staff assigned to work on the NPR were given responsibilities for agencies other than their own, emphasizing a generic approach to change and minimizing the use of specific knowledge of the unique worlds of those agencies. In some cases, individuals who played a major strategy role came directly from the private sector. Even when career officials played a leadership role, they relied on private sector experience as their model. This approach emphasized internal aspects of change, using the concept of a chief executive officer as the focal point.

The private sector experience leads one to adopt a more managerial approach, which avoids politics and the conflict that is usually found as a result of dealing with Congress and interest groups.[15] Sometimes, however, the apolitical managerial mindset actually serves to support a political agenda. Ironically, as the NPR unfolded, it had to deal with a Congress controlled by Republicans who sought to oppose the policies and substantive agenda of the Clinton administration.

Alternative Approaches to One Size Fits All

Despite the reliance on the private sector model, those who focus on public organizations do find it difficult to argue that all organizations are the same and that one strategy for change would work similarly in all of them. Yet there is a powerful argument that is contained within the framework of private sector organizations that is attractive and alluring to those within the public sector. That, of course, is the power of the bottom line of profit. With profit as the bedrock for the private sector, there can be attention to the different pathways that can be taken within different settings to achieve significant profit. Students of the public sector have attempted to find surrogates for profit, and the results are not always clear or appealing.

Perhaps the most successful attempt to find a way to describe the variety of agencies has been accomplished by James Q. Wilson in his now classic volume *Bureaucracy: What Government Agencies Do and Why They Do It*. Wilson argues that agencies differ in two main respects: (1) Can their activities be observed and (2) can the results of those activities be observed? He notes that "[t]he first factor involves *outputs*—what the teachers, doctors, lawyers, engineers, police-officers, and grant givers do on a day-to-day basis. . . . The second factor involves *outcomes*—how, if at all, the world changes because of the outputs. Outcomes can be thought of as the results of agency work. . . .

The outcomes (or results) are the changes, if any, in the level of safety, security, order, and amenity in the community."

Wilson writes that outputs can be hard to observe in some situations (when the work done is esoteric or out of sight) and outcomes may be difficult to ascertain because "the organization lacks a method for gathering information about the consequences of its actions." Because he finds that observing both outputs and outcomes is variable, Wilson details four kinds of agencies. They are

> Agencies in which both outputs and outcomes can be ob-
> served; agencies in which outputs but not outcomes can be
> observed; agencies in which outcomes but not outputs can
> be observed; and agencies in which neither outputs nor
> outcomes can be observed. . . . I have called the first kind
> of agency a *production* organization, the second a *procedural*
> organization, the third a *craft* organization, and the fourth a
> *coping* organization.[16]

Wilson's description of each of these types of agencies indicates that each has both strengths and limitations. For example, managers in production agencies may give most of their attention to the outcomes that are easily measured and ignore those less easily observed or counted.[17] Managers in a procedural bureaucracy are faced with a situation in which there is often no result, or one that occurs in the distant future. Wilson notes that this type of agency is ripe for management that encourages the development of professionalism.[18] (See discussion of professionalism in chapter 4.) Craft organizations involve situations in which staff either produce an outcome or do not. These staff are highly decentralized or dispersed, and managers are not attentive to the way in which outcomes are achieved. Wilson notes that because public agencies produce many kinds of outcomes, managers are concerned not only about "progress toward the primary goal of the agency, but also conformity to the contextual goals and constraints in which the agency is enmeshed." The last type—coping organizations—is viewed by Wilson as constituting a difficult situation. Managers, he writes, "can try to recruit the best people (without having much knowledge about what the 'best person' looks like), they can try to create an atmosphere that is conducive to good work (without being certain what 'good work' is), and they can step in when complaints are heard or crises erupt (without knowing whether a complaint is justified or a crisis symptomatic or atypical)." Wilson notes that "Where both outputs and outcomes are unobservable there is likely to be a high degree of conflict between managers and operators in public agencies, especially those that must cope with a clientele not of their own choosing."[19]

Wilson's typology clearly suggests that it would be legitimate and understandable that some agencies would find it very difficult—if not impossible—to report on the outcomes of their work. Yet the requirements of many performance measurement initiatives do not acknowledge this possibility.

During the early years of implementation of the Government Performance and Results Act (GPRA), at least one office within the U.S. Government Accountability Office (GAO) did suggest that some agencies would find it difficult to respond to the requirements of the Act. In a series of three reports issued in 1998, GAO's program evaluation office within the General Government Division sought to advise the Congress on the problems involved in balancing flexibility and accountability in federal grant programs. In the first report titled *Balancing Flexibility and Accountability: Grant Program Design in Education and Other Areas*, GAO focused on the differences between a range of programs. Three design features were emphasized:

> Whether the national objectives involved are performance-related or fiscal; whether the grant funds a distinct "program" or contributes to the stream of funds supporting state and local activities; and whether it supports a single activity or diverse activities. In combination, these features are associated with differences in flexibility, accountability, and the level of government that is accountable for performance.[20]

The second GAO report continued the analysis that emphasized diverse features. It described the difficulties of balancing flexibility and accountability in some program forms, noting that programs that focus on a single activity with a national program focus have the clearest accountability structure but the least flexibility. Conversely, programs that provide funds to states or localities but not program specificity have the most flexibility but least accountability.

> Design features also have implications for the availability of performance information. Although most reported simple activity or client counts, relatively few flexible programs collected uniform data on the outcomes of state or local service activities. Collecting such data requires conditions (such as uniformity of activities, objectives, and measures) that do not exist under many flexible program designs, and even where overall performance of a state or local program can be measured, the amount attributable to federal funding often cannot be separated out.[21]

The third GAO report was issued following the submission of the first annual performance plans submitted by federal agencies as required by GPRA. GAO noted that "many of these first performance plans faltered at the central task: developing measurable goals for the results or outcomes that their programs are intended to achieve. A common challenge faced by many federal agencies is developing goals for outcomes that are the results of phenomena outside of federal government control." GAO found that their review of the first plans identified a common weakness—"namely, that few performance goals were outcome-oriented."[22]

Despite this advice and analysis from GAO, it was difficult for management reformers to find ways to deal with programs on anything but an aggregate basis. The management effort that was put into place by the George W. Bush administration did try to organize its Program Assessment Rating Tools (PART) effort into categories by different mechanisms and approaches. The effort, orchestrated out of OMB, defined seven categories of federal programs. They were:

1. Competitive Grant Programs: programs that distribute funds to state, local, and tribal governments, organizations, individuals, and other entities through a competitive pro-

cess. Examples include Empowerment Zones and the Safe Schools/Healthy Students program.

2. Block/Formula Grant Programs: programs that distribute funds to state, local, and tribal governments and other entities by formula or block grant. Examples include the Preventive Health and Health Services Block Grant, Medicaid, and Housing for People with AIDS.

3. Regulatory Based Programs: programs that employ regulatory action to achieve program and agency goals. More specifically, a regulatory program accomplishes its mission and goals through rulemaking that implements, interprets, or prescribes law or policy or describes a procedure or practice requirements. An example is the EPA's Office of Air and Radiation (Clean Air Program).

4. Capital Assets and Service Acquisition Programs: programs where the primary objective is to develop and acquire capital assets (such as land, structures, equipment, and intellectual property) or to purchase services (such as maintenance, and information technology) from a commercial source.

5. Credit Programs: programs that provide support through loans, loan guarantees, and direct credit. Examples include the Small Business Administration 7A loan program and FHA Multifamily Development.

6. Direct Federal Programs: programs where support and services are provided primarily by employees of the federal government. Examples include the Federal Mint, Diplomatic and Consular programs, the National Wildlife Refuge System, FEMA, and the Indian Health Service.

7. Research and Development Programs: programs that focus on the creation of knowledge or on the application of that knowledge toward the creation of systems, devices, methods, materials, or technologies. R&D programs that primarily develop specific systems or other capital assets would most likely fall under Capital Asset and Service Acquisition.[23]

On paper, it appeared that OMB was planning to acknowledge that performance measurement requirements had to be crafted to meet differences between programs. Yet when one examined the

specific questions and the weighting that determined the score under each category, the one-size-fits-all mindset continued to prevail.
All programs were subject to the same distribution of weights: program purpose/relevance federal role was given 20 percent; strategic
planning 10 percent; program management 20 percent; and program results 50 percent.

The questions that were asked concerning research and development programs indicate that OMB was not really willing to view
these programs as significantly different from other program forms.
Research and development programs often involve multiyear grants,
support of uncertain scientific procedures, ability of grantees to determine the details of expenditure of funds, and the use of peer review processes to determine which grantees will be funded. The nature of scientific inquiry means that research can yield as much from
surprises and negative findings as from achievement of hypothesized
findings. The questions that were listed during the FY 2002 Spring
Review did not appear to be sensitive to the program construct. But
even though OMB seemed to move to differentiate between program types, these questions suggest that there was a strong tendency
to think about research programs as efforts to meet specific and annual goals and avoid acknowledging the uncertainties involved in
scientific endeavors. The questions that were used in this process for
research and development programs included the following:

> Does the program demonstrate proposed relevance to presi-
> dential priorities, agency mission, relevant field of science,
> and other "customer" needs?
> Is a research program the most effective way to support the
> federal policy goals compared to other policy alternatives
> such as legislation or regulation?
> Does the program have a limited number of specific, ambitious,
> long-term performance goals that focus on outcomes and
> meaningfully reflect the purpose of the program?
> Does the program track and report relevant program inputs
> annually?
> Does the program have annual performance goals and out-
> come and output measures that they will use to demon-
> strate progress toward achieving the long-term goals?

Does the program (including program partners) achieve its
   annual performance goals?
Were program goals achieved within budgeted costs and established schedules?[24]

While Wilson, GAO, and OMB sought to sort programs by establishing a typology that distinguished one type from another, others attacked the sentiment behind the search for principles or science
of administration that often led to the one-size-fits-all approach.

Herbert Simon's article "The Proverbs of Administration" set
forth a critique of rules of thumb that some (e.g., Luther Gulick)
devised in their quest to define a science of administration. Simon
began his argument by noting that proverbs "almost always occur
in mutually contradictory pairs. 'Look before you leap!'—but 'He
who hesitates is lost.'" Simon wrote:

Most of the propositions that make up the body of administrative theory today share, unfortunately, this defect of
proverbs. For almost every principle one can find an equally
plausible and acceptable contradictory principle. Although
the two principles of the pair will lead to exactly opposite
organizational recommendations, there is nothing in the
theory to indicate which is the proper one to apply.[25]

He applies his argument to four administrative principles: specialization, unity of command, span of control, and organization by
purpose, process, clientele, and place. He finds that

[a]dministrative description suffers currently from super-
ficiality, oversimplification, lack of realism. It has confined
itself too closely to the mechanism of authority and has
failed to bring within its orbit the other, equally important, modes of influence on organizational behavior. It has
refused to undertake the tiresome task of studying the actual allocation of decision-making functions. It has been
satisfied to speak of "authority," "centralization," "span of
control," "function," without seeking operational definitions of these terms.[26]

Simon's approach clearly resonated with practitioners who sought ways to link organizational theory with their practical experience. In 1966, Harvey Sherman, director of the Organizations and Procedures Department of the Port of New York Authority, published a book that was based on five lectures given at the University of Alabama in 1962. In the book, he argues that the ideal of clear-cut responsibility is difficult to attain. He frames his argument within the Simon approach, showing that the traditional principles of organization are variable. He wrote: "In each case, we would find that under some conditions the principle is valid, while under other conditions it is not."[27]

> I suggest that the task of organization theory is not to lay down "principles," but to determine as precisely as possible what effects different arrangements of structure or process will have for a particular enterprise, staffed with real people, over a specified time period. This does not imply any evaluation of these effects in terms of universal ideals. Whether the effects are good or bad depends on the value system of those who are making the judgment. Organizational decisions require hard choices; and what favors certain groups or individuals usually penalizes others.[28]

Sherman warns about a series of what he calls "pitfalls" that result from the search for easy answers to complex problems.[29] These pitfalls include "pendulumitis" (or faddism), "doctrinairism" (or sloganitis), "oversimplification," a passion for planning (plans rather than action), the "economy/efficiency cult," a "conflict-phobia," a "total systems approach," "aesthetics" (tendency to make an organizational virtue of symmetry, balance, and uniformity), and a belief that communications follow the chain of command.[30]

In his conclusion, Sherman makes a strong argument against the one-size-fits-all approach:

> The more we study the problem of organization, the more we recognize its complexity, its dynamics, its variety, its pluralism, its paradoxes, and its contradictions. One might even say that organization, like war, is essentially disorderly.

Organizational decisions are, and will be, based on probabilities, not absolutes. And generalizations about organization are notable for the number of qualifications, limitations, and exceptions to them. In recognition of these facts, we no longer search for "the one best organization"; we recognize that different types of organization may be appropriate for different types of work, different kinds of people and different environmental conditions; and we acknowledge that what is the best organization today may be much less than the best tomorrow.[31]

Conclusion

This chapter has argued that a significant part of the performance measurement movement lies within that element of organization theory that searches for a science of organizations. While there are alternative ways to think about organizations, the contemporary performance measurement movement largely falls within the one-size-fits-all and generic orientation. The attempt to rationalize the aspects of organizations that produce outcomes clearly ignores the uniqueness of programs or agencies. While there have been a number of theorists and practitioners who suggest that it is important to acknowledge the differences between organizations, government-wide management reform efforts do not seem to be able to deal with this variety.

As Raymond Wilson was appreciating the diversity of the programs within his department, he also had to respond to a very different set of imperatives—the GPRA requirements defined by individuals who wanted to view the entire federal government as a single system. Wilson is dealing with three hundred programs in multiple forms that make it difficult to apply a single strategy to measuring performance. Some of the programs in the department accentuate flexibility to grantees (particularly state and local governments). Others establish clear goals and expectations that lead to stricter accountability to the federal govern-

ment. Still others establish research and development programs or regulatory efforts. One would hope that Wilson
would be able to convince both OMB and the Congress
that the "one-size-fits-all" strategy is neither appropriate
nor effective as a way to make change.

Notes

1. See Beryl A. Radin, "The Government Performance and Results Act
   (GPRA) and the Tradition of Federal Management Reform: Square Pegs
   in Round Holes?" *Journal of Public Administration Research and Theory* 10
   (January 2000).
2. H. George Frederickson and Kevin B. Smith, *The Public Administration Theory Primer* (Cambridge, Mass.: Westview Press, 2003). These frameworks are
   largely from the public sector but also represent more generic approaches.
3. Luther Gulick, "Notes on the Theory of Organization," in Jay M. Schafritz,
   Albert C. Hyde, and Sandra J. Parkes, eds., *Classics of Public Administration:
   Fifth Edition* (Belmont, Calif.: Wadsworth-Thomson Learning, 2004), 97.
4. Judith E. Gruber, *Controlling Bureaucracies: Dilemmas in Democratic Governance* (Berkeley: University of California Press, 1987), 18.
5. Ibid., 22.
6. James W. Fesler and Donald F. Kettl, *The Politics of the Administrative Process:
   Second Edition* (Chatham, N.J.: Chatham House Publishers, Inc., 1996),
   21–23.
7. Ibid., 113. See Frederickson and Smith, *The Public Administration Theory
   Primer*, 123.
8. James G. March and Johan P. Olson, "Organizing Political Life: What Administrative Reorganization Tells Us about Government," *The American
   Political Science Review* 77 (1983): 283.
9. Fesler and Kettl, *The Politics of the Administrative Process*, 288.
10. Modified from Beryl A. Radin, "Balancing Policy and Administrative
    Change," in Yong Hyo Cho and H. George Frederickson, eds., *The White
    House and the Blue House: Government Reform in the United States and Korea*
    (Lanham, Md.: University Press of America, 1997), 13.
11. George W. Downs and Patrick D. Larkey, *The Search for Government Efficiency:
    From Hubris to Helplessness* (Philadelphia: Temple University Press, 1986), 3.
12. See Beryl A. Radin, "Balancing Policy and Administrative Change in the
    Clinton Administration: The National Performance Review and the Gov-
    ernment Performance and Results Act," in Cho and Frederickson, *The
    White House*, 15–25.

13. David Osborne and Ted Gaebler, *Reinventing Government* (Reading, Mass: Addison Wesley Publishing, 1992).

14. See Donald F. Kettl and John J. DiIulio, Jr., eds., *Inside the Reinvention Machine: Appraising Governmental Reform* (Washington, D.C.: Brookings Institution, 1995).

15. Radin, "Balancing Policy and Administrative Change in the Clinton Administration," 20.

16. James Q. Wilson, *Bureaucracy: What Government Agencies Do and Why They Do It* (New York: Basic Books, 1989), 158.

17. Ibid., 161.

18. Ibid., 163.

19. Ibid., 168–69.

20. Susan S. Westin, associate director, Advanced Studies and Evaluation Methodology, General Government Division, USGAO, *Balancing Flexibility and Accountability: Grant Program Design in Education and Other Areas* (Testimony before the Education Task Force, Committee on the Budget, U.S. Senate, February 11, 1998, GAO/T-GGD/HEHS-98-94), 1.

21. USGAO, *Grant Programs: Design Features Shape Flexibility, Accountability, and Performance Information* (Report to Congressional Requesters, GAO/GGD-98-137, June 1998), 2.

22. USGAO, *Managing for Results: Measuring Program Results That Are under Limited Federal Control* (Report to the Committee on Labor and Human Resources, U.S. Senate, GAO/GGD-99-16, December 1998), 1, 4.

23. OMB, "Instructions for the Program Assessment Ratings Tools," April 18, 2002.

24. OMB, "OMB Program Assessment Rating Tool (PART), Research and Development Programs," Draft, FY 2002 Spring Review.

25. Herbert A. Simon, "The Proverbs of Administration," *Public Administration Review* 6, no. 1 (Winter 1946), 53.

26. Ibid., 63.

27. Harvey Sherman, *It All Depends: A Pragmatic Approach to Organization* (University, Ala.: University of Alabama Press, 1966), 51.

28. Ibid., 57.

29. Ibid., 97.

30. Ibid., chapter 4.

31. Ibid., 158.

DEMEANING PROFESSIONALS: THROWING OUT THE BABY WITH THE BATHWATER?

4

Dr. Robert Peacock is currently the head of the family practice unit at a large health maintenance organization (HMO) that has several clinics in urban areas as well as in rural sections of the state. Dr. Peacock joined the practice after completing an assignment at an Indian reservation as a part of the Health Services Corps. He became a family practice physician because of his commitment to providing services to the underserved within U.S. society. He has spent much of his career attempting to improve the performance of the health system to meet the needs of this often neglected population.

During the past several years, Dr. Peacock has found it difficult to balance his commitment to patient-defined performance with the performance requirements that are emerging from the HMO. He knows that the HMO cannot continue to operate without achieving a sound financial base. However, the performance requirements that have been devised for the organization do not seem to him to apply equally to all of the diverse settings in which the HMO operates nor to the range of patients that he sees. He has been given specific expectations in terms of the length of each appointment, the requirements that would allow him to prescribe specific tests and referrals, and the types of prescriptions that are reimbursed by the HMO. His patient pool includes individuals from various ethnic and racial groups, some people who are not fluent in English, and individuals who live in highly congested urban settings as well as remote rural communities. He is very concerned that the "one-size-fits-all" approach to performance assessment devised by the HMO does not allow him to respond appropriately to the specific needs of his patients nor to apply the professional judgment that results from his years of training and experience.

One of the characteristics of U.S. society in the post-Vietnam era has been a strong skepticism about reliance on "experts." Whether this skepticism is directed at a foreign policy expert, a military strategist, a teacher, or a medical doctor, it blends with a general decline in the status of and reliance on a range of institutions within the society. Experts were once viewed as specialists who could be trusted to deal with issues in a fair, balanced, and effective manner.

According to public opinion polls, almost all economic, political, and professional institutions have experienced dramatic drops in their status. One recent poll taken by the Pew Research Center for the People and the Press asked people their opinion of some people and organizations. The highest rating that was received in a June 2004 survey found that the military received a very favorable rating from 48 percent of the respondents. No other institution came anywhere near that score; all were below 16 percent very favorable ratings, and the Congress and the news media received only a 7 percent very favorable rating.[1]

Given this backdrop, it is not surprising that one of the threads in the performance movement centers around an attack on what have been characterized as professional monopolies. These monopolies, it is argued, are not only mechanisms for protecting members of the profession, but they are also methods of removing those members from the normal accountability mechanisms that one expects in the expenditure of public (or, indeed, private) monies. The argument highlights issues of financial greed, inability to focus on the needs of the citizens or customers that they serve, and conflicts of both financial and policy interest.

One recent popular book titled *Trust Us, We're Experts*, centers on the relationship between researchers and corporate interests. The authors detail the habits and practices of experts who manage the perceptions of those in the broader society. They argue that the negative views of experts reflect "a set of elitist values that have become all too common in modern society. Functioning at a philosophical and psychological level, it amounts to a kind of anti-popular prejudice that is dangerously corrosive of democratic values." According to these authors, experts are individuals whose training allows them to present their analysis as rational, objective, and reasonable. Others find that experts are "deluded, prejudiced, and even emotionally unbalanced."[2] Rampton and Stauber believe that experts trade in a kind of arrogance and this has been used to evoke a role that leads to problematic behaviors. This arrogance helps to explain the failure of medical doctors to make the Hippocratic Oath come alive. It has been used to detail the failure of elementary school teachers to believe that students from lower socioeconomic status families can learn. And it has been used to explain the behaviors of biomedical researchers who undertake research projects that support the perspective of those who pay for that research (such as pharmaceutical companies).

At the same time that these concerns are being voiced within the general public, others have pointed to the role that is played by professional experts who "speak truth to power." These individuals—whether they are intelligence experts, engineers, researchers, or physicians—use the norms and values of their professions to counter demands for political or bureaucratic compliance.

In their important study of accountability expectations in the Challenger space shuttle disaster, Romzek and Dubnick define professional accountability systems as one of four important sources of agency control. They note:

> Professional accountability occurs with greater frequency
> as governments deal increasingly with technically difficult
> and complex problems. Under those circumstances, public

officials must rely on skilled and expert employees to provide appropriate solutions. Those employees expect to be held fully accountable for their actions and insist that agency leaders trust them to do the best job possible. If they fail to meet job performance expectations, it is assumed they can be reprimanded or fired. Otherwise they expect to be given sufficient discretion to get the job done. Thus, professional accountability is characterized by placement of control over organizational activities in the hands of the employee with the expertise or special skills to get the job done.[3]

The decisions to override concerns of engineers about ice on the launch pad or weather conditions and the O-rings clearly were factors contributing to the disaster. Romzek and Dubnick note that a "a return to professional accountability calls for establishment of explicit guidelines and criteria for use in making launch decisions."[4] These guidelines and criteria can help—but not assure—that professional judgments can be made independently of the agendas of those in power.

These conflicting views within the American society suggest that to some degree both perceptions are true. There are professionals who use their expertise to avoid accountability and believe that the society should defer to them because of their training and knowledge. In some of these instances, the professionals are in conflict with expectations and demands of citizens. And yet there are situations in which experts provide assistance to citizens who push for change and challenge decisions made on other grounds (such as saving money or supporting powerful interests in the society). In addition, many programs cannot be implemented without the active involvement of professionals who make policy and deliver services. But professionals may be in conflict with those who call for performance measurement and have the power or authority to define outcomes for performance. This is of concern to those who deal with measures of performance because the performance movement has set up many expectations and processes that demean professional autonomy.

Onora O'Neill, a well-known British academic who has written widely on political philosophy and ethics, commented on professionalism in the BBC Reith lectures in 2002. She described what she called "the new accountability" as containing detailed control, conformity to procedures and protocols, and "sharp teeth." She noted that the new accountability distorts "the proper aims of professional practice" and "[damages] professional pride and integrity. Much professional practice used to centre on interaction with those whom professionals serve: patients and pupils, students and families in need. Now there is less time to do this because everyone has to record the details of what they do and compile the evidence to protect themselves against the possibility not only of plausible, but of far-fetched complaints."[5]

Concern about professionalism has been one of the areas of study within the field of sociology. This literature, while rarely tapped by those concerned about performance, provides a way to understand the conflict often experienced between the proponents of performance measurement and spokespeople for various professions. Eliot Freidson, one of the premier students of the professions, helps us understand what he calls "the logic" of professionalism and contrasts it with the logic of the market and bureaucracy.[6] As a result, the drive to hold professionals accountable to a particular set of standards creates dynamics and pressures that can lead to ineffective and inappropriate behaviors. Examples of these behaviors that illustrate the conflict between different approaches to professional identity are found in the world of public school teaching, in the practice of medicine, in scientific research, and in university faculties.

Professionals vs. Managers vs. Consumers

Freidson begins his argument by stating that the professions have not defended themselves well. He notes that the professions are divided by different vested interests and inclined to attack each other. "When they do defend themselves they rely primarily on a rhetoric of good intentions which is belied by the patently self-interested character of many of their activities. What they almost never do is spell out the principles underlying the institutions that organize and support the way they do their work and take active responsibility for their realization."[7] His book seeks to establish a framework to understand these principles.

Freidson contrasts "professionals" with consumers or managers. He notes that professionalism is a way for individuals to arrange their own work in a way that gives them the ability to organize that work themselves. By contrast, "market" is a way of organizing work around consumer preferences. And in bureaucracy, managers have the authority to organize their work. As such, he notes that professionalism exists when "an organized occupation gains the power to determine who is qualified to perform a defined set of tasks, to prevent all others from performing that work, and to control the criteria by which to evaluate performance."[8] Professionals—not consumers or managers—have the right to choose or determine the criteria for the choice of the workers or evaluate their work against standards defined by the occupation.

Professionalism, according to Freidson, has two core ideas: "that certain work is so specialized as to be inaccessible to those lacking the required training and experience, and the belief that it cannot be standardized, rationalized or . . . 'commodified.'"[9] Some of the skills involved in professional work are formal, codified and defined in the course of training. Others are tacit—unverbalized or even unverbalizable but not part of a formal or codified technique. For the professional, specialization leads to working and practical knowledge. As is obvious, this leads to a situation in which the profession has what approximates monopolistic control.[10]

Unlike the rhetoric of both the market and bureaucratic perspectives, efficiency is not the primary goal of a professional. It is not clear what is efficient and what is not, and the belief that there is "one best way" to organize work is viewed as problematic. Freidson gives attention to the organization of the bureaucratic labor market that is created and administered neither by consumers nor by workers. He describes it as a labor market that is created by staff members who are responsible to the ultimate authorities of the bureaucratized state, industrial sector, or firm rather than to the producers or consumers of their products. "Their duty is to advance the policies of their superiors, whatever they may be."[11]

Further, he notes, "performance is difficult to assess and ability even more so. In addition to direct testing of an individual's performance of an actual task, some kind of indirect or inferential information must be used if one is to avoid essentially random selection."[12] Training is often the substitute for the performance assessment. Training is usually under the control of the occupation and the faculty providing training provides an important source for sustaining professionalism.[13]

Freidson argues that professions have within them claims, values, and ideas; he writes that these constitute professional ideologies and that these ideologies are the primary tools available to a profession for gaining the political and economic resources needed to establish and maintain their status.[14] This ideology leads to a focus on productivity, not efficiency; an emphasis on quality of work; and the importance of service.

The professional ideology of service goes beyond serving others' choices. Rather, it claims devolution to a transcendent value infusing its specialization with a larger and putatively higher goal, which may reach beyond that of those they are supposed to serve.[15]

He notes that professionals are different from what he calls "mechanical specialization," which emphasizes the production of quantities of goods and services. The specialization that is found in professions emphasizes a "capacity to be flexible and adaptive in dealing with qualitative differences among individual tasks."[16] By contrast, market control's ideology is consumerism, and bureaucratic control's ideology is managerialism. And managerialists prefer generalists over specialists. They also claim the authority to "command, organize, guide, and supervise both the choices of consumers and the productive work of specialists."[17] Freidson reminds his readers that "the ideal-typical ideology of professionalism is one that denies the sovereignty of both the state and lesser clients, asserting independence in serving some transcendent value."[18] He focuses on qualified members of a profession as well as on professional associations as he analyzes professionalism.[19]

Thus, for Freidson, professionalism has five components:

- a body of knowledge and skill based on abstract concepts and theories and requiring the exercise of considerable discretion;
- a division of labor controlled by the needs of the profession;
- a labor market that requires training credentials for entry and career mobility;
- training programs that create credentials for the profession that are separate from those of the ordinary labor market;

- an ideology serving some transcendent value and asserting greater devotion to doing good work than to economic
  gain.[20]

Freidson concludes his work by noting that there is an assault
on the credibility of the professional ideology. He argues that the
assault has created "an atmosphere of distrust that has weakened the
credibility of professional claims to an independent moral voice in
evaluating social policies." By focusing on the monopoly aspect of
professionalism, critics have ignored "the fact that the institutions of
professionalism are grounded not only in an economy but also in
a social enterprise of learning, advancing and practicing a body of
specialized knowledge and skill."[21] While acknowledging that some
degree of monopoly can be subject to abuse, he pleads for a recognition that the professions are not "merely masks for self-interest
and illegitimate power."[22] Further, he notes that the professional
ideology is committed to the quality of work.

Freidson returns to the role of both the market and the bureaucracy. He argues that "[g]reater control by capital and the state over
both performance and cost is likely to be gained in part by inten-
sifying the trend toward a two-tier professional system composed
of a permanent, relatively small elite corps of professionals who do
research and set standards of performance in practice organizations
and an often floating population of qualified practitioners who may
be employed on a temporary and sometimes part-time basis."[23]

Three consequences will result from this two-tiered system.
First, the quality of service to individual clients will change due to
the minimization of discretion in everyday disciplinary work. This
will result in dissatisfaction of line practitioners with their work.
Second, this will lead to the diminution of curiosity and theoretical
interest. And third, if the activities of members become organized
around immediately practical service, they will loss the spirit of
professionalism.[24]

He argues that hierarchical control and standardization of procedure and production is actually "intrinsically at odds with professionalism, since its aim is to reduce discretion as much as possible
so as to maximize the predictability and reliability of its services or
products."

Where service is being provided to individual humans in need, standardization runs the risk of degrading the service to some and failing to serve appropriately those who fall outside the norm. Where research and development are involved, rational-ideal administration may gain its immediate ends but, due to its constraints, point nowhere further than management can imagine. Unanticipated knowledge will be lost.[25]

A few other authors have applied the sociological analysis of writers like Freidson to contemporary developments in democratic theory related to the performance movement. In his important book on the transformation of public bureaucracies around the world, Ezra Suleiman argues that the changes in bureaucracies do occur as a result of reforms "willed by governments under pressure from citizens who insist on better performance." But they are also combined with what he calls the "gradual deprofessionalization of their upper echelons." He comments:

We find that even in European societies with strong traditions of administrative professionalism—Germany, France, Spain, Britain—the encroachment of politics into the administrative domain has been considerable. The reinvention of government, or the introduction of a corporate culture into public administration, needs to be analyzed in conjunction with other transformative forces, some of which have no link to managerial techniques. This is the case with the phenomenon of what I have chosen to call deprofessionalization.[26]

Freidson and Suleiman's analyses suggest a number of issues that are illustrated by current conflicts between performance measurement efforts and professional norms. These conflicts appear to lead to gaming, creaming, and other nonproductive behaviors by professionals. They tend to accentuate conflict between professional norms and bureaucratic approaches, particularly those related to cost-cutting. In the name of accountability, they seem to increase politicized stances that lose sight of the goals of programs and policies. And they illustrate how different professionals are able to deal with performance measurement requirements because of their status within the society. Four examples are discussed that relate to these issues: teachers and the No Child Left Behind program; health professionals and the Health Plan Employer Data and Information Set; academic researchers and the Committee on Science, Engineering, and Public Policy of the National Academy of Sciences, the National Academy of Engineering, and the Institute of Medicine; and higher education and the Research Assessment Exercise in Great Britain.

Controlling Teachers with No Child Left Behind (NCLB)

Three days after taking office in January 2001, George W. Bush announced *No Child Left Behind,* his framework for bipartisan education reform that he described as "the cornerstone of my administration." President Bush emphasized his deep belief in our public schools, but an even greater concern that "too many of our neediest children are being left behind," despite the nearly $200 billion in federal spending since the passage of the Elementary and Secondary Education Act of 1965 (ESEA). The president called for bipartisan solutions based on accountability, choice, and flexibility in federal education programs. According to the Department of Education, "The new law reflects a remarkable consensus—first articulated in the President's *No Child Left Behind* framework—on how to improve the performance of America's elementary and secondary schools while at the same time ensuring that no child is trapped in a failing school."[27]

The department emphasized what they called four "pillars" of the act; the first was termed "stronger accountability for results."

> Under *No Child Left Behind,* states are working to close the achievement gap and make sure all students, including those who are disadvantaged, achieve academic proficiency. Annual state and school district report cards inform parents and communities about state and school progress. Schools that do not make progress must provide supplemental services, such as free tutoring or after-school assistance; take

corrective actions; and, if still not making adequate yearly progress after five years, make dramatic changes to the way the school is run.[28]

In addition, the other pillars involved "more freedom for states and communities," use of "proven education methods," and "more choices for parents."

The legislation was constructed on top of the existing federal program for elementary and secondary education—Title I of the Elementary and Secondary Education Act (ESEA), originally enacted in 1965. The effort was described as a way to impose national accountability standards on a decentralized educational system that had high levels of discretion at both the state and local levels of government. The standards would be contained in standardized tests that would be given to students across the nation. In addition, it included a focus on teachers. The program requires states to measure the extent to which all students have highly qualified teachers (particularly minority and disadvantaged students). Qualified teachers are defined as individuals with subject matter competency, years of experience, past and current training and flexibility. It also requires them to adopt goals and plans to ensure that all teachers are qualified and to report their plans and progress in meeting these goals.

According to the Department of Education:

> The NCLB Act will strengthen Title I accountability by requiring States to implement statewide accountability systems covering all public schools and students. These systems must be based on challenging State standards in reading and mathematics, annual testing for all students in grades 3–8, and annual statewide progress objectives ensuring that all groups of students reach proficiency within 12 years. Assessment results and State progress objectives must be broken out by poverty, race, ethnicity, disability, and limited English proficiency to ensure that no group is left behind. School districts and schools that fail to make adequate yearly progress (AYP) toward statewide proficiency goals will, over time, be subject to improvement, corrective action, and restructuring measures aimed at getting them

back on course to meet State standards. Schools that meet or exceed AYP objectives or close achievement gaps will be eligible for State Academic Achievement Awards.[29]

When the legislation was debated and developed, it received the support of both of the two largest and most powerful organizations (usually described as unions) representing the teaching profession. The American Federation of Teachers (AFT) supported the legislation, noting that "the legislation—though far from perfect—embraced a number of positive measures the AFT has long championed, particularly accountability for the progress of all students and high standards around core academic subjects." Further,

> The AFT remains firmly committed to NCLB's goals and supportive of the framework that embraces standards and accountability and the guarantee of a high-quality education for all of our children. We support quality assessments, disaggregation of data that focuses attention on the needs of children who require additional help, the requirement that all children be taught by highly qualified teachers and that paraprofessionals be well prepared to assist in the classroom (ibid).[30]

Similarly, the National Education Association (NEA) supported the goals of the program, commenting that "[a]ccountability in education is important, and the NEA and its affiliates are working with parents and policy makers at all levels to make sure that state assessments provide regular, reliable feedback on how students, teachers, and schools are faring under the new ESEA."[31]

While committed to the general goals of the legislation, the teachers' organizations have identified a series of problems that were viewed as obstacles to what they believed to be the goals of NCLB. These concerns largely stem from the professional values and perspective of classroom teachers. Perhaps the most public and professional concern focuses on the role of testing in this process.

NEA actually developed its own accountability system that sought to address their concern about testing. The organization commented that "educators are concerned that a solitary focus on testing ignores important opportunities to help all students achieve at high levels. Over-reliance on testing could have the unintended consequence of hurting more than helping. . . . Instead of just applying more tests, NEA calls for smarter testing that also provides students and schools the tools they need to succeed."[32]

In addition, the NEA's proposal—called Testing Plus—called for:

- More thorough measures that reflect the complexity of school organizations. They called for multiple indicators that include dropout rates, absenteeism, number of students taking advanced placement courses, and parental involvement.

- Improved tests and assessments that include alternatives to the "less than perfect measures of student or school progress." These tests should be developed in cooperation with teachers. And classroom assessment practices should include the use of portfolios, projects, and performance assessments that are included in professional development efforts.

- Comprehensive reporting to parents that expands the report data, including information on multiple indicators of success.

- Alternatives to a test as the sole means of accountability. This would expand the accountability process to include school accreditation, visiting teams, and displays of student work to the public. Test scores give little data to improve school operation.[33]

The AFT also listed a number of problems that they described as "serious flaws in the law and its implementation that must be fixed." These included the following:

- The adequate yearly progress formula does not give schools sufficient credit for improvements in student achievement.

- Many of the so-called failing schools and districts are being identified more for statistical than educational reasons. Many of the students started further behind, and the system does not acknowledge the progress that has been made.

- A large number of students with disabilities who are performing well below grade level are to be measured against grade-level standards.

- The "highly qualified" teacher requirements are unworkable for some teachers and do not apply to all individuals who teach public school students.

- The public school choice provision is designed in a way that can undermine schools rather than improve student achievement.[34]

AFT also proposed its own program even before the NCLB legislation; the Redesigning Schools to Raise Achievements (RSRA) program places a priority on low-performing schools. It helps AFT locals forge partnerships with school district leaders to turn around low-performing schools and provides technical assistance in applying the proven approaches it recommends.[35]

Because public education is a highly visible and intense policy issue, many of the concerns that were voiced by the NEA and the AFT actually became a part of a public debate over NCLB. Daily newspapers as well as public policy periodicals became the source for the concerns. Some teachers expressed apprehension that the NCLB requirements would not allow them to behave in a way that was consistent with their training and professional norms and removed their ability to exercise their individual judgment.

Education writer Jay Mathews of the *Washington Post* asked his readers for stories about how NCLB was affecting children in public school classrooms. The response pointed to both strengths and weaknesses of the law, but the negative messages far outnumbered the positive ones. His article summarizing the response included almost a dozen instances of teachers around the country expressing concern about the implementation of the law. Mathews also cited a survey by the Council for Basic Education that documented the squeeze on social studies, civics, geography, languages, and the arts because teachers had to prepare for tests in reading, writing, and math that forced cancellation of other pursuits that some teachers and parents considered valuable.[36]

Much of the criticism about NCLB focused on the role of standardized tests. At the same time, critics of the status quo argued that the exercise of individual judgment by teachers was not addressing the needs of poor and disadvantaged children and that defining specific requirements through standardized tests removed ineffective discretion and would thus lead to improved performance.

One researcher, Richard Rothstein, wrote about standardized tests; while he acknowledged that they had a place in evaluating both schools and students, he noted that "they are of little use in assessing creativity, insight, reasoning and the application of skills to unrehearsed situations—each an important part of what a high-quality school should be teaching. Such things can be assessed, but not easily and not in a standardized fashion." He also argued that "its incentives are functioning instead to lower state sights to existing levels of student achievement . . . and are distorting teaching as well."[37] According to the American Educational Research Association, studies have shown "that teachers reallocate their time to emphasize the subjects on state tests at the expense of nontested subjects. Even within content areas, teachers shift the focus of lessons to stress the material on the state exams."[38]

A teacher in a Northern Virginia public school classroom at the time when the state's Standards of Learning (SOLs) were instituted described his teaching in a low-scoring school. "I taught learning-disabled kids, then English as a second language (ESL), then 'regular' classes and eventually in an International Baccalaureate program. I can trace my evolution—from a creative young teacher to one straightjacketed by SOLs—through the strata of marbled composition books stacked in my shed. . . . More frequent SOL 'reviews' consisting of multiple-choice questions had all but wiped out the in-class writing that had been the basis of my class."[39]

A number of the critics of the requirements found that they operated as a blunt instrument and were not sensitive to the realities of a particular classroom or school. A principal in another northern Virginia school that was among the top public schools in America found it disturbing that his school was ranked as failing to make adequate yearly progress. "That's the problem with the NCLB," the principal commented. "We are generally acknowledged to be one of the best schools in the country, and yet we got graded as failing. We were going to appeal this in some way, and I think we could have prevailed. But we wanted people to see the ridiculousness—the lack of flexibility—in the approach."[40]

The responses to standardized tests and the data requirements did not always evoke what its proponents expected. In Virginia, the state-defined Standards of Learning exams seem to have contributed to an increase in the dropout rate in the state's high schools. An increase of approximately 4 percent has been anticipated and became the basis for a request that state educators investigate graduation rates and their connection to the SOL exams.[41] However, the number of students who did not graduate from high school in the spring of 2004 solely because of their performance on state standardized tests appeared to be fewer than some expected.[42]

A report by The Education Trust, usually one of the major supporters of NCLB, found that states were not honest in the way that they reported graduation rates. The Trust found that some states rely on ludicrous definitions of graduation rates and resulted in "extremely unreliable graduation-rate information that erodes public confidence in schools and their leadership and threatens to undermine the important work of high school reform."[43]

In Texas, Houston public schools were put on probation for severely underreporting high school dropouts. A state audit of sixteen schools found that fifteen had vastly underreported dropout numbers. This was particularly sensitive because Rod Paige, the federal education secretary who ran the Houston schools as superintendent from 1994 to early 2001, reported sharp drops in the dropout rate. As a result of the audit, state officials required the city to hire an outside consultant to address the way it tracked students who quit school and assigned a state monitor to oversee their effort.[44]

In Florida, the number of youngsters who must repeat third grade is about five times greater than students who repeat second grade because of a policy that bases promotion largely on the Florida Comprehensive Assessment Test. One Florida principal commented: "These children will either become so angry they're going to be aggressive and discipline problems, or be so demoralized and heartbroken and depressed. . . . This is real to me, because this is my life's work. This is what I do. I know that these children are going to drop out."[45]

A retired Iowa elementary school principal described the legislation as generating "increasing amounts of fear, anger and unjust blame." He commented, "It's hard to tell whether this law is more a product of arrogance or ignorance, but either way it's shaping up to be a spectacular train wreck of a collision between bureaucracy and reality."[46]

Although the NCLB legislation establishes specific requirements for transfer of students who have low test scores, fiscal limitations have limited the ability of a number of school districts to carry out those requirements. For example, 68 of the 149 schools in the District of Columbia failed for the second time in a row to make adequate yearly progress in reading and math. NCLB stipulates that students must be offered the option of transferring to another school. However, there are not enough open slots at higher-performing schools to make this possible because of budget limitations.[47] One commentator described the failure of the governor of New York to support additional resources for students in New York City as "hypocrisy" as he raised academic requirements but fought against additional resources.[48] According to one study of transfers in New York City, about a third of the 8,000 transfers "—children often traveling over an hour to attend crowded schools—have been moved from one school labeled failing under the law to another failing school."[49]

A study of public schools in California also indicated that schools with diverse student populations are far more likely than those with homogeneous populations to be labeled as failing. PACE, Policy Analysis for California Education, found that many teachers and principals agree with NCLB. "Yet the complicated regulations pushed into schools to accomplish this virtuous goal have come to resemble, in the minds of many educators, a mine field—a harrowing set of trip wires that can easily detonate consequential explosions." These may "bring down their school, even when performance is rising, differing only in demographic diversity."[50] There are instances in which students who have limited English speaking ability improve their English but, as a result, move into another category, which makes it "virtually impossible for districts to demonstrate progress."[51]

When a school district or state educational system confronts widespread failure in the exams, there has been a tendency for those districts to change the test substance or to set aside the results.[52] In some cases, the emphasis on tests has led to cheating by teachers, where teachers "read off answers during a test, sent students back to correct wrong answers, photocopied secure tests for use in class, inflated scores and peeked at questions then drilled those topics in class before the test."[53]

Other impacts of the type of performance system found in NCLB have been documented by researchers who have examined how an accountability system is likely to affect the ability of schools with large proportions of low-performing students or that are labeled as low performing to attract and retain high-quality teachers. This study of North Carolina's schools found that the state's accountability system has "exacerbated the problems that low performing schools face in attracting and retaining high quality teachers, to the detriment of the students they serve."[54]

While the testing requirements are the key component of the No Child Left Behind Act, another requirement involves a stipulation that all of the nation's teachers be "highly qualified" by the 2005–2006 school year. These requirements have created what one observer called "a massive paperwork shuffle." Further, according to this observer, "Teachers are also grimacing at the law's requirements, taking the act's 'highly qualified' demands as something of an insult. They largely view the problems facing schools as systemic and don't like the idea that they are being held accountable for problems beyond their control."[55]

There is a range of problems that were faced by teachers with the NCLB. They included problems of implementation, impacts that appear to lessen the creativity of teachers, "gaming" processes, and policies that require teachers to teach to the test. While these problems did not appear in all of the nation's school systems, they were found in many places around the country. For some teachers, the reliance on standardized tests did accentuate conflict between professional norms and what became bureaucratic requirements. During the second term of the Bush administration, resistance by some states has led to measures to ease up on federal requirements. While these changes did provide opportunities for more flexibility for school districts, in some instances they fed a growing sense of cynicism by teachers that did not lead to more effective teaching.

The first nationwide test to permit an appraisal of NCLB indicated that there were mixed results from the law's implementation and that even some supporters of the law were expressing disappointment with the results. Indeed, by some measures, students were making greater gains before the law was put into effect.[56]

Health Professionals: Assessing Performance Inside the Profession

The experience of the teaching profession involving performance assessment is clearly embedded in the perceptions of the larger society about teachers. It is rare for U.S. citizens to perceive public school teachers as high-status individuals who possess valuable specialized skills that warrant deference and discretion. In addition, because of local tax systems that collect separate monies for education, most citizens are aware of the relationship between their tax dollars and the educational sector.

Health professionals—particularly medical doctors—provide a contrast with educators.[57] Physicians have high status within the society; not only does the profession establish barriers to entering and remaining in the profession, but patients have a special relationship with their doctors because these individuals are viewed as the gatekeepers to life or death. And, until recently, many individuals were actually unaware of the cost of medical care because their costs were buried within insurance coverage. Given this, it is not surprising that the experience of the medical profession regarding performance assessment is quite different from that of public school teachers.

Much of the activity involving performance measurement in health parallels the development of the managed care approach to paying and delivering health services. In 1990, the National Committee for Quality Assurance was formed to fill what was identified as an accountability and accreditation void in the health field. It defined its mission as the improvement of the quality of health care for all and sought to become the trusted source of information driving health care quality improvement. In 1992, NCQA created a national system to develop and provide standardized performance measures. Known as the Health Plan Employer Data and Information Set (HEDIS), the system was designed to allow employers and consumers to make comparisons of performance among health care organizations. More than three hundred health plans across the country now provide data for the system.

One observer, writing in 1998, noted,

> Our attempts to systematically measure the quality of care are less than a decade old and still very much in their

methodological adolescence. The delay in getting started can be explained by a variety of factors: a general assumption that quality was high, the implied insult to the medical profession and discomfort to the public that comes with measuring performance, and the fact that substandard performance is largely invisible except through a statistical lens. It took exposés of poor quality and questions from purchasers about what they were getting for their money to push performance measurement ahead.[58]

In 1998, three of the nation's preeminent health care accrediting organizations—the American Medical Association's Accreditation Program (AMAP), the Joint Commission on Accreditation of Healthcare Organizations (JCAHO), and NCQA—announced a collaborative effort designed to coordinate performance measurement activities across the entire health care system. The three groups established the Performance Measurement Coordinating Council, a fifteen-member group that "seeks to ensure that measurement driven assessment processes are efficient, consistent and useful for the many parties that rely on them to help make important decisions about health care."[59]

Each of the three organizations involved in the collaborative effort defined performance measurement at different levels of the health care system. The AMAP focused on standards of quality for the individual physician; JCAHO accredits a range of health care facilities including organizations providing acute care, home care, clinical laboratory services, long term care, and managed care; NCQA had already been involved in an accreditation and performance measurement program through HEDIS for groups such as health maintenance organizations.

A consensus statement titled "Principles for Performance Measurement in Health Care" outlined

- the rationale behind performance measurement efforts;
- appropriate uses of performance data;
- specific areas on which measures should focus;
- guidelines for using performance data for comparative purposes;

- general requirements for cost-effective measurement; and
- specific opportunities for collaboration.[60]

Others were also involved in the effort to assess and improve the nation's quality of care. The Institute of Medicine of the National Academy of Sciences began an effort in 1996; "Crossing the Quality Chasm" documented the serious and pervasive nature of health quality through a series of reports and meetings. The Agency for Healthcare Research and Quality in the U.S. Department of Health and Human Services was designed to support research that would help improve the quality, safety, efficiency, and effectiveness of health care.

The collaborative effort represented an attempt by the health care industry to accomplish multiple purposes. First, it was a way to develop and publish norms for clinical behavior in a wide range of fields. As such, it served as a strategy for the industry to address public concern about health care quality, including questions about medical errors, and to increase the level of transparency and accountability in medical practice. It provided a way of comparing the quality of care being delivered by different entities. Second, it was a way to highlight the importance of clinical competence in the health profession. As the American College of Physicians wrote, "As we consider better ways to recognize and compensate physicians who care for patients with multiple and chronic diseases, performance measures could provide the mechanism by which we reward and foster higher quality care."[61] Third, the effort provided the information for HMOs and insurance companies to establish specific expectations about what will be reimbursed and allowed. Fourth, performance measurement also provides information that is useful to researchers who are attempting to describe the effect of some intervention on a specified group of patients. Jha et al. have noted that "[h]ow good a measure is depends heavily on its purpose. One common error is to take a measure that was designed to track outcomes . . . and try to use it to compare plans."[62]

There is significant dispute about the impact of the guidelines that have been developed to assist practitioner and patient decisions about appropriate health care. One study published in the *Journal of the American Medical Association* argued, "Despite wide promulgation, guidelines have had limited effect on changing physician behavior. In general, little is known about the process and factors responsible for how physicians change their practice methods when they become aware of a guideline." The review of the literature in this article found that physicians may not follow clinical practice guidelines because of lack of awareness, lack of familiarity, lack of agreement, lack of self-efficacy, lack of outcome expectancy, the inertia of previous practice, and external barriers.[63]

Despite some skepticism, it was not surprising that the availability of this data created a set of dynamics that moved beyond the original concerns of those involved in creating a set of performance measures. Originally focused on behaviors in the private sector, the availability of the HEDIS measures moved them to be used in the public sector both for performance requirements and for reimbursement policies. Some of the measures became the basis for the federal government in the Centers for Medicare and Medicaid Services to issue reporting requirements in Medicare. And some states used them as requirements for health plans participating in Medicaid programs. Efforts to modify the Veterans Health Administration in the U.S. Department of Veterans Affairs relied on the HEDIS measures as well as the measures used by the Joint Commission on Accreditation of Healthcare Organizations for inpatient care.[64] The government organizations varied in their use of HEDIS; some used them to create standards for service while others used them as a way to limit costs.

As the years have progressed, the quality focus of the measures seems to have been overpowered by a concern about cost savings. This agenda has pushed away clinically sensitive measures and highlighted measures devised by individual companies and some government agencies. Health practitioners who are concerned about quality and service to their patients complain about bluntness, distortion, incompleteness, and cost of the measures.[65] For example, a typology known as the DSM typology is being used by insurance companies that are third parties designated by government agencies or other medical payers to actually determine whether psychiatrists are providing appropriate treatment. However, this typology was developed for research purposes, not for determining reimbursement.

In addition, the Global Assessment of Function requires a psychiatrist to provide a specific numerical score that is difficult for some clinicians to apply (especially if they know that a specific score will determine whether the treatment will be reimbursed). The doctor is required to provide detailed proposed treatment based on a code that provides estimates of time as well as medication. Increasingly, the review of these treatment plans is not done by doctors but by nurses who do not have the same expectations about professional autonomy.

One physician commented on the situation:

> The pressures are fierce for doctors to compromise their professionalism, their humane instincts, for business reasons. . . . While it is true that we still make a decent living, at the same time we must hire more and more staff members to handle certifications, precertifications and referrals while also accepting lower payments. . . . But it's not just about doctors' incomes. Even if physicians decided not to worry about profit margins but simply to concentrate on giving all their patients the kind of attention [they need] . . . the HMOs would not stand for it. Never mind that, in my experience, it takes at least half an hour to legitimately address a patient's problems and handle the required paperwork. The HMOs make their payments on the basis of 10- to 15-minute patient visits on the average.[66]

Cost control mechanisms have also been created on top of the performance measures by government agencies. One such effort is the PATH project—Physicians at Teaching Hospitals. It is an initiative designed by the federal government to verify compliance with Medicare rules governing payment for physician services provided in the teaching setting and to ensure that claims accurately reflect the level of service provided to patients. Some university-based hospitals argue that the system that was put in place is "an unfair application of vague federal guidelines regarding physician presence and imprecise evaluation and management codes."[67]

Increasingly, as the public sector is focusing on cost savings, the HEDIS and other health performance measurement systems will be attached to reimbursement decisions. At the same time, enforcement of such standards appears to be uneven and reflects political decisions about imposition of penalties. A decline of 18 percent in the number of nursing homes penalized for violations of federal standards, a decline of 12 percent in the number of monetary penalties imposed, and a decline of 47 percent in the number of nursing homes denied Medicare or Medicaid payment for new admissions are evidence of improved quality to some, and, to others, evidence of less emphasis on enforcement.[68]

Thus, despite the high status of health professionals in the society, their effort to focus on quality seems to have collided with imperatives of cost savings and cost control. This conflict between quality and efficiency has led to the beginnings of gaming within the system. Unlike teachers with NCLB, the health professionals were more active participants in the standards devised through the HEDIS program. Those standards emerged from definitions of good medical practice within the profession. In that sense, they did not represent a conflict between professional norms and formal requirements. However, the use of those standards moved from practice recommendations to bureaucratic efforts to control costs. The HEDIS experience suggests that performance standards do have a life of their own, and even when professionals are engaged in their development and definition, they may be used in unanticipated ways.

Researchers and Performance Management

While it is not unusual for federal government agencies to have difficulties complying with the Government Performance and Results Act (GPRA; see chapter 6), federal organizations that are engaged in research have been able to develop alternative approaches to the GPRA requirements largely because of a stipulation in the federal legislation. The legislation contains a proviso that allows an agency (in consultation with OMB) to determine that it is not feasible to express performance goals in an "objective, quantifiable, and measurable form."[69] The legislation gives an agency an opportunity to describe a minimally effective and successful program and to state why the agency cannot express a performance goal in any way for the program activity.

It became clear to research agencies that it was difficult to link results with annual investments in research. In 1998, the Committee on Science, Engineering, and Public Policy (COSEPUP) of the National Academy of Sciences, the National Academy of Engineering, and the Institute of Medicine began a study to identify and analyze the most effective ways to assess the results of research; help the federal government determine how its agencies can better incorporate research activities in strategic and performance plans; and develop mechanisms to evaluate the effects of implementing GPRA on agency program decisions and on the practices of research. The activities of this committee were detailed in a report, *Evaluating Federal Research Programs*, issued in February 1999.[70] It drew on the experience of ten federal agencies that had significant research activities within their portfolios.

In its report, COSEPUP reported that it had heard two distinct and conflicting viewpoints on approaches to measuring basic research.

> One is that it should be possible to measure research, including basic research, annually and provide quantitative measures of the useful outcomes of both basic and applied research. The other is that, given the long-range nature of basic research, there is no sensible way to respond to the GPRA annual measurement requirement and that the best that can be done is to provide measures that appear to respond but in fact are essentially meaningless, such as a list of an agency's top 100 discoveries of the preceding year.[71]

COSEPUP defined a position that was different from both of these viewpoints. It argued that outcomes of basic research cannot be measured directly on an annual basis "because the usefulness of basic research is inherently too unpredictable; so the usefulness of basic research must be measured by historical reviews based on a much longer time frame." At the same time, the committee found that there are "meaningful measures of quality, relevance, and leadership that are good predictors of eventual usefulness, that these measures can be reported regularly, and that they represent a sound way to ensure that the country is getting a good return on its basic research investment."[72] For example, the National Institutes of Health often presents its performance in what are called "stories of discovery." These "stories" define performance in terms of the process of scientific analysis rather than in terms of anticipated outcomes. This method is particularly useful in instances in which scientists find that negative findings lead them to unanticipated discoveries.

The committee found that the most effective way to evaluate federally funded research programs is expert review. This included quality review, relevance review, and benchmarking.[73] The report noted that "peer review is the method by which science exercises continuous self-evaluation and correction. It is the centerpiece of many federal agencies' approach to evaluating proposed, current, and past research in science and engineering. Peer review, like all human judgments, can be affected by self-interest, especially the favoritism of friendship and prejudice of antagonism. However, those distortions can be minimized by the rigor of peer selection, the integrity and independence of individual reviewers, and the use of bibliometric analysis and other quantitative techniques to complement the subject nature of peer review."[74]

These activities represented an effort by the research community to speak with one voice and, while acknowledging the differences among various research enterprises, to highlight the professional norms surrounding the research enterprise, particularly peer review and what is called "sound science." In the early years of the twenty-first century, however, the language of the research community appeared to some to be reinterpreted in quite a different way. According to one commentator,

> the phrases "sound science" and "peer review" don't necessarily mean what you might think. Instead, they're part of a lexicon used to put a pro-science veneer on policies that most of the scientific community itself tends to be up in arms about. In this Orwellian vocabulary, "peer review" isn't simply an evaluation by learned colleagues. Instead, it appears to mean an industry-friendly plan to require such exhaustive analysis that federal agencies could have a hard time taking prompt action to protect public health and the environment."[75]

The peer review proposal that had been issued by OMB was eventually modified and its prescriptive and restrictive requirements were reduced after an outcry from researchers, advocacy groups, and some federal agencies.[76] These groups found that the OMB-proposed process was a way to impose a political agenda defined by the White House on what they believed to be scientific issues.

But perhaps the strongest criticism of the policies of the Bush administration related to research came from a report issued by the Union of Concerned Scientists and signed by sixty leading scientists, including twenty Nobel laureates. The report called for restoring scientific integrity in policymaking.

> When scientific knowledge has been found to be in conflict with its political goals, the administration has often manipulated the process through which science enters into its decisions. This has been done by placing people who are professionally unqualified or who have clear conflicts of interest in official posts and on scientific advisory committees; by disbanding existing advisory committees; by censoring and suppressing reports by the government's own scientists; and by simply not seeking independent scientific advice. Other administrations have, on occasion, engaged in such practices, but not so systematically nor on so wide a front. Furthermore, in advocating policies that are not scientifically sound, the administration has sometimes misrepresented scientific knowledge and misled the public about the implications of its policies.[77]

The report provoked a response both from the president's science advisor and from visible members of science advisory groups, both of whom argued that the document was more political than scientific.

In December 2004, a report from the Committee on Science, Engineering, and Public Policy of the National Academy of Sciences also argued that candidates for federal advisory panels on science and technology should be chosen for their expertise and not for their politics. It wrote:

Many factors—including societal values, economic costs, and political judgments—come together with technical judgments in the process of reaching advisory committee recommendations. . . . Scientists, engineers and health professionals nominated primarily to provide S and T [Science and Technology] input should be selected for their scientific and technical knowledge and credentials and for their professional and personal integrity . . . . [I]t is no more appropriate to ask S&T experts to provide nonrelevant information, such as hair color or height, than to ask them for other personal and immaterial information, such as voting record, political-party affiliation, or position on a particular policy.[78]

Although researchers were able to use their high status within the society to be treated differently within the GPRA process, the budgetary demands and ideological approaches led to a range of problems that had the impact of politicizing the "scientific" process. This example indicates that a political agenda can be imposed on what is viewed as the purview of the professionals. In the name of accountability, the discretion of the professional researcher has been challenged using the highly regarded process of peer review. Professional norms have been subjected to bureaucratic approaches, particularly those related to cost-cutting.

Auditing Higher Education

For more than a decade, a growing number of institutions both in the United States and in other countries have developed an approach to achieve quality improvements through academic audits. These audits are one of the ways that performance measurement has been used to become a part of the decision-making process involving both policy changes and budget allocations. As such, they provide an example of the spread of performance measurement in the higher education sector beyond the United States. The effort began in Great Britain around 1990 and has spread across the globe. According to one of its advocates: "The objective of an academic audit is to elicit thoughtful conversations about how to produce tangible improvements in education quality without having to spend more money. . . . [A]cademic auditors evaluate what are coming to be called 'education-quality processes'—the key faculty activities required to produce, assure, and regularly improve the quality of teaching and learning."[79]

In 2003, Burke and Minassians conducted the seventh annual survey of state higher education finance officers and found that performance reporting had spread to all but four states. Burke and Minassians had distinguished between three behaviors in the field—performance funding, performance budgeting, and performance reporting. Performance funding ties state funding directly and tightly to the performance of public campuses; performance budgeting allows governors, legislators, and others to consider campus achievement on performance indicators as one factor in determining allocations for public campuses; and performance reporting provides periodic reports on priority indicators but has no formal link to allocations. In Freidson's terms, the process moved away from a bureaucratic approach to one that reflected professional norms as well as market principles.[80]

The survey found that performance reporting is the preferred approach to accountability for higher education. At the same time that performance funding and performance budgeting slipped in states, performance reporting increased from 30 to 46 programs from 2000 to 2003. The authors suggest that performance reporting allows a longer list of indicators than performance budgeting and funding; that reports are sent to a broad range of stakeholders both on campuses and in the larger political environment; and that these reports rely on information and publicity rather than funding or budgeting to encourage colleges and universities to improve their performance.[81]

Unlike the United States, where public higher education has historically been the purview of states and is often eclipsed by the practices of private universities and colleges, higher education policy in Great Britain has been a national policy effort. In the 1990s, Britain became concerned about the use of its scarce resources to support high-quality research.[82]

Each university is expected to use the resources allocated on research-based criteria primarily for research and not teaching, which is financed separately. Institutions prepare standard statistical and narrative material for submission to central panels for assessment; this information is purely documentary and there are no site visits and no appeals of the panel decisions. A five-point criterion referenced scale was established and panels considered all types of research: applied, strategic, and basic.[83]

Each individual faculty member is required to report research production within twelve categories:

- Authored books
- Edited books
- Short works
- Conference contributions, refereed
- Conference contributions, other
- Editorships
- Papers in academic journals
- Papers in professional journals
- Papers in popular journals
- Reviews of academic books
- Other publications
- Other public output.

Called the Research Assessment Exercise (RAE), the exercise is designed to enable funding to be allocated selectively but also to promote high quality. The government department charged with implementing higher education policy (the Department for Education and Skills) defined three goals for the process: (1) to target resources in the best research institutions; (2) to make sure that the very best individual departments are not neglected; (3) to encourage the formation of consortia and collaborative work.[84] The process operates through sixty assessment panels whose members are nominated by a range of organizations, including research associations, learned societies, professional bodies, and those representing industrial, business, and other users of research.[85]

Another round of this process is scheduled for 2008. It has provoked significant criticism in the British higher education community. According to one observer:

Research is at a crossroads in British universities. The government recognizes its importance for the knowledge economy but even though funding is being increased, there will never be enough for all the avenues of new knowledge that academics want to explore.

The upshot is another bruising round in the contest between the perfectionists, who insist that only the best research deserves to be funded—if it's not world class, its not worth doing—and the pragmatists, who want research effort to be widely diffused on the grounds that (a) it's essential for university-level teaching and (b) research does not have to be world class to benefit the local or regional economy of the university concerned.[86]

Members of the Association of University Teachers (AUT) criticized the RAE for contributing to the closure of departments in subjects like chemistry and engineering, pointing to difficulties comparing pure and applied research. An organization called Save British Science argued that the process was pushing scientists into safe research and that many departments had improved their grades but received less money. [87]

The AUT argued that universities were "games playing" by transferring staff that were seen as weak researchers onto teaching-only contracts or easing them out. It was reported that funding had become increasingly concentrated in fewer institutions and academics are fighting to retain their research links. A representative of the AUT commented that there was an impact of "strategic exclusions on women and ethnic minority staff. In particular, there is the impact of producing research publications on those staff who have taken career breaks or women staff on maternity leave.[88]

At this writing, there is growing pressure for the postponement of the 2008 process and rethinking the use of metric data, particularly as it applies to arts and humanities subjects. Although higher education has a tradition of high status in Britain, there are alternative pressures on the system, particularly the demand for spreading resources across the range of both elite and nonelite institutions. Thus the impact of this process—leading to creaming of the top institutions—became a problem, particularly for a Labour government. This example illustrates the difficulty in turning a highly formalized set of standards into a mechanized decision process. The process in Britain produced distributional results that were not a part of the government's game plan. While the elite institutions were able to do well within the decision rules because their faculty were already productive in terms of research, the rules actually created results that over-measured research to the detriment of teaching. Thus some of the academic professionals did well but others were penalized for their investment in particular subject areas and inability to meet defined outcome measures.

Conclusion

Eliot Freidson's typology provides a useful way to think about the behaviors of these four performance efforts that all involve professional identity. These examples illustrate the conflict between professionalism and bureaucratic behaviors, especially efforts to control service delivery for both substantive but—more important—for cost savings and control agendas. The irony remains, however, that all of these examples require the active involvement of professionals in order for desired performance to occur.

No Child Left Behind involved diminished discretion for teachers (and some would argue lessening of creativity for teachers), use of standardized tests across different classrooms and schools, a verbal commitment to children who had not been high achievers, and an increased role for the federal government. NCLB did not emerge as a result of interaction or even involvement of representatives of teachers' organizations; rather, it was imposed on a profession that did not have high status in the society. Various types of problems emerged from this process; many of them involved gaming by teachers and school systems to meet requirements.

The health professionals' activity began with an effort to establish norms that would improve the quality of health care. The medical establishment (such as the AMA) was intimately involved in the development of the standards and seemed to view the HEDIS measures as a way of assuring that these standards met the profession's view of best practices. However, as the effort was used by those who paid for health services, there was a conflict between a quality effort and expectations of cost savings and control. It appears that various games are being played out in a conflict between quality and efficiency.

The research example suggests that even when a profession has developed its own definition of accountability, those efforts can be politicized. The peer review process has been used by the research community as a way to assure that quality standards of research are met. However, when those in positions of power do not agree with the results of peer review, they can redefine who is a "peer." They can make sure that individuals who share their views are appointed to review committees and can establish procedures that constrain the traditional research values. The high status of the research community has meant that there has been public criticism of these efforts.

The higher education example provides evidence of difficulties and unanticipated consequences of moving performance information into a structured and technocratic decision process. Relying on one set of indicators (even those that seem to represent professional values) does not allow decision makers to look at a range of other goals and objectives beyond research productivity. Even when professionals were involved in establishing the indicators, they were unable to think about other factors that would be considered in the allocation of resources.

These examples indicate that professionals vary in terms of their status within the society, and the norms of each profession lead to a range of problems. However, it appears that the imperative of cost savings and fiscal control that is associated with the bureaucratic approach appears to be overpowering the role of professionals.

In addition, these examples illustrate a number of other issues. First, in all four cases, professional organizations have played an important role but have had difficulty keeping bureaucratic (and political) pressures at bay. Second, professionals seek to maximize their discretion and space to innovate that usually flows from their training and role. They are clearly uncomfortable with efforts to establish "one best way" practices that minimize their ability to try new things, to adapt and be creative. Third, while supporting the goals of performance measurement, professionals live in a world of complex goals where they are often faced with conflict between quality standards and efficiency standards. Fourth, it appears that efforts to establish bureaucratic control over performance assessment have created a new set of internal problems within the profession as well as differential impacts that may conflict with the norms of the profession. These norms include values of service as well as ethical independence. And finally, these efforts may give rhetorical attention to consumers and the market approach, but the reality of the economy and social structure make efforts to rely on consumer choice seem hollow.

Dr. Robert Peacock has to live with these competing demands. He may attempt to draw on the norms that are found within the HEDIS system as a way to discuss alternative approaches with the HMO management. He may also try to contact other practitioners who deal with comparable patient pools to show the HMO that in the long run it makes more sense to respond to the problems today than to wait until they require even more expensive hospitalization and tests.

Notes

1. Pew Research Center for the People and the Press, "Institution Approval Trends." Data received 30 July 2004.
2. Sheldon Rampton and John Stauber, *Trust Us We're Experts!* (New York: Jeremy P. Tarcher, Putnam, 2002), 3–4. The book focuses on the role of the public relations industry in this set of behaviors.
3. Barbara S. Romzek and Melvin J. Dubnick, "Accountability in the Public Sector: Lessons from the Challenger Tragedy," *Public Administration Review* 47, no. 3 (May–June 1987): 229.
4. Romzek and Dubnick, "Accountability in the Public Sector," 233.
5. Onora O'Neill, "A Question of Trust," BBC Radio, Reith Lectures, 2002, http://www.bbc.co.uk/radio4/reith2002/lecture3.shtml. Italics in original removed.
6. Eliot Freidson, *Professionalism, The Third Logic: On the Practice of Knowledge* (Chicago: The University of Chicago Press, 2001).
7. Ibid., *Professionalism*, 3.
8. Ibid., *Professionalism*, 12.

9. Ibid., *Professionalism*, 17.

10. Ibid., *Professionalism*, 33.

11. Ibid., *Professionalism*, 67.

12. Ibid., *Professionalism*, 80.

13. Ibid., *Professionalism*, 92, 96.

14. Ibid., *Professionalism*, 105.

15. Ibid., *Professionalism*, 122.

16. Ibid., *Professionalism*, 111–12.

17. Ibid., *Professionalism*, 115–17.

18. Ibid., *Professionalism*, 134.

19. Ibid., *Professionalism*, 142.

20. Ibid., *Professionalism*, 180.

21. Ibid., *Professionalism*, 197–98.

22. Ibid., *Professionalism*, 208.

23. Ibid., *Professionalism*, 210.

24. Ibid., *Professionalism*, 212–13.

25. Ibid., *Professionalism*, 217–18.

26. Ezra Suleiman, *Dismantling Democratic States* (Princeton, N.J.: Princeton University Press, 2003), 17.

27. See information on the program on the Department of Education website, http://www.ed.gov/nclb/overview/intro/edpicks.jhtml (accessed July 23, 2005).

28. Ibid.

29. Department of Education, Executive Summary, NCLB, http://www.ed.gov/nclb/overview/intro/execsumm.html.

30. American Federation of Teachers, "NCLB—Let's Get It Right." http://www.aft.org/topics/nclb/index.htm (accessed July 23, 2005).

31. National Education Association, "Adequate Yearly Progress." http://www.nea.org/esea/eseaayp.html (accessed July 23, 2005).

32. NEA, "Testing Plus: Real Accountability with Real Results." http://www.nea.org/accountability/testplus.html (accessed July 23, 2005).

33. Ibid.

34. AFT Teachers Policy Brief, "NCLB: Its Problems, Its Promises," No. 18, (July 2004): 1–3.

35. AFT, "Questions and Answers about the No Child Left Behind Act (NCLB)" p. 5. See also AFT, "Redesigning Schools to Raise Achievement." www.aft.org/topics/school-improvement (accessed July 23, 2005).

36. Jay Mathews, "Examining No Child Left Behind," *Washington Post*, March 9, 2004, A 4.

37. Richard Rothstein, "Testing Our Patience," *The American Prospect* (February 2004): 45–46.

38. American Educational Research Association, "Standards and Tests: Keeping Them Aligned," *AERA, Research Points: Essential Information for Education Policy* 1, no. 1 (Spring 2003): 1.

39. Emmet Rosenfeld, "The Weakly Standards," *The American Prospect* (February 2004): 48.

40. Quoted in William Raspberry, "Giving 'No Child' a Chance," *Washington Post*, June 7, 2004, A 23.

41. Rosalind S. Helderman, "SOL Tests Spurring Dropouts, Group Says," *Washington Post*, June 15, 2004, B 1.

42. Rosalind S. Helderman, "Tests Keep Few in N. Va. from Graduating," *Washington Post*, August 3, 2004, B 7.

43. The Education Trust, "Getting Honest about Grad Rates: Too Many States Hide behind False Data" (press release, June 27, 2005).

44. Diane Jean Schemo, "Texas Lifts Its Probation on Schools in Houston," *New York Times*, August 5, 2004, A 12.

45. Brendan Farrington, Associated Press, "5 Times More Fla. Kids to Repeat 3rd Grade," *Washington Post*, August 24, 2003, A 12.

46. Jerry Parks, "No Illusion Left Behind," *Washington Post*, September 21, 2003, B 7.

47. Sewell Chan and Valerie Strauss, "Despite 'No Child' Law Few Transfer Slots in D.C. Schools," *Washington Post*, August 3, 2004, A 1.

48. Bob Herbert, "The 'Iota' Standard," *New York Times*, July 1, 2002, A 19.

49. Michael Winerip, "In 'No Child Left Behind,' A Problem with the Math," *New York Times*, October 1, 2003, A 21.

50. John R. Novak and Bruce Fuller, "Penalizing Diverse Schools," policy brief, PACE (December 2003), 1–2.

51. Sam Dillon, "School Districts Struggle with English Fluency Mandate," *New York Times*, November 5, 2003, A 21.

52. Karen W. Arenson, "New York Math Exam Trials Showed Most Students Failing," *New York Times*, August 27, 2003, C12, and Karen W. Arenson, "Scores on Math Regents Exam to be Raised for Thousands," *New York Times*, August 30, 2003, B 3.

53. "NY Teachers Cheated in Testing of Students," *New York Times*, October 27, 2003, A 20.

54. Charles T. Clotfelter, Helen F. Ladd, Jacob Vigdor, and Roger Aliaga Diaz, "Do School Accountability Systems Make It More Difficult for Low Performing Schools to Attract and Retain High Quality Teachers?" (paper prepared for the annual meeting of the Association for Public Policy Analysis and Management, Dallas, Texas, November 2002, p. 24).

55. Brian Friel, "No Teacher Left Behind," *National Journal* (September 11, 2004): 2714.

56. Sam Dillon, "Bush Education Law Shows Mixed Results in First Test," *New York Times*, October 20, 2005, sec. A.

57. This discussion focuses on physicians. Other health professionals—such as nurses—do not enjoy the same high status as physicians.

58. David M. Eddy, "Performance Measurement: Problems and Solutions," *Health Affairs* (July/August 1998): 8.

59. National Committee for Quality Assurance, "Nation's Three Leading Health Care Quality Oversight Bodies to Coordinate Measurement Activities," May 17, 1998. http://www.ncqa.org/communications/news/co-labrel.htm (accessed July 23, 2005).

60. NCQA, "Principles for Performance Measurement in Health Care," *NCQA News*. http://www.ncqa.org/communications/news/prinpls.htm.

61. American College of Physicians:"Performance Measures Should Help, Not Punish, Doctors," *ACP Observer* (November 2003). http://www.acponline. org/journals/news/nov03/president.htm (accessed July 23, 2005).

62. Ashish K. Jha, M.D., et al., "Effect of the Transformation of the Veterans Affairs Health Care System on the Quality of Care," *New England Journal of Medicine* (May 29, 2003): 2225.

63. Michael D. Cabana et al., "Why Don't Physicians Follow Clinical Practice Guidelines? A Framework for Improvement," *JAMA* 282, no. 15 (October 20, 1999): 1458, 1463.

64. Ibid., "Why Don't Physicians...," 1463.

65. Eddy, "Performance Measurement," 21.

66. Marc Siegel, "I'm Sorry, Your Illness Is Coded for Only 15 Minutes," *Washington Post*, September 14, 2003, B 3.

67. Jack J. Chielli, "Teaching Hospital Audits Hit Region," *Physician's News Digest* (May 1998). http://www.physiciansnews.com/cover/598wp.html (accessed July 23, 2005).

68. Robert Pear, "Penalties for Nursing Homes Show a Drop in Last 4 Years," *New York Times*, August 6, 2004, A 11.

69. *Government Performance and Results Act of 1993*, 103rd Cong., Section 1115 (b).

70. NAS, NAE, IOM, *Evaluating Federal Research Programs: Research and the Government Performance and Results Act* (Washington, D.C.: National Academy Press, 1999).

71. Ibid., 1–2.

72. Ibid., 2.

73. Ibid. Benchmarking is the process of determining who is the very best, who sets the standard, and what the standard is. The process involves deciding what to benchmark, how to measure it, and how the top performer achieved those results. Others use the benchmark as a way to develop their own agenda.

74. Ibid., 20–21.

75. Chris Mooney, "Beware 'Sound Science,' It's Doublespeak for Trouble," *Washington Post,* February 29, 2004, B 2.

76. Rick Weiss, "OMB Modifies Peer-Review Proposal," *Washington Post,* April 16, 2004, A 19.

77. Union of Concerned Scientists, "Restoring Scientific Integrity in Policy Making," February 19, 2004, p. 1.

78. Committee on Science, Engineering, and Public Policy, The National Academy of Sciences, *Science and Technology in the National Interest: Ensuring the Best Presidential and Federal Advisory Committee Science and Technology Appointments* (Washington, D.C.: National Academies Press, 2004), 41.

79. William F. Massy, "Auditing Higher Education to Improve Quality," *Chronicle of Higher Education,* June 20, 2003, B 16.

80. Joseph C. Burke and Henrik Minassians, *Performance Reporting: "Real" Accountability or Accountability "Lite": Seventh Annual Survey 2003* (Albany, N.Y.: The Nelson A. Rockefeller Institute of Government, 2003), 3.

81. Ibid., 1–3.

82. William J. Patrick and Elizabeth C. Stanley, "Assessment of Research Quality," *Research in Higher Education* 37, no. 1 (1996): 23–42.

83. Ibid., 24–25.

84. The Department for Education and Skills, "The future of higher education and the Higher Education Bill 2004: Regulatory Impact Assessment," Chapter 2: Research Excellence. http://www.dfes.gov.uk/hegateway/up loads/final%20RIA%20V8.pdf.

85. "A Guide to the 2001 Research Assessment Exercise," RAE 2001, p. 3. http://www.hero.ac.uk/rae/Pubs/Index.htm.

86. Alok Jha, "Going Metrics," *Guardian,* January 7, 2003.

87. Donald MacLeod, "Universities Hit by Research 'Snobbery'," *Guardian,* June 8, 2004.

88. Donald MacLeod, "Universities 'Bullying Weak Research Staff'," *Guardian,* June 9, 2004.

COMPETING VALUES: CAN THE PERFORMANCE MOVEMENT DEAL WITH EQUITY?

5

George Hawthorne has spent the last five years of his life teaching in a section of a West Coast city that has one of the lowest socioeconomic populations in the country. He came to this city after two years in the Teach for America program and, following that, a year-long academic program that awarded him a teaching certificate. He is committed to a teaching career that provides educational opportunities for children who have been "left behind."

Despite the problems that stem from the poverty that is a part of the reality of the children in his school, he has made some progress in terms of their basic educational achievements. Children have become interested in reading when he is able to provide them with materials that are a part of their out-of-school interests. Articles on rap performers and other singers engage them and provoke their attention. Similarly, he has found that the boys in his fifth-grade class are interested in math when he gives them problems related to sports statistics. The absentee rate in the classroom has dropped significantly. He has also found ways to get parents involved; he meets with them in small groups and lets them know what he is trying to do in the classroom. Most of the parents have been very impressed with his work.

But while he has devised a program and approach that he thinks is responsive to the needs of his students, he is under pressure from his principal to focus on the standardized tests that are given to the students. His students do not do well on these tests, although they have improved marginally over the past several years. His colleagues in the school tell him that the only way his students will really improve is if he "teaches to the test," preparing the students throughout the year to take the end-of-the-year tests.

Based on his experience, George Hawthorne does not think that his students will respond to that approach. He expects the absentee rate to increase, leading to a significant dropout rate. And most importantly, he does not think that the performance measured by the tests will actually improve. Since the state has adopted a policy that requires students to pass competency tests before they are allowed to graduate from high school, he is afraid that teaching for the required performance tests will actually increase the disparity between the educational achievement of his students and their life chances for success.

Despite the tendency of the American society to worship the gods of efficiency, the values that emerge from a democratic system constantly set up roadblocks to efficiency norms. As economist Arthur Okun wrote,

> American society proclaims the worth of every human being. All citizens are guaranteed equal justice and equal political rights. . . . Yet at the same time, our institutions say "find a job or go hungry," "succeed or suffer." . . . Such is the double standard of a capitalist democracy, professing and pursuing an egalitarian political and social system and simultaneously generating gaping disparities in economic well-being.[1]

Few government programs are designed to accomplish a single goal. Rather, embedded in most programs is a complex combination of efficiency, effectiveness, and equity goals. Sometimes this occurs because the citizens of a democracy do not have a single set of expectations about the program's objectives and, even more frequently, do not agree on what should be done to achieve a goal.

Program administrators are confronted with the need to devise schemes to trade off what are often conflicting values and goals. The programs and policies that they are charged with implementing often are embedded in multiple objectives. They are frequently expected to serve specific client groups who had never been a part of the service system, maintain existing service systems, deliver quality services, and spend the least amount of money. Further, sometimes programs are designed to provide services in a field in which there is not agreement about the best way to deliver those services. This is particularly true in those policy areas that seek to target previously underserved individuals.

Program administrators thus are likely to focus on specific processes used to administer programs as well as the level of inputs (the resources used). They avoid emphasizing outcomes of an intervention because the outcomes are hard to specify. If this were not difficult enough, some programs are designed to achieve symbolic rather than literal action. It is extremely tricky to find a way to measure what is conceptualized as symbolic activity.

Like so many other aspects of the performance movement, balancing conflicting goals and values sets up a paradoxical situation. Program managers are attempting to achieve multiple and often antithetical goals. When they move in one direction to achieve particular goals, they diminish their ability to achieve other goals. As Deborah Stone has commented in her important work *Policy Paradox and Political Reason*, "Paradoxes are nothing but trouble. They violate the most elementary principle of logic: Something cannot be two different things at once. Two contradictory interpretations cannot both be true. Paradox is just such an impossible situation, and political life is full of them."[2]

Stone argues that the world of political reasoning provides the setting for dealing with these paradoxes. Through the processes of decision making, political actors use both conflict and cooperation to deal with multiple perspectives and find ways to hammer out agreement. The process is temporal and messy but moves along relatively predictable paths toward temporary closure. But these temporary closures are hardly the basis for defining clear and explicit outcomes.

The problems involved in trading off and balancing values are not unique to the performance measurement field. Weimer and Vining emphasize the importance of value conflicts within the policy analysis profession. They write:

> Policy analysis, like life itself, forces us to confront conflicts among competing values. Often conflicts arise inherently in the substantive question being considered. For example: Should a policy that will yield a great excess of benefits over costs for society as a whole be selected even if it inflicts severe costs on a small group of people? Our answers will depend on the relative weights we give to the values of efficiency (getting the greatest aggregate good from available resources) and equity (fairness in the way it is distributed). These values, along with others, such as the protection of human life and dignity and the promotion of individual choice and responsibility, provide criteria for evaluating specific policy proposals.[3]

The process of trading and balancing competing values is one of the attributes of the U.S. democratic system. As Judith Gruber has noted in her work *Controlling Bureaucracies: Dilemmas in Democratic Governance*, this leads to a conflict between control and democracy. She highlights the structural limitations of control mechanisms that are imposed by the complexity of the system as well as the costs of control on bureaucrats. Reform, she notes, has both costs and benefits. She also emphasizes the need to create control mechanisms that are appropriate for different settings, moving quite far away from the "one-size-fits-all" advice found in other commentators.[4]

The type of advice that flows logically from the Gruber analyses collides with the management competence approach that is found in the writings of Luther Gulick. According to Gulick,

> [i]n the science of administration, whether public or private, the basic "good" is efficiency. The fundamental objective of the science of administration is the accomplishment of the work in hand with the least expenditure of manpower and materials. Efficiency is thus axiom number one in the value

scale of administration. This brings administration into apparent conflict with certain elements of the value scale of politics, whether we use that term in its scientific or in its popular sense. But both public administration and politics are branches of political science, so that we are in the end compelled to mitigate the pure concept of efficiency in the light of the value scale of politics and the social order.[5]

The efficiency values that are embedded in the contemporary performance movement are very similar to the values that have motivated reformers for more than a century. In this sense, they share mindsets and approaches that have been found in past management reform. The contemporary performance movement clearly follows the tradition of past reform efforts within the federal government. The U.S. Government Accountability Office (GAO) examined the legacy of government-wide activity involving performance budgeting since World War II, particularly the Planning, Programming, and Budgeting System (PPBS) system begun in 1965 by President Lyndon Johnson; the Management by Objectives (MBO) effort initiated in 1973 by President Richard Nixon; and Zero-Based Budgeting (ZBB), initiated in 1977 by President Jimmy Carter.

To some degree, the contemporary interest in performance management reflects the public attention to management that was a characteristic of the 1990s and continues today. It was embraced by the Clinton administration and viewed as complementary to the Gore reinvention effort called the National Performance Review.[6] This interest—often called the reinvention movement—has been labeled as New Public Management and stands as another attempt to move toward a science of management such as that outlined by Luther Gulick.

There is an assumption by many of the advocates in the performance movement that the analytic process embedded in performance measurement activities provides a way for agencies to sort through the competing values nested in their enabling legislation and budgets and select what they—not the legislative enablers—believe are the most important. It appears to be assumed that through this analytic process, agencies will be able to avoid making the trade-offs that are placed in front of them.[7]

H. George Frederickson compared the reinvention movement with an earlier effort in the 1960s to deal with change and the substance (rather than the process) of management.[8] That effort was called the New Public Administration. His analysis provides a useful discussion of the differences in value preferences between the two efforts:

> The value preferences of the two movements are both similar and different. Both movements place a high value on better, more innovative, more creative, more sensitive management. Both movements hold to the view that organizational structure and design make a difference. Both movements emphasize clients, citizens or customers, albeit in somewhat different ways.
>
> The most important difference in values between the two movements is political and philosophical. In new public administration, politics, democratic government, issues of majority rule–minority rights, and associated issues were central. . . . In contrast, the reinventing government movement claims to have little to do with politics. By the generous use of symbols such as governance, total quality, entrepreneurial, and reinventing, the movement attempts to skirt fundamental political issues. Put in harsh terms, reinventing government begs basic philosophical political questions and is politically naïve. Put in positive terms, reinventing government tries to be smart enough not to get trapped politically.[9]

Frederickson's analysis emphasizes the difficulty of raising issues that emerge from the political process within the reinvention framework. Much of the reinvention agenda is borrowed from the private sector, where efficiency is the prevailing value. Equity concerns usually arise from the political process and not from an emphasis on efficiency. Attention to these issues has been raised by Edward Jennings, who reviewed the performance reports and plans of sixteen federal departments. He found that there was "little attention generally to social equity under GPRA."[10]

What makes this debate more than an academic exercise is the reality that many government programs are designed to increase equity and establish processes that meet a sense of fairness. As we know, measuring results has consequences beyond the measurement exercise, and those elements not measured often suffer in terms of allocation of resources. Given the classic value conflict between efficiency and equity in the management field, it is extremely difficult to include equity concerns in the performance movement. This is true for a number of reasons. First, the definition of equity is neither clear nor something that is shared by all. To some, equity calls for the fair, just, and equitable management of all institutions serving the public, directly or indirectly, and the fair, just, and equitable distribution of public services and implementation of public policy.[11] Other definitions equate equal access with equal opportunity, highlight simple equality, allocate resources based on some specific factor, focus on resources that will compensate for past inequalities, look to equality between groups, or focus on equal results or performance. Second, there is resistance to including equity questions in the measurement of performance and a strong tendency to rely on efficiency measures for judgments about performance. And third, even when individuals attempt to deal with equity within performance measurement, there are significant difficulties involved in including equity measurements. These difficulties relate to data issues, problems of the extent of bounding these questions, and—perhaps most important—the conflict within the society about these issues.

Efforts to Deal with Equity Questions

Several examples illustrate these problems. They include efforts by the National Academy of Sciences, the National Academy of Public Administration, and the State of Oregon; an analysis of the conflict within the civil rights community as members of the community were confronted with the No Child Left Behind initiative; and the effort within the Office of Management and Budget (OMB) to implement the Bush administration's PART program without attention to any equity-related issues. While touted as a value neutral enterprise, the PART effort has a heavy overlay of ideology built into it. Efforts by groups within the advocacy community to raise equity questions have been largely ignored by players within OMB.

*The Complexity of Measuring Racial Discrimination: The National
Research Council of the National Academy of Sciences*

In 2001, the Committee on National Statistics of the National
Academy of Sciences convened a panel on methods for assessing
discrimination. It sought to define racial discrimination; review and
critique existing methods used to measure such discrimination; and
recommend the most promising methods to deal with differences
among racial and ethnic groups in the United States. As the panel
wrote in the preface to its final report, the diversity of the group
of experts involved in the effort "added a great deal to the creative
debates among the panel members but also added to the difficulties
in writing this report. It took time to develop a language and an
intellectual framework with which we were all comfortable." Further, the report noted that "[a]ll of the panel members recognize
the difficulties in defining racial discrimination in a clear way and
in finding credible ways to measure it. There are different types of
discrimination, different venues in which it can occur, and different
ways in which it can have an effect."[12]

The report sought to provide examples of differential outcomes
among racial groups in five areas: education, the labor market, the
criminal justice system, the housing market and mortgage lending,
and health care. These served as "examples of the large and persistent differential outcomes by race in various social and economic
domains that make racial discrimination an important topic."[13]

The panel concluded that "[f]or the purpose of understanding and measuring racial discrimination, race should be viewed as a
social construct that evolves over time. Despite measurement problems, data on race and ethnicity are necessary for monitoring and
understanding evolving differences and trends in outcomes among
groups in the U.S."[14] It also recommended that program agencies
should support research that cuts across disciplinary boundaries,
make use of multiple methods and types of data, and study racial
discrimination "as a dynamic process. . . . Program agencies can not
only support the addition of relevant questions to ongoing cross-
sectional and longitudinal surveys but also work to improve the
research potential of agency administrative records data."[15]

While this report focused on the technical problems involved
in measuring racial discrimination, its scope of study did not in-

clude a discussion of the implications of these findings for the performance movement. But its acknowledgement of the difficulties of this task could be extrapolated to problems related to resources for new data collection schemes and what could be viewed as a paperwork burden on those who would have to collect these data. It is interesting that the report of the panel did not include specific recommendations for policy changes or directions related to data collection. The somewhat narrow scope of the report may have been a way for the committee to avoid issues that tended to generate conflict within its membership.

The Problem of Establishing Boundaries for Equity Measurement: The Equity Panel of the National Academy of Public Administration

In 2002, the Standing Panel on Social Equity in Governance of the National Academy of Public Administration (NAPA) acknowledged that there were important linkages between social equity and the contemporary performance measurement movement. The key question that linked the two efforts was defined as "Performance for whom?" A committee was established within the panel that focused on measurement issues. It began by creating a framework for each policy area under discussion and reviewed the role of government agencies from all levels of government in specific policy areas and the nature of their contribution. In addition, the committee included the contribution of nonprofits and businesses to providing services.[16]

Six areas were defined within this framework. They are:

1. *Access.* This is defined as distributional equity and includes a review of programs that deal with simple equality, differentiated equality, targeted intervention, redistribution, and equal results.
2. *Procedural Fairness.* This involves examination of problems or issues in procedural rights (due process), treatment in a procedural sense (equal protection), and determination of eligibility within existing policies and programs.
3. *Quality.* This involves process equity and looks to the level of consistency in the quality of existing services delivered to groups and individuals. It assumes that a commitment to equity entails a commitment to equal quality.

4. *Outcomes.* This looks to define disparities in outcomes for population groups (e.g., by race or income) and how social conditions and individual behavior affect outcomes or limit the impact of government services.

5. *Assessment.* This seeks to define the key issues or concerns for a policy area.

6. *Implications for public administrators.* This involves stipulation of the implications for agencies directly involved in the policy area as well as agencies indirectly involved. It also focuses on the responsibility of the public administration community in this policy area.[17]

The comprehensive nature of this framework sets out an extensive agenda for both analysis and change. While the breadth of the agenda is intellectually appealing, its scope does create significant problems for those who want to focus on specific sectors that are "ripe" for change. The NAPA framework does not highlight areas that are priorities for constituent groups and others outside of government. As a result, it could turn out to be difficult to move to substantive change.

Creation of an Honest Scorekeeper: Oregon Benchmarks Report on Oregon's Racial and Ethnic Minorities

In 1988 a new governor of the State of Oregon decided to focus on a process involving nearly two hundred business, labor, education, and government leaders to help plan a strategy for the state's economic development. The state is known for a tradition of innovation as well as a reliance on participatory democracy. By 1996, more than five hundred community leaders were involved in a process of defining specific outcomes in individual sectors that would be viewed as indicators of progress within the state. These were called benchmarks and became the basis for what was termed "results-driven government." Called Oregon Shines, it was the responsibility of a group called the Oregon Progress Board.

The benchmarks were not limited to government accomplishments; rather they were a way of measuring progress toward broad societal outcomes. Benchmarks were both short term and long term. For example, preventing teenage pregnancy was viewed as a short-term goal, while increases in per capita income were long term. As the process evolved over time, it focused on jobs, community, and environment. The state defined successes in the process in increased per capita income; statewide job growth; forest, agricultural, and wetland preservation; air quality; and health insurance coverage.

While the process was highly touted around the globe, its original agenda was not easy to maintain. Fiscal problems within the state, a change in political leadership, and a proliferation of the number of benchmarks (from 158 in 1991 to 272 in 1993) modified the original plan. By the mid-1990s, the effort moved from a comprehensive planning strategy to become an instrument of public sector accountability.

Most efforts to devise benchmarks do not provide information or goals that focus on the accomplishments of racial and ethnic minorities within a jurisdiction. But the approach adopted by the State of Oregon included an assessment of how well the racial and ethnic minorities in the state were able to meet the benchmarks and targets established by the Oregon Progress Board. The first report was issued in July 2000 and summarized changes in Oregon Benchmarks by race and ethnicity in the period from 1990 to 1998. The report examined trends in eight areas, including education, health, and community, for each of Oregon's minority communities: African American, Asian American, Native American, and Hispanic. The executive director of the Oregon Progress Board noted that compared to state averages, Hispanics and African Americans lost ground in this period. He commented, "For almost every indicator we looked at, African Americans and Hispanics improved less rapidly than the state average. If this trend continues, these Oregonians will fall farther and farther behind the rest of the population."[18]

In 2002, the Board issued a report on racial and ethnic parity between Oregon's population and elected and appointed officials. It found minorities and women underrepresented in both elected and appointed positions at the state and local levels. The most dramatic example of this underrepresentation was found in the Hispanic population, who make up 8 percent of Oregon's population but comprise only 1.1 percent of all locally elected officials.[19]

Also in 2002 the Progress Board issued another report analyzing trends in education, health and safety, and financial status.
Again comparing Oregon's four races, the report found that African
Americans and Native Americans generally lag well behind whites
in the benchmark areas examined. Asian Americans, however, are
at or above white rates for college completion, eighth-grade reading, eighth-grade math, and high school retention rates. The report
noted that Hispanic Oregonians are far behind their non-Hispanic
counterparts in all of the benchmarks examined and, in many cases,
Hispanics were further behind non-Hispanics than they were a decade ago.[20]

In many ways, the Oregon activity can be viewed as the exception that proves the rule. The willingness of the Progress Board to
issue reports that focus on outcomes by race and ethnicity is very
unusual. The state has been able to devise a process that is viewed as
neutral and to serve as an honest scorekeeper in a way that is trusted
by the state "establishment" as well as by advocates for the minority groups whose performance is reported in what is viewed as an
evenhanded manner. To my knowledge, there is no other jurisdiction that has been able to produce this type of data. The Oregon
example stands as an exception but does indicate that it is possible
to ask equity and distributional questions within a performance
measurement framework.

The Dilemma of Advocacy: Civil Rights Advocates and No Child Left Behind

For many years, civil rights advocacy groups have been concerned
about educational chances for children who had been denied equal
opportunities because of historical patterns of discrimination by
race and ethnicity. Moving to supplement legal and judicial change
strategies, an important aspect of a policy strategy involved the
collection of data that was able to report on the performance of
children disaggregated by race, ethnicity, and other characteristics.
These data were viewed as the first step in determining whether
school systems were being held accountable for providing equal
opportunities for all children, regardless of race and ethnicity. Issues of accountability were initially developed within Title I of the

Elementary and Secondary Education Act (ESEA), first enacted in 1965 as the first large-scale federal support of education. Title I supported funds for the education of disadvantaged children. But concern about federal control of public school education—viewed as a prerogative of local and, increasingly, state government decisions— kept federal policy from creating national standards of expectations for performance. (See chapter 7 for a discussion of the federalism and intergovernmental questions involved in performance measurement activities.)

National attention to the performance of children in the public schools began in 1983 with the publication of a report titled *A Nation at Risk*. It was followed by an education summit in 1989 at which both then-president George H. W. Bush and the nation's governors set performance goals for U.S. schools. These goals were viewed as a way to begin to assure that variation in educational performance would not be subject to the vagaries of geography and that children throughout the United States would be expected to meet national standards. These performance goals would be measured by performance in standardized tests. Andrew Rudalevige has written that President Bush's 1991 proposal to include voluntary national testing tied to international standards led to a filibuster by Republicans in the Senate.[21] In 1994 President Clinton supported a law providing grants to help states develop academic standards. Advocates of standards came from various perspectives; some focused on education achievement as the key to developing a skilled labor force, while others highlighted the disparities in achievement between population groups. Advocates of this latter position frequently pointed to failures of school systems to meet the needs of racial and ethnic minorities or students with special needs.

The national commitment to standards-based reform came through the 1994 reauthorization of the Elementary and Secondary Education Act (ESEA). While the reauthorization required states to develop specific curriculum content and achievement of performance standards for public schools, there were no sanctions for any state that did not make progress toward the goal of academic proficiency for all its students. Civil rights advocates, best represented by a group called the Citizens' Commission on Civil Rights, were concerned about the failure of the Congress to hold schools accountable for the performance of all of their students. The Citizens' Commission noted that "[t]he outcome of the debate [over reauthorization] will determine whether schools will be accountable for the progress of all their students, particularly those who have been poorly served in the past, and whether schools have an incentive to improve performance at a rapid pace."[22] The Commission and others, such as the Education Trust, highlighted what they called the achievement gap. They noted that between 1970 and 1988, the difference in performance between white and minority students fell 50% for African Americans and 33% for Latinos. However, the gap held steady during the 1990s and even grew slightly among seventeen-year-olds in reading and among thirteen-year-olds in mathematics.[23]

Others, largely researchers who analyzed the provisions of the proposed legislation, found the provisions flawed and warned that they would result in large numbers of schools labeled as failing for reasons that are unrelated to the quality of education they provide. The Commission criticized these warnings because it felt that they did not hold schools accountable for the performance of all their students. They wrote:

> Every approach that deviates from that goal—for example, by allowing students to be considered successful even if they are not helping a significant group of students achieve proficiency—is an admission of failure. If Congress takes a fearful approach that allows many failing schools to escape accountability and improvement, there will be no remedy for the students who need it, and the hard struggle for reform may come to naught.[24]

The civil rights community was particularly concerned about proposals to turn the large Title I ESEA program into a block grant, giving up any attempt to hold local school districts accountable for performance of all children regardless of race or ethnicity or other characteristics (such as limited English ability or disability or gender).

Apprehension about the possibility of federal control of education continued until George W. Bush assumed the presidency in

2001 and proposed the No Child Left Behind legislation. Bush had borrowed the phrase (without permission) from the rhetoric of the Children's Defense Fund, who had termed its mission as "to leave no child behind."

According to Andrew Rudalevige,

> As Congress opened its doors in January 2001, "No Child Left Behind" emerged not as a piece of draft legislation but as a 30-page legislative blueprint. The proposal, released just three days after the inauguration, closely tracked Bush's campaign agenda. It included a broad block-grant program providing new spending flexibility to "charter states," and it consolidated categorical grants into five areas of focus. . . . It called for the annual testing of students in grades 3–8 and the release of state and school report cards showing the performance of students disaggregated by ethnic and economic subgroups. . . . [S]chools receiving Title I compensatory-education funds would be required to show that disadvantaged students were making adequate yearly progress.[25]

In other words, the Bush proposal had elements within it that represented some of the proposals advocated by the civil rights community while it also had elements that were anathema to it. Gary Orfield, the codirector of the Civil Rights Project at Harvard University, commented that the Bush bill "was the most important thing to affect the education of minority young people over the next five years."[26] He noted that the legislation that was enacted was mostly fads, not facts, and that none of the researchers who had serious knowledge about the effects of legislation on poor children were invited to testify. He commented:

> What emerged was an 1,100-page document calling for impossible achievements that have never been accomplished anywhere. . . . Some of these sanctions are going to take hold this fall for thousands of schools and the states are utterly unprepared to implement them. (There is nothing in the law that will equalize the schools before they are sanctioned.)[27]

Orfield noted that congressional players such as Senator Ted Kennedy supported the bill because there was thought to be more money for poor schools, more concentrated funds than before, and support of a reading program.

The Citizens' Commission on Civil Rights issued its own analysis of the Bush proposal, highlighting the concern about the availability of public reporting requirements:

> While the President's proposals do not go as far as others in providing information to parents and the public, they are improvements over current law. Parents need to have good information on their children's schools. They also want to understand how their own child's school compares to other schools and school districts and whether the school is progressing or moving backwards. When a school's overall achievement is substandard, parents need to understand that their own child's academic struggles may not be the child's or parent's fault, but the result of deficiencies in the school as a whole or in the system.[28]

By the end of 2003, many problems became clearer to civil rights advocates. Dropout rates were increasing, especially for disadvantaged children, as schools were able to raise test scores by getting rid of low-achieving students. Teachers and administrators argued that the law's sanctions harm struggling schools instead of helping them. Groups such as the NAACP expressed their concern about the effort.[29] Education researchers found that "[d]espite policies calling for equal 'opportunities to learn,' minority students often do not have a chance to study as rigorous a curriculum as more privileged students, and they also are less likely to be taught by teachers with high levels of experience."[30]

The dilemma was described by the executive director of the National Center for Fair and Open Testing:

> If the law were designed to make significant progress toward this goal [of ensuring access for all children], every supporter of equity and excellence in education would applaud it. However, for multiple reasons, the actual provi-

sions of NCLB, particularly Title I of the Act, contradict its professed aims. This leaves advocates for high-quality education with the complex problem of opposing the law without giving support to those who will seize upon its inevitable failure as a way of promoting privatization and continuing the push for high stakes testing.[31]

At the same time, the Education Trust issued a statement from more than one hundred African American and Latino school district superintendents from across the country urging Congress to "stay the course on accountability." The director of the Education Trust commented:

> There is a battle raging for the soul of American education. In our work around the country, we often hear local educators talk about the progress they are seeing *as a result of* the new accountability. These education leaders are especially concerned with the messages communicated by those opposed to accountability. Too often, the critics imply that students from low-income families and students of color simply cannot be expected to be taught to high levels.[32]

In an attempt to reclaim its language and agenda, the Children's Defense Fund (CDF) proposed a new piece of legislation, "The Act to Leave No Child Behind," to develop a single, comprehensive measure with specific policy objectives that aim to improve the lives of children. A long list of organizations endorsed the act.[33] The proposed legislation represented an attempt by groups such as CDF to refocus the debate and look at the performance reporting requirements in a less restrictive manner.

The case of NCLB and the civil rights community illustrates the difficulties involved in focusing on equity questions within a complex policy environment. Despite agreement about the importance of dealing with problems of differential treatment of students of color and others whose needs had not been addressed in the existing system, divisions developed within the civil rights community over the best way to achieve those equity goals.

Ignoring Equity Altogether: The OMB Program Assessment Rating Tool (PART)

The Program Assessment Rating Tool (PART) being used by the Bush Office of Management and Budget is viewed as a part of the Bush management agenda—the effort to integrate the budget and performance assessments. The effort has been described as including four purposes:

1. to measure and diagnose program performance;
2. to evaluate programs in a systematic, consistent, and transparent manner;
3. to inform agency and OMB decisions for management, legislative or regulatory improvements, and budget decisions; and
4. to focus program improvements and measure progress compared with prior year ratings.

PART started as a small-scale effort and reported information on sixty-seven programs as a part of the FY 2003 presidential budget. Following that, it expanded the process to include 20 percent of all federal programs each succeeding year. The OMB budget examiner for each program plays the major role in evaluating the assessments.

Each of the programs included in a special volume of the budget documents was rated along four dimensions: program purpose and design; strategic planning; program management; and program results. Agencies received questionnaires that were theoretically fine-tuned to respond to the program type; thus different questionnaires were given for competitive grant programs; block/formula grant programs; regulatory-based programs; capital assets and service acquisition programs; credit programs; direct federal programs; and research and development programs. Five categories of ratings were used: effective, moderately effective, adequate, results not demonstrated, and ineffective.

The patterns of rating programs are not very clear, largely because of variability among the OMB budget examiners. However, there appears to be little if any attention to equity issues within the rating process. Rather, ratings emphasized issues dealing with efficiency values. The more than three-hundred-page document that was issued as a part of the White House budget does not give attention to protected groups (such as specific racial or ethnic groups, or women) within the society. Few of the performance measures that have been devised collect data on the way that programs may disproportionately affect racial and ethnic minorities.

A word search of the section of the 2004 budget report on the PART activity produced the following information.

- The word *equity* was only used once in the document, and that was in relation to benefit equity in the Federal Employees Compensation Act in the Department of Labor.
- The words *African American* never appeared in the document.
- The word *Hispanic* never appeared.
- The word *Indian* appeared in thirteen programs, most of which had the word Indian or tribal in the name of the program.
- The word *woman* appeared in four programs. Two of them were Health and Human Services programs specifically focused on women. The other two involved Department of Defense recruiting and U.S. Agency for International Development development assistance programs. This word usage suggests that OMB staff were not concerned about protected groups in the society.

When one examines specific programs that had compensatory goals or goals with one form or another of equity, it appears that efficiency measures really drive the process. Several examples from the FY 2005 budget document illustrate this pattern:[34]

Food Stamp Program: The measures are not disaggregated by population group. They include participation rates as an aggregate and error rates.

National School Lunch: The long-term measure involves the percentage of calories from fat, and annual measures involved percentage of schools in compliance with rules. Again, these data do not include disaggregated reports by population group.

Independent Living Programs: The annual measure focuses on percentage of goals achieved by consumer but does not disaggregate by population group.

Cluster of Individuals with Disabilities Education Act (IDEA) Programs: There are five IDEA programs that were designed to provide a range of services for individuals with disabilities. They are:

> *IDEA Grants for Infants and Families*: Performance measures are reported on an aggregate basis.
>
> *IDEA Grants to States*: The measures report percentage of students with disabilities who meet or exceed basic levels in reading, math, and science; they also report percentage of students who earn a high school diploma. All of these data are reported on an aggregate basis.
>
> *IDEA Part D—Personnel Preparation*: No measures are reported as key performance measures.
>
> *IDEA Part D—Research and Innovation*: The measures include percentages of program priorities that respond to critical needs of children; the use of evaluation research and methods; and the percentage of practitioners who use the products developed under this program. Again, none of these measures is disaggregated by population.
>
> *IDEA Preschool Grants*: No performance measures were reported.

Head Start: The key performance measures included gain in word knowledge and percentage of parents that report reading to their children. None of these measures are disaggregated by population group although the program was designed to meet the needs of low-income children.

Health Professions: This program was designed to provide support to minority and low-income students but the measures that they use involve proportion of persons who have a source of healthcare, proportion of health professions completing programs serving in medically underserved communities, and proportion of health professionals completing training who are from underrepresented minorities. While this last measure does provide some disaggregated information, it is reported as an aggregate percentage.

Low Income Home Energy Assistance Program: The measures presented here do include disaggregated data by age of recipient (over 60 years and under 5 years) as well as the ability of the program to leverage other resources.

Several public interest groups have been critical of the way that OMB has used the PART process to further substantive policy directions. OMB Watch, a nonprofit research and advocacy organization dedicated to promoting government accountability and citizen participation in public policy decisions, has commented on the process.[35] They focused on a range of programs that were designed to serve the needs of the poor and received recommendations for budget cuts from the White House. They wrote: "But there is little evidence in the FY 2006 budget to support the presidential rhetoric that results are the basis of funding decisions. The president's rhetorical focus on performance and results seem to be just that— merely a smokescreen providing political cover for a Bush agenda that seeks to promote particular ideological policies while drastically reducing the size of the federal government."

Further, according to OMB Watch:

Despite all the hype, the PART cannot be characterized as a refined or sophisticated effort to gauge government performance. Rather, it gives the impression of the grade-school sticker method used to reward good work or punish bad work. Its very simplicity, however, makes it a potentially powerful method to justify budget cuts or increases. In spite of vocal protests that the President's agenda is not to downsize government or reduce its role, there are clear indications to the contrary. . . .

While no one can argue that every government program is useful and operating at peak effectiveness, determining performance is a difficult process fraught with ambiguity. Linking performance evaluations with budget decisions brings into play underlying ideological positions about the role of government and the role of various programs according to which side of the aisle you sit.

Conclusion

This chapter has attempted to explore some of the dimensions of finding a way to deal with equity and fairness questions within the parameters of the performance movement. The balancing of multiple values is not an easy one, even though we know that many government programs are designed to increase equity and establish processes that meet a sense of fairness. The examples that have been used illustrate the difficulty involved in defining equity even when there is commitment to deal with those values, as well as problems involved in trying to use equity measures. They also illustrate the forms of resistance that can have an impact on this process and the continued reliance on efficiency measures that do not capture the needs and realities of specific elements of the population. Given the conflict within the society at large about these issues, it is not surprising that these problems loom large.

The problems faced by George Hawthorne do illustrate the pulls and tugs of dealing with equity as well as the dangers faced in dealing with it. Ignoring equity values is at once politically appealing and, at the same time, often cancels out decisions arrived at democratically through our elected representatives. Hawthorne does not want to be in a situation where he seems to believe that his students cannot learn. Yet he knows that the tests that will be given to the students will not provide them with confidence in themselves. Hawthorne's best allies may be the parents of the students or others who are able to act as spokespeople for their interests. This may involve community organizations or other nongovernmental organizations. It's clear that he will have limited opportunities to change this situation on his own.

Notes

1. Arthur M. Okun, *Equality and Efficiency: The Big Tradeoff* (Washington, D.C.: The Brookings Institution, 1975), 1.
2. Deborah A. Stone, *Policy Paradox and Political Reason* (Glenview, Ill.: Scott, Foresman and Company, 1988), 1.

3. David L. Weimer and Aidan R. Vining, *Policy Analysis Concepts and Practice, Second Edition* (Englewood Cliffs, N.J.: Prentice Hall, 1992), 16.

4. Judith E. Gruber, *Controlling Bureaucracies: Dilemmas in Democratic Governance* (Berkeley: University of California Press, 1987), 192.

5. Luther Gulick, "Science, Values and Public Administration," in Louis C. Gawthrop, ed., *The Administrative Process and Democratic Theory* (Boston: Houghton Mifflin, 1970), 100.

6. See the discussion of the National Performance Review in chapter 4.

7. I am indebted to George Frederickson for this point.

8. H. George Frederickson, "Comparing the Reinventing Government Movement with the New Public Administration," *Public Administration Review* 56, no. 3 (May–June 1996): 263–70.

9. Ibid., 268.

10. Edward T. Jennings, Jr., "Social Equity and the Government Performance and Results Act" (paper prepared for presentation at the 8th Public Management Research Conference, Veterans Administration, Los Angeles, September 29–October 1, 2005).

11. From National Academy of Public Administration Standing Panel on Social Equity in Governance Issue Paper and Work Plan, November, 2000.

12. Panel on Methods for Assessing Discrimination, Committee on National Statistics, Division of Behavioral and Social Sciences and Education, National Research Council of the National Academies, *Measuring Racial Discrimination* (Washington, D.C.: National Academies Press, 2004), xvii.

13. Ibid., 14.

14. Ibid., 3.

15. Ibid., 12–13.

16. Jim Svara, Measurement Committee, NAPA Equity Panel, "Proposed Outline for Assessment of Equity by Policy Area" (September 12, 2003), 1.

17. Ibid., 1–2.

18. Jeff Tryens, Oregon Progress Board, "Report Documents Minority Progress toward Oregon Benchmarks" (press release, July 19, 2000).

19. Jeff Tryens, Oregon Progress Board, "Study Finds Minorities and Women Are Underrepresented in Elected and Appointed Positions" (press release, July 9, 2002).

20. Rita Conrad, Oregon Progress Board, "Oregon Benchmarks: A Progress Report on Oregon's Racial and Ethnic Minorities" (November 2002), 1.

21. See Andrew Rudalevige, "The Politics of No Child Left Behind," Hoover Institution, *Education Next*, http://www.educationnext.org/20034/62.html (accessed July 23, 2005).

22. Citizens' Commission on Civil Rights, "ESEA Policy Brief #4: Adequate Yearly Progress: Analysis and Recommendations" (September 1, 2001), 1.

23. See North Central Regional Educational Laboratory, "Closing the Achievement Gaps," http://www.ncrel.org/gap/library/text/schoolsmatter.htm (accessed May 2005).

24. Citizens' Commission, "ESEA Policy Brief #4."

25. Rudalevige, "Politics," 4.

26. Gary Orfield, Harvard Graduate School of Education, "No Child Left Behind?: A Faculty Response to President Bush's Education Bill," *HGSE News*, September 1, 2002, p. 1.

27. Orfield, "No Child," 2.

28. Citizens' Commission on Civil Rights, "Analysis of President George W. Bush's Education Plan," March 1, 2001.

29. Linda Perlstein, "The Issue Left Behind," *The Nation* (October 21, 2004).

30. The American Educational Research Association, "Closing the GAP: High Achievement for Students of Color," *Research Points* 2, no. 3 (Fall 2004): 1.

31. Monty Neill, "Leave Children Behind: How No Child Left Behind Will Fail Our Children," *The Phi Delta Kappan* (November 2003): 225.

32. The Education Trust, "Don't Turn Back the Clock: Over 100 African American and Latino Superintendents Voice Their Support for the Accountability Provisions in Title I (NCLB)" (press release, November 18, 2003).

33. Children's Defense Fund, "The Act to Leave No Child Behind," http://www.childrensdefense.org/theact (accessed November 2003)

34. See the Program Summaries of the Program Assessment Rating Tool, 2005 Budget Document, OMB. This analysis uses the key performance measures detailed in the document.

35. See "Program Assessment and Budget Cuts Ahead," *OMB Watcher* 4, no. 3 (February 10, 2003): 2. OMB watch centers on four main areas: the federal budget; regulatory policy; public access to government information; and policy participation by nonprofit organizations. Located in Washington, D.C., OMB Watch was founded in 1983 to lift the veil of secrecy shrouding the powerful White House Office of Management and Budget (OMB).

THE REALITY OF FRAGMENTATION: POWER AND AUTHORITY IN THE U.S. POLITICAL SYSTEM

6

Enid Brown is a senior executive service official in the U.S. Environmental Protection Agency (EPA). She is a career civil servant who started her career as a Presidential Management Intern in EPA and worked her way up to the top rungs of the civil service. She is the director of an important component in the agency—the Office of Research and Development. This is an office that is staffed with a variety of individuals, including scientists, program managers, and individuals who are able to deal with both public and private players in the environmental policy area.

Ms. Brown knows that the program she manages has been controversial in the past. It has been subject to various political pressures over the years, resulting in staff demoralization and the loss of talented individuals. Before she became the director of the unit, she served in several capacities within the office and experienced the results of budget cuts, political appointees who were not committed to the program's goals, and pressure from a range of interest groups. Although the legislation creating the program seems to be relatively clear in terms of the goals and objectives, the political pressure from outside of the unit creates a cloud of uncertainty over its operations.

When she took over the office, Ms. Brown committed herself to creating a working environment for her staff that allowed them to focus on the goals of the program and fostered relationships based on collegiality and mutual respect. It was especially important for the office to maintain close relationships with the scientific community. She believed that if she could protect the staff from many of the outside pressures, they would be able to perform more effectively than they had in the past. After two years she believed that she had achieved many of her objectives. The staff worked well together, they respected the different perspectives that they each brought to the task, and she felt that the program was being implemented in a collegial and creative fashion.

However, when the Office of Management and Budget developed its performance effort called PART, the Program Assessment Rating Tool, Enid Brown found that it was difficult to maintain her management plan—attention to her staff and specific program needs—and meet the OMB requirements. All three of her programs that were rated through the PART process were categorized as "results not demonstrated." The comments from OMB did not appear to be appropriate for her research programs. The ecological research program, the pollution prevention and new technologies program, and the particulate matter research program were told to establish efficiency measures, annual measures, and outcome-oriented long-term measures, and to devise a metric for uncertainty reduction.

In order to protect her budget (because PART is linked to the OMB budget process), she was required to achieve the PART stipulation that she focus on program outcomes in a manner that was acceptable to the OMB budget examiners. That process took a lot of time, energy, and resources, and she knew that these expenditures would not be important to crucial members of the congressional appropriations committees and subcommittees. While she was attentive to the OMB process, she was not able to spend the time that she felt was needed to continue to work with her staff.

Although there are examples of the performance movement in both the for-profit and the nonprofit sectors, more attention has been paid to performance measurement involving public policies in one way or another. In part this is because the private sector can use the profit margin as a way to determine successful performance and does not need to establish performance measures that are crafted for individual activities. The efforts called Managing for Results are found in both state and local government settings in the United States. A number of these efforts provide information to managers of programs and allow them to modify their activities. Some provide information to the political "masters" (such as city or county councils, mayors, governors, or legislators). While these efforts as implemented differ from one another around the country, they tend to use a common language and often employ common strategies.

But the most visible performance activities at the end of the twentieth and beginning of the twenty-first centuries involve the U.S. national government. The two main efforts are the Government Performance and Results Act (GPRA) and the Program Assessment Rating Tool (PART). Neither of these federal performance management activities fits easily into the institutional structures, functions, and political relationships found in the American political system. The attributes of that system often lead to a misfit between it and the approaches developed as a part of the federal performance movement. The tension that emerges from this misfit is experienced by a number of federal cabinet departments, especially those that include a variety of programs, are relatively large and complex in their structures, and include programs in which there is not agreement within the society about goals and implementation strategies.

The Dimensions of the "Misfit": Fragmentation and Complexity

Political institutions in the United States, wherever they are found and whatever they are called, are constructed to minimize or, if possible, avoid the exertion of concentrated power. Power and authority are separated and shared across all aspects of the political landscape. This occurs horizontally through the delineation of separate institutions charged with executive, legislative, and judicial functions as well as vertically through the assumption of shared or separate powers among the national, state, and sometimes local levels of government. The principle of fragmentation is carried on within institutions (e.g., bicameral legislatures and separation of authorizing and appropriations functions within the legislative branch) as well as across most levels of government (e.g., shared powers between a state governor and a state legislature or between a city mayor and a city council).

As a result, unlike in a parliamentary system, there is no institutional actor with authority to look at the government as a whole. Except in emergency situations such as wartime, the American system would not create a national planning commission, as have many countries, or even a body charged with allocating funds within program areas to the separate states. The political process, with its vagaries, determines the allocation pattern.

There are a number of aspects of the American institutional setting that have an impact on the implementation of reform efforts such as GPRA and PART. These include the institutional conflict between the legislative and executive branches; the fragmentation of responsibilities within the legislative branch; tension between OMB and departments and agencies; and differentiated responsibilities and roles inside agencies and departments.

Performance Requirements by Legislation: The Government Performance and Results Act (GPRA)

The Government Performance and Results Act is the legislation passed by Congress in 1993 that requires all federal agencies to develop strategic plans, annual performance plans, and performance reports. These stipulations are implemented within the constraints and realities of the annual budget process. All of these requirements are supposed to elicit a focus on the outcomes that have been achieved in the use of federal resources and to justify requests for dollars in terms of both promised and actual outcomes.[1]

On its face, the GPRA legislation seems quite straightforward—indeed, almost innocuous. It clearly follows the tradition of past reform efforts within the federal government. In a report on the historical antecedents of the performance budgeting movement, the General Accounting Office concluded that GPRA "can be seen as melding the best features of its predecessors. . . . Nonetheless, many of the challenges which confronted earlier efforts remain unresolved and will likely affect early GPRA implementation efforts."[2]

At the same time, there are differences between GPRA and earlier efforts. Its enactment as legislation (rather than as executive orders) has built in a role for Congress that is relatively unusual in government reform efforts. In addition, GPRA's inclusion of pilot projects and its provision for a number of years for start-up are not the usual way for reform efforts to be conceptualized. Most efforts emerge full-blown and do not provide time for agencies to work out details of the implementation. Although GPRA was enacted in 1993, its real requirements did not take effect until 1997.

The multiple aspects of the legislation—particularly its emphasis on the relationship between budgeting and performance—can be viewed as an attempt to respond to public concerns about the ways that public monies have been expended. The report from the Senate Committee on Governmental Affairs attached to the legislation noted that "[p]ublic confidence in the institutions of American government is suffering from a perception that those institutions are not working well. . . . [T]he public believes that it is not getting the level and quality of government service for which it is paying."[3]

John Mercer, the acknowledged "father " of GPRA, brought his management reform experience garnered at the local level in Sunnyvale, California, to the legislative development process within the U.S. Congress. Advising the Republican members of the Senate Committee on Governmental Affairs, Mercer's agenda was to craft a piece of legislation that provided the mechanism for performance budgeting. He believed that the efforts in Sunnyvale could inform the federal government, leading to tightly constructed cost accounting systems that would yield technically driven budget decisions. The transfer of local government experience to the federal level can be viewed as a leap of faith. Indeed, there are differences between the experiences at the three levels of government—local, state, and federal—that continue to characterize the movement.

Although his proposals were modified by some of the Democrats on the committee, the legislation that was enacted did accentuate the belief that "congressional policymaking, spending decisions, and oversight are all seriously handicapped by the lack both of sufficiently precise program goals and of adequate program performance information. . . . The legislation will provide the information necessary to strengthen program management, to make objective evaluations of program performance, and to set realistic, measurable goals for future performance."[4]

The Senate committee made a number of assumptions about the GPRA requirements. First, it argued that past and current attempts at performance measurement and reporting had been successful. Second, the report reflected a belief that GPRA would not impose a major additional cost or paperwork burden on federal programs. And third, it argued that at least some federal agencies were already moving toward the development of performance measure systems for results-oriented decision making. There was no acknowledgement in this congressional report that there was a conceptual conflict between these assumptions and a concern about diminishing what some viewed as the "heavy hand" of the federal government where the federal level would impose its agenda on state and local jurisdictions (this is often referred to as federal preemption).

Indeed, the only cautionary note that was sounded in the Senate report came from Arkansas Democratic Senator David Pryor. He wrote: "My concern is that by mandating yet another very specific layer of internal management controls, performance measures and strategic plans, we are building in even more rigidity. I realize that the legislation seeks to allow flexibility in some pilot programs, but after years of watching these well intended reforms transform into routine reports written by contractors using largely boilerplate language, I am not convinced that this legislation will actually enable federal agencies to improve their performance."[5]

The rigidity that was feared by Senator Pryor actually took form within the confines of a highly polarized Congress. GPRA was embraced by the Republican leadership in both the House and the Senate as a means of putting pressure on the Democratic administration. House Majority Leader Richard Armey established a grading system to rate the "progress" of federal agencies as they submitted both their strategic plans and their annual performance plans to the Congress as well as the White House. The Senate Governmental Affairs Committee used the GPRA framework to highlight problems of waste, fraud, and mismanagement within federal agencies. Neither setting focused on the difficulties that federal agencies had in establishing measures of performance for programs designed as block grants or with high levels of discretion provided for third-party implementers, particularly state agencies. It looked at the federal government as one system, utilizing a one-size-fits-all mindset.

In fact, when one examines the GPRA legislation and its history, there is little in that background that provides real guidance regarding federal agency dependence on other levels or other branches of government. The only specification of consultation with "external" parties is found in fairly vague language regarding the development of the agency strategic plans. Agencies are not required to deal with these external parties as they devise their annual performance plans. Some have actually been concerned that state and local governments who act as agents for the federal government are relegated to the category of "external" parties. Similarly, there has been little attention to the form that the program takes (e.g., whether it is a competitive grant program, a block grant, or some other form of formula funding).

Over the past several years, at least some federal agencies have been pressured by Congress and some of its agents to take direct responsibility for the performance outcomes achieved through federal programs, whether or not the federal agency actually delivers the services provided through federal funding. In some instances, this has moved the agency away from a focus on performance that values state flexibility and discretion and back to a more traditional compliance-oriented posture. GPRA has tended to highlight the federal role of defining goals at a national level rather than leaving it to states (often termed the Laboratories of Democracy) to bargain about specific goals and outcomes for their jurisdictions. (See chapter 7 for a discussion of the intergovernmental issues.)

The Bush Administration Discovers Performance Management: The Program Assessment Rating Tool (PART)

Most presidential administrations seem to want to put their own imprint on management reform efforts. In this respect, the George W. Bush administration is no different from many that preceded it. Although some believed that the passage of the Government Performance and Results Act (GPRA) in 1993 established an approach to management reform that involved both the Congress and the White House and was bipartisan in nature, the current administration has created its own approach to performance management within the executive branch. This approach is implemented by the Office of Management and Budget alongside the GPRA requirements.

This effort is called the Program Assessment Rating Tool (PART) and is viewed as a part of the Bush management agenda—the effort to integrate the budget and performance assessments.[6] While PART shares some perspectives with GPRA, it does differ from the earlier effort in a number of ways. Its focus is different; it is located only in the executive branch; it has more of a top-down than a bottom-up approach; it does not attempt to include all programs every year; it focuses only on performance measures; and it emphasizes efficiency approaches. Table 6.1 summarizes the differences:

PART started as a small-scale effort and reported information on 67 programs as a part of the FY 2003 presidential budget. Following that, it expanded the process to include 20% of all federal programs within the FY 2004 budget document (231 programs). The process further expanded to include 20% more federal programs for the FY 2005 budget. Some changes were made in the requirements, but the general format remained fairly consistent. Unlike GPRA, which focused on agencies and departments, the PART analysis focuses on specific programs. The OMB budget examiner for each program plays the major role in evaluating the assessments.

Each of the programs included in a special volume of the budget documents was rated along four dimensions: program purpose and design (weight 20%); strategic planning (weight 10%); program

Table 6.1 A Comparison of GPRA and PART

Area of Difference	GPRA	PART
Focus	Focuses on offices and organizational units	Focuses on programs
Branch of government involved	Both Congress and the executive branch	Only in executive branch, centered in OMB
Organizational approach	Bottom up, begins with program units	Top down, OMB must approve measures
Requirements	Multiple; strategic plan, performance plan, performance report	Performance measures
Approach to measures	Multiple types, but highlights outcomes	Focuses on efficiency outcomes

management (weight 20%); and program results (weight 50%). Questionnaires were available to agencies (but completed by the OMB budget examiners) that were theoretically fine-tuned to respond to the program type; thus different questionnaires were given for competitive grant programs; block/formula grant programs; regulatory-based programs; capital assets and service acquisition programs; credit programs; direct federal programs; and research and development programs. Five categories of ratings were used: effective, moderately effective, adequate, results not demonstrated, and ineffective. Of the programs included in the FY 2004 budget document, 14 were rated as effective, 54 moderately effective, 34 adequate, 11 ineffective, and 118 results not demonstrated.[7] In the FY 2005 budget document, 11% of the programs were rated effective, 26% rated moderately effective, 21% adequate, 5% ineffective, and 37% results not demonstrated.[8]

The patterns of rating programs are not very clear regarding the FY 2004 process, largely because of variability among the OMB budget examiners. This variability was pointed out by GAO in its assessment of the process. In addition, there appears to be a pattern of rating block grant programs as "results not demonstrated."

Congressional reaction to the PART activity has been variable. Some members of the House have introduced legislation that would make PART a statutory obligation. Called the Program Assessment and Results Act, the proposed legislation, according to its sponsor, would call on OMB to review and assess each federal program at least once every five years.[9] By contrast, however, the House of Representatives appropriations subcommittee that has authority for the OMB budget put in a limitation on OMB's authority and approach to PART. This required OMB to provide a detailed description of programs, methodology, data, and responsible agencies' involvement. The subcommittee report stipulated that if the subcommittee did not agree with OMB's plans for PART, it prohibited OMB from using information from PART in its budget requests.[10]

OMB Watch, a nonprofit organization that has been monitoring the PART process, commented on the process:

> In his recent efforts to further promote a "good-government" approach, the president often referred to a list of 154 programs slated for deep cuts or elimination in his FY 06 budget because those programs were "not getting results." OMB Watch has analyzed this list and other sections of the FY 06 budget and compared program funding requests to the ratings received under the PART. This analysis has yielded some interesting and puzzling results. Out of the list of 154 programs to be cut or eliminated, supposedly for lack of results, more than two-thirds have never even been reviewed by the PART. It is unclear what kinds of determinations, if any, the president used to identify these failing programs when the White House budget staff has yet to assess them. . . .
>
> A quick review of programs rated under PART since its inception finds no logical or consistent connections with budget requests. Of the 85 programs receiving a top PART score this year, the president proposed cutting the budgets of more than 38 percent, including a land management program run by the Tennessee Valley Authority and the National Center for Education Statistics. . . .
>
> However, this is not the only illogical aspect of the PART. Another puzzling situation is how the PART relates

to and is integrated with the Government Performance and Results Act (GPRA) of 1993. GPRA, which was fully implemented in 1997, set out to establish a system for measuring each agencies [sic] performance—both on a whole and for specific programs—that could be tied to the congressional appropriations process. . . .

OMB Watch's current analyses of the PART have produced more questions than answers about its value and purpose. It is unclear how the PART scores impact budgeting decisions within OMB as there are no consistent patterns to follow. It is hard to determine whether the PART is measuring programs accurately, consistently and in a value-neutral way. Even if it achieves these, there has been little attention paid to the question of whether the PART is measuring the right kinds of outcomes.[11]

Pressures That Emerge from the American Political Structure

There are structural characteristics of the American political structure that make the implementation of both GPRA and PART difficult. These include the institutional conflict between the legislative and executive branches, the fragmentation of responsibilities within the legislative branch, tension between OMB and departments and agencies, and differentiated responsibilities and roles inside agencies and departments.

Institutional Conflict between the Legislative and Executive Branches

Because GPRA has established a set of expectations for both the legislative and executive branches, this reform effort directly collides with the institutional design of separation of powers. The U.S. institutional structure rarely provides the means for a smooth path from one institutional setting to another. The system of shared powers within the national political setting creates tensions and frequently leads to conflict between the two ends of Pennsylvania

Avenue. And rarely have administrative reforms been designed to accommodate the separation of powers.[12]

GPRA calls for the development of information (in the form of strategic plans, performance plans, and performance reports) that will be used by these very different institutions with diverse cultures and responsibilities. These institutions include the political actors in both the legislative and executive branches as well as the top, middle level, and program managers within departments and agencies. The literature on the stages of the policy process provides strong evidence of different perspectives that are at play when a policy issue moves from the policy adoption stage to the policy implementation stage.[13] These differences are directly linked to the different perspectives that flow from the very different institutional settings. While these differences are often a source of frustration (when a policy or program does not emerge from implementation activities in a form that meets the original expectations of the policy adopters), they can lead to more useful accountability relationships and are also a source of creativity and new ideas.

The GPRA legislation did establish a formal set of shared responsibilities between the two branches of government with a requirement in the legislation that called for the involvement of Congress in the strategic plan development.[14] The majority leader in the House effectively took the legislative language over, creating a far more contentious environment than some of the GPRA architects had imagined.

The appellation used to title the Government Performance and Results Act offers some of the strongest evidence of the different perspectives on GPRA held by the Congress and the executive branch. The Congress (particularly the Republicans in Congress) calls the legislation "The Results Act," while the Executive Branch tends to call the legislation "GPRA" or use its entire name.

There is some evidence that the difference in institutional perspectives has led to a compliance perspective and bred cynicism.[15] For example, the Department of Education surveyed its staff and found that they were "doing GPRA" simply because it was required by Congress.

There are differences between the GPRA approach and PART in terms of the relationship between the legislative and executive branches. Because the PART process focuses only on the executive branch and its authority, there is an implicit conflict between the Congress and the White House in that process. One subcommittee of the House Appropriations Committee actually complained about OMB's reliance on PART-like information in the budget justification. The report accompanying the FY 2005 spending bill for the departments of Transportation and Treasury and general government accounts noted that "[t]he committee is disturbed to note the serious decline in the quality of budget justification material submitted this year." Further, the committee complained that the kinds of information they traditionally wanted (such as information on finances and staffing) "have been minimized or eliminated." The report said that "agencies are directed to refrain from including substantial amounts of performance data within the budget justifications themselves, and to instead revert to the traditional funding information previously provided."[16]

GAO commented on the difficulties of balancing the GPRA and PART approaches, especially as they sought to inform the congressional decision-making process. The congressional agency noted that "[t]he PART was designed for and is used in the executive branch budget preparation and review process; as such, the goals and measures used in the PART must meet OMB's needs. GPRA is a broader process involving the development of strategic and performance goals and objectives to be reported in strategic and annual plans." The GAO report further noted:

> Most congressional committee staff we spoke with did not find either the PART information or the way it was communicated suited to their needs. Many had concerns about the usefulness of the goals and measures OMB used to assess program performance and some questioned the "units of analysis" used for the PART as well as the design of the tool itself. [17]

The Fragmentation of Responsibilities within the Legislative Branch
    Although we have a tendency to speak of Congress as if it operated as a unified, monolithic institution, the fragmentation in the

structure of the legislative branch does not allow it to speak with a single voice. It is difficult to expect a body with a combined membership of 535 individuals to operate in lock step, particularly in a country where political party discipline has been historically much weaker than that in a parliamentary system.[18]

The differentiation between the roles of the authorizing and appropriations committees is perhaps the most formal expression of the reality of multiple voices. The authorizing committees focus on the substance of programs, while the appropriations committees look at programs from a budgetary perspective. Despite the increased role of the appropriations committees over the past decades, the authorizing committees often look at programs and policies in different ways (including reauthorizing and oversight responsibilities) than do the appropriators. Even these categories mask the complexity within the committees, as separate subcommittees often operate quite independently.

In addition, most of the government reform efforts have been on the agenda of the government operations committees—the committees in both the Senate and the House that tend to look at government-wide efforts. While they have the ability to focus on the general dimensions of these efforts, when the policy questions are raised in specific agencies and programs, the jurisdiction is not in those committees but in specific authorizing and appropriations committees.

During the early years of GPRA implementation, an additional complicating factor was established as the Republican leadership (particularly in the House of Representatives) attempted to speak for the entire legislative body. As a result, rhetoric emerged from then Majority Leader Richard Armey suggesting that there is a single, unified voice in the Congress evaluating the GPRA submissions of the executive branch agencies. Although there was a series of letters, press releases, and other forms of communication from the majority leader and other members of the Republican leadership in both houses, during the first years of GPRA implementation there was very little evidence that these communiqués played an important role in the decisions of either the appropriations or authorizing committees. One such letter was sent to the director of

OMB in July 1999 in response to the draft OMB guidance with regard to the performance reports. The letter was signed by four members of Congress—none of whom had positions on the appropriations committees or important authorizing committees of either the House or Senate.[19] That rhetorical response has clearly not translated to action across the board in the work of the multiple committees involved in appropriating, creating, or examining specific programs and policies.

Although GPRA has been constructed with close linkages to the budget process, staff and time limitations as well as existing relationships in the appropriations committees and subcommittees make it very difficult to move in the direction that was originally envisioned. And PART focused only on the Executive Branch budget process. In at least a few instances, agency and department officials have actually pleaded with Hill appropriations staffers to use performance plans in their decision-making process but have had very little success in that setting. Some appropriations committee staff do believe that GPRA may eventually provide them information that they can use to minimize the power of interest groups who do not tend to talk about the effectiveness of programs they are supporting.

By contrast, there are a few examples of the use of the GPRA submissions; the concept of performance measures has emerged in new legislation that has come from several authorizing subcommittees. But GPRA's concentration on performance outcomes—to the exclusion of other elements of the decision process such as processes and outputs—is not always agreed to by the appropriating committees. As one individual put it, while GPRA wants to move beyond counting beans, in many programs Congress wants to count beans and focus on the detailed processes of implementation.

Tension between OMB and Departments and Agencies

Historically, federal government-wide management reform has been located in the management staff at the Office of Management and Budget, reflecting the effort from the White House to approach management issues from the perspective of the government as a whole. Although the management side of OMB has been effectively eliminated (or at least drastically reduced) since the reorganization of the agency early in the first Clinton term, there continues to be a small staff within OMB that deals with GPRA as a whole. In addition, GPRA's close attachment to the budget process provides OMB with an opportunity to make tradeoffs across programs and organizational units and to deal with management issues as an aggregate.

The Republican leadership in the Congress attempted to hold OMB responsible for the early stages of GPRA implementation, ignoring the decentralized nature of budget decision making both in OMB itself and in Congress. They held the Clinton OMB accountable for efforts such as the development of performance budget pilots (specified in the GPRA legislation). In turn, OMB played into that role even though the staff is very limited and lacks the ability to follow through on issues. OMB convened regular conference calls with participation across all federal government agencies. While providing some semblance of coordination, these efforts tended to be superficial and did not provide a venue for agency staff to discuss substantive experiences with one another.

OMB's niche in the process is built around the budget process—a process that has always involved a set of tensions between the executive office of the president and individual departments and agencies. The budget process provides limited opportunities for the discussion of specific aspects of programs and policies. In addition, OMB itself is actually quite decentralized. Budget examiners within OMB have been given both budgetary and management responsibilities for a specific set of programs and have significant autonomy to deal with agencies. And these budget examiners play the crucial role in assessing the PART submissions and have varied considerably in the way they have applied the requirements. As a result, some OMB staff have given serious attention to the GPRA submissions, while others have only dealt with them in a broad-brush fashion. OMB staffers describe the agency as the preeminent government agency that already uses performance information in the process of developing the budget. In that sense, the view that GPRA *began* an interest in performance actually demeans what long-time OMB staffers view as their past history and contributions.

Differentiated Responsibilities and Roles inside Agencies
and Departments

There are several institutional tensions at play within the agencies and departments that affect the GPRA implementation effort. Although the GPRA legislation links the requirements to the budget process, a number of agencies and departments chose to give responsibility for the development of the strategic plan, performance plans, and performance reports to the offices responsible for planning (and sometimes evaluation). While some of these offices are involved in the budget process, more often they operate very separately from the budget staffs. As a result, the development of the documents—although they are usually attached to the budget itself—is a separate and parallel process.

In addition, whether found in the planning staffs or the budget staffs, the GPRA implementation may be located in decentralized program units or in centralized offices within the office of the secretary. In at least a few departments, the GPRA documents do not reflect significant input from program staff and are, instead, the work of centralized planning or budget offices.

GPRA also inherits the structural tension between short-term political appointees and long-term career staff. While political appointees may be committed to the concept of performance accountability, they have limited opportunities to integrate the process into standard operating procedures. The Clinton administration's commitment to flattened organizations and reinvention processes actually may have minimized these opportunities even further. From the perspective of the long-term career staff, as long as the process is viewed in compliance terms (largely satisfying the Congress), it has limited ways of changing the agency culture and decision processes.

The actual process of responding to the GPRA requirements involves a number of steps that are common to a classic rational planning approach. First, agencies are expected to define and get agreement on goals. Second, they are required to set objectives. Third, they are expected to devise a management strategy for reaching those objectives. Fourth, performance measures will be established. Fifth, they will establish who is responsible for achieving results. Sixth, they are expected to monitor and report on their achievements based on defined performance measures. And seventh, they will develop a reward system linked to the agreed-upon objectives.

Definitions of activity were laid out that established rules for proceeding. Agencies were told that they should focus on longer range outcomes of activity as they defined their performance goals and that attention to input or process measures were not appropriate. These requirements ignored the reality that in many instances program managers were told (by OMB and sometimes by GAO) to focus on specific methods of delivering a service or implementing a policy, in terms of both who was involved in the process and the resources used to achieve it (including the types of staff involved and stipulations about expenditure of specific resources). Outputs—defined as immediately observable products and services produced by a program and delivered to customers—were allowable as long as they led to outcomes. As a result, there was very little attention to process measures and the relationship between process activities and output or outcome performance. A few caveats were noted (e.g., problems involved in applying the framework to research activities, block grants, or policy advice) but were largely ignored as the instructions matured. Performance measures could include quantity, quality, timeliness, and cost as well as outcomes. Improvement of efficiency and effectiveness were highlighted as the basis for the activity. Examples of PART requirements are provided in the next section of the chapter.

Performance Management in a Federal Department: The Case of the Department of Health and Human Services (HHS)

In the years between the enactment of GPRA in 1993 and its implementation in 1997, various components of the Department of Health and Human Services (HHS) were involved in a range of activities that were viewed by staff as related to the GPRA implementation. These included development of a department-wide strategic plan and a number of pilot projects that were viewed as first steps toward the development of the first performance plan that would be submitted by the department along with its FY 1998 budget.

Because the GPRA submissions were seen as meeting both the needs of the executive branch through the White House Office of Management and Budget (OMB) and those of the Congress, HHS received instructions about the process from OMB as well as from the GAO, an investigative arm of Congress. Both organizations viewed the requirements of GPRA as department-wide in scope and communicated them to offices within HHS that they believed exerted centralized control over the components within the department.

For HHS, however, this was difficult. Few public agencies in the world are as complex as the U.S. Department of Health and Human Services. The management challenges that are posed by this public organization have worried administrators and policymakers since it was officially created as the Department of Health, Education, and Welfare in April 1953. The department was responsible for the implementation of more than three hundred programs, covering a vast array of activities in medical and social science research, food and drug safety, financial assistance and health care for low-income, elderly, and disabled Americans, child support enforcement, maternal and infant health, substance abuse treatment and prevention, and services for older Americans. The range of these programs means that the activities found within the department affect the health and welfare of nearly all Americans. The FY 2005 budget is $580 billion, implemented by approximately sixty-six thousand employees. The department's programs are administered by eleven operating divisions in both headquarters locations, as well as by ten regional offices.

This complexity has created a set of management challenges for department secretaries over the department's life. One of these challenges has been the definition of the role of the office of the secretary and its relationship to the operating components of the agency. For at the same time that the secretary is the official head of the agency and held publicly accountable for the actions of the programs within it, the Congress and the public have frequently focused on the operating components when specific action is demanded. Thus the department is expected to respond to two sets of expectations that call for inconsistent strategies: *centralization* in the office of the secretary and *decentralization* to the operating programs.[20]

The communications from OMB and GAO, however, assumed that the units within the office of the secretary (particularly the budget office) exerted direct control over the operating programs and that the program units were in the role of a supplicant to the centralized offices. While past secretaries had tried to use this approach, Donna Shalala, the secretary during the early GPRA period, adopted a conscious management strategy that was very different from those attempted in the past. She began with the assumption that the department contains many decentralized elements and that it is not possible to change them. She described the department as composed of units that have their own history, needs, cultures, and constituencies. She used the professional credibility of the subunits within the office (especially those dealing with the health world) as an important source of public and political support. She downsized the office of the secretary and delegated many different functions to the operating components.

After the passage of the Government Performance and Results Act in 1993, the HHS response to the requirements of the legislation was found within the separate program units within the department. This strategy acknowledged the size and decentralized nature of the department. While it was charged with the implementation of approximately three hundred programs, the size and disparate functions of these programs lent themselves to a decentralized approach to program management and performance measurement.[21]

Although the specific requirements of the legislation did not go into effect until 1997, several of the HHS program agencies decided to devise pilot projects (a possibility included in the law) that might serve as demonstrations or examples for others. The assistant secretary for management and budget requested that each program component develop a pilot annual performance plan for a minimum of one program activity and establish a strategy for aggregating program activities in its FY 1999 Annual Performance Plan. Two pilots were actually developed in the department: a performance plan for the Child Support Enforcement Program in the Administration for Children and Families, and a plan for the Food and Drug Administration's Prescription Drug User Fee Act (PADUFA) program. However, there was limited attention to these pilot efforts within other parts of the department since the two major requirements of the legislation—a five-year strategic plan and annual performance plans—were not immediate demands.

In 1996, work began seriously on the HHS strategic plan, led by the Office of the Assistant Secretary for Planning and Evaluation (ASPE). Although a staff-level work group had been formed in early 1994 to develop a department-wide plan and provide technical assistance to the program units as they developed their own plans, these efforts were disrupted by attention to other initiatives, especially the health care reform initiative and reinvention activities. The guidelines that had been established for that staff-level work group called for a two-part plan—a section that attempted to identify broad, crosscutting goals and objectives that seemed appropriate to all parts of the department, and plans that were specific to each individual component within the department that would supplement the crosscutting goals.

In the fall of 1996, concerns were expressed about the strategic plan that was emerging through this process. Its critics argued that the plan lacked vision and a strategic focus. The two-level approach was thought to create multiple layers and large numbers of goals, objectives, and strategies that were uncoordinated, duplicative, and did not flow from one another. It was described as the product of a staff-level process, resulting in goals, objectives, and strategies that satisfy major program and constituent interests but fail to articulate a vision or priorities. As a result of these criticisms, the secretary and deputy secretary decided that a document would be written by a few top staffers in ASPE and circulated within the department before it became final. Thus a bottom-up approach was replaced by a document developed in a top-down fashion.

While this document did present a picture of a unified department, held together by six overarching goals, the strategic plan did not easily fit into the fragmented decision-making structure that is a part of the HHS reality. Both appropriation and authorizing committees in the Congress focus on specific program areas, not on broad goals. Even the staff of the Office of Management and Budget only scrutinizes specific elements of the department's programs, since a number of separate budget examiners have responsibility for specific program areas. And the approach did not seem consistent with the management approach taken by the secretary and deputy secretary.

In part in reaction to the more centralized ASPE process, which attempted to emphasize approaches that were department-wide, the Office of the Assistant Secretary for Management and Budget (ASMB)—the unit within the office of the secretary that was given responsibility for the development of the annual performance plans required by GPRA—developed a strategy that emphasized the unique nature of the individual HHS program components. Because the performance plans were attached to the budget submissions, their development was clearly a bottom-up process. GPRA activity within the department was undertaken by the budget staff in ASMB, by the planning and evaluation staff in ASPE, by the legislative staff in the Office of the Assistant Secretary for Legislation, and by the program management staff from specific program areas.

During the first several years of the process, the role of ASMB was that of a gentle facilitator, attempting to provide opportunities for representatives of program units to raise questions and discuss their experiences. The annual performance plans that were devised were very different from one another. While most of the program units made some reference to the themes established by the strategic plan, their performance plans—as did the budgets—emphasized quite diverse goals and objectives.

While the deliberations within the congressional appropriations process did not indicate that members of Congress were focused on the problems stemming from the diversity of these documents, there was strong criticism of the HHS submissions by the General Accounting Office and by the Republican leadership in the Congress. The model of decision making that was employed by these critics assumed that HHS was managed as a centralized, command and control department. While this model was not realistic for a department the size and scope of HHS (nor did it comport with the secretary's personal approach), there was a danger that the criticism of the GPRA submissions could cause problems for the department.

Thus the staff of ASMB was faced with a dilemma: how could it respect the diversity and autonomy of the program units and, at the same time, find ways to address the critics who sought a unified, single document? In addition, there clearly was a range of GPRA-related competencies within the department, and it would be useful for program unit staff to find ways to learn from one another.

The strategy that was employed within ASMB contained several aspects. The ASMB staff developed a performance plan summary document that did provide a more unified picture of the department. It focused on the linkage between program unit goals and objectives, departmental initiatives, and the HHS strategic plan. It highlighted crosscutting areas, drawing on the individual performance plans to illustrate shared areas. It set out the HHS approach to performance measurement and the close relationship between the department's budget development process and the GPRA performance plans.

In addition, the ASMB staff held a series of conference calls that provided an opportunity for program unit staff to discuss issues, share experiences, and develop a collegial (almost collective) approach to the task. These calls (and some face-to-face meetings) were constructed to provide methods of active rather than passive involvement in the process.

Finally, the ASMB staff worked closely with a subgroup of the GPRA program unit staff to develop a standardized format, which all program components agreed to use for their FY 2001 performance plans and their FY 1999 performance reports. This format established a consistent "order of presentation" of information required by the law and OMB for performance plans and reports. While the program units followed the standardized format to ensure that they met all of the requirements of the law, significant flexibility remained to ensure that the units were able to tailor their performance plans and reports to meet their individual needs. Some components chose to present certain types of performance information at the agency level; others chose to present information at the program or goal levels. For the reader who was required to assess all of the HHS performance plans, this shared format painted a picture of some level of consistency across the program units and did make the job of reading the documents somewhat easier.

The GPRA process provided the department with the space to define and organize its process and substantive response to requirements. While OMB, GAO, and the Republican majority leader's office had the ability to respond to and comment on the GPRA documents released by HHS, the department did have a measure of control over this process. This was not true for the PART process. In contrast, the essential control over PART rested with the OMB budget examiners. Individual budget examiners could actually determine the content of specific performance measures. The process involved direct negotiations between agency staff and OMB; the office of the secretary's budget office would sit in during these negotiations, but they were not the main players in the process. The department budget staff often sought to provide support to the agencies within this process and to help them strategize about approaches. Participants in the process describe the experience as generating a high workload and being very subjective in terms of the expectations of an individual OMB budget examiner.

HHS Deals with OMB

The instructions for the 1998 budget that were given in September 1995 to the heads of executive departments and independent agencies by Alice Rivlin, then director of OMB, offered the first indication of the formal GPRA implementation process. As the September 1997 deadline approached, the OMB examiners began to play a more important role in assessing preliminary submissions by agencies based on draft strategic plans and stipulation of performance measures. This shift placed what had been a relatively flexible and often symbolic set of pronouncements into a highly formalized and stylized budget process. The budget calendar is clear and rigorous, and agencies are attentive to its requirements. At the same time, however, placing much of the responsibility for GPRA in the hands of individual OMB examiners acknowledges the somewhat decentralized nature of that operation, with individual examiners making judgments about a specific and limited set of program areas. This shift emphasized the budgetary face of GPRA, minimizing its importance for meeting agency management needs and definitions of program effectiveness.

Because the HHS GPRA activity was tracked along the budget process, the requirements developed by OMB to structure the development of the president's budget organized the GPRA process. Unlike smaller and less diverse agencies, the HHS budget was developed in separate components and was sent both to OMB and to the Congress in these separate tracks, mirroring the separate budgets submitted to the department, OMB and the Congress. The instructions for completing the budget came to HHS from OMB through circular A-11; that document specified a detailed format to be used to submit budget requests. Thus while individual program components developed their own budgets, they used a standardized format that would eventually become the basis for the president's budget.

Once the GPRA requirements became operative, each element of the decentralized HHS budget included a performance plan for the past year and one for the coming year; in addition, by FY 2001 it also included a performance report comparing planned and actual performance for all goals and measures in the Revised Final Fiscal Year 1999 Performance Plan. Relationships between HHS officials and OMB proceeded along two tracks: the small management staff within OMB served as the procedural adviser for the GPRA process. HHS staff from the office of the secretary participated in regular government-wide conference calls that reviewed the general requirements for submitting the GPRA documents. However, the detailed discussion and negotiations about the substantive elements of the budget and performance plans occurred among OMB budget examiners assigned to particular program areas, budget staff from the program agency, and the budget office staff within the office of the secretary. Because OMB budget examiners operate in a relatively autonomous fashion, the review of performance plans and discussion of specific measures varied significantly from program to program.

At the same time that agencies have the responsibility for implementing GPRA, they are also charged with the implementation of a number of other management requirements. More than half of these requirements stem from legislation and the rest from executive branch requirements. Each of these requirements has its own internal logic; however, these requirements sometimes are unintentionally incompatible and often lead to different decisions. While they may be theoretically reinforcing of one another, they are often given to different staff units with different perspectives on issues. One HHS analysis of the requirements that also impacted the process listed them as follows:[22]

Federal Managers Financial Integrity Act of 1982. Legislation that seeks to improve the accountability and effectiveness of federal programs and operations. This requires annual assurance of the adequacy of controls and a report on material weaknesses of management controls.

Chief Financial Officers Act of 1990. Legislation focused on improvement of accounting and financial management systems and internal controls to reduce waste. It requires the specification of a chief financial officer in each agency and annual financial statements as well as audited financial statement reports. Agencies are expected to issue annual accountability reports that document compliance with these requirements.

Government Management Reform Act of 1994. This legislation seeks to expand the Chief Financial Officers Act to support more informed spending decisions. It requires an annual financial statement report to OMB.

Information Technology Management Reform Act of 1996. Legislation that seeks to achieve efficient and effective acquisition and use of modern information technology. It establishes a chief information officer and requires annual reports in budget submissions on how information technology is used to help programs achieve their goals.

The Paperwork Reduction Act of 1995. This legislation focuses on the elimination of unnecessary paperwork burden. It requires agencies to prepare and implement an information streamlining plan and an information collection budget.

Federal Financial Management Improvement Act of 1996. Legislation that seeks to increase accountability by implementing financial accounting standards in financial management systems and increases the capability of agencies to monitor execution of the budget. It requires reports on financial system compliance by agency heads, OMB, and inspector generals.

Customer Service Executive Order of 1993. An executive order that asks agencies to establish and implement customer service standards, to establish customer service plans and surveys.

REGO III of the National Performance Review, 1996. This policy requirement asks agencies to convert to performance-based organizations, to improve customer service, to increase the use of regulator partnerships, to create performance-based partnership grants, and to transform the federal workforce. Annual reports are required.

Reinvention Impact Center Initiative of the National Performance Review, 1997. This initiative is focused on approximately thirty agencies that deliver services to the public (either directly or indirectly). It asks these agencies to develop a one-page presentation of goals that will lead to the achievement of goals of the NPR by the year 2000. (The GPRA strategic plan is a five-year plan focused on the year 2001.)

Annual OMB Budget Instructions to Agencies (Circular A-11). In addition to general instructions on budget submissions and GPRA, this circular also established guidelines for better management and performance of fixed assets. In addition to these requirements, individual departments and agencies may have also devised their own programs related to quality of work life, other personnel issues, and other management initiatives that have an impact on GPRA implementation.

The PART Process. With the change of administration in 2001, OMB's concern about performance issues revolved around PART. As a result, the HHS budget process effectively substituted concern about GPRA with the PART effort. OMB described the PART process in 2005 as including 60 percent of programs within the federal program (since PART evaluations were made of some programs in FY 2003, 2004, and 2005). However, only 63 of the HHS programs were assessed by the development of the FY 2005 budget. Since there are approximately 300 programs in HHS, this was far from the 60 percent mark. Of those programs, 6 were rated "effective," 15 as "moderately effective," 24 as "adequate," 2 as "ineffective," and 16 as "results not demonstrated." Of the "results not demonstrated" programs, 7 were block grant/formula programs and 7 were competitive grant programs. The Substance Abuse Prevention and Treatment block grant was rated as "ineffective"; however, the president's budget did not reduce the budget request for that program. The Health Professions program, the other program rated as "ineffective," had a history in which OMB called for its elimination, but the Congress continued to fund it.

In some cases, OMB budget examiners were willing to deal with multiple elements of programs as a package; in other cases, the examiner insisted that small programs would require individual PART submissions. It was not always clear to HHS staff why a particular program received the rating it was given; OMB policy officials did not appear to have a consistent view of the PART process. The process appeared to reflect both the individual idiosyncrasies of budget examiners and the political agenda of the administration. While the process was touted as "objective evaluation," it clearly echoed these two elements and served to highlight programs over which OMB wanted control. Unlike the GPRA process (which began with the reality of program managers) PART, in contrast, did not appear to provide any information that would actually help managers. In addition, as GAO commented about the PART entire process, there did not appear to be a clear relationship between the rating that a program received and the budget that was submitted for it by the White House.[23] By the third year of the PART process, that performance activity took shape as a control/management tool and not as a process that would be helpful to managers who sought to improve performance.

HHS Deals with Congress

Unlike a number of other cabinet departments, HHS appropriations authority is dispersed among several subcommittees in both the House and the Senate.[24] The range of committees is documented in a listing of congressional testimony of officials from January to July 2004.[25] The full committees are:

Senate Committee on Health, Education, Labor, and Pensions
Senate Committee on Governmental Affairs
Senate Committee on Energy and Natural Resources
Senate Committee on Aging
Senate Committee on the Budget
Senate Committee on Appropriations
Senate Committee on the Judiciary
Senate Committee on Indian Affairs
Senate Committee on Foreign Relations
Senate Finance Committee
House Select Committee on Homeland Security
House Committee on Financial Services
House Committee on Energy and Commerce
House Committee on Government Reform
House Committee on Ways and Means
House Committee on Science
House Committee on Armed Services

Three separate appropriations subcommittees in each of the chambers have authority over parts of the HHS budget. As a result, although the department's budget is prepared as a whole, it is not evaluated by the congressional players in its entirety. The subunits within the department each have hearings before the appropriations subcommittees, responding to specific questions and concerns about their programs and policies. The Food and Drug Administration budget is presented to subcommittees of the appropriations committee that largely deal with the Department of Agriculture while the Indian Health Service budget is presented to the subcommittees that also deal with the Department of Interior. The remainder of the HHS budget is presented to the subcommittees that deal with labor, education, human services, and health. Congress can also focus on units within units; for example, the budget of the National Cancer Institute (NCI) is described as a bypass budget. Congress has stipulated that the NCI director should present a budget that does not go through the regular department review and, instead, bypasses both the HHS secretary and the National Institutes of Health (NIH) director.

Each of the HHS program units presents its budget to the relevant appropriations committee following an overall presentation by the secretary (usually limited to the House and Senate subcommittees with authority over most of the programs). These hearings vary tremendously in their style and dynamics, often reflecting the level of controversy involving programs. In a few instances, the Congress is a champion of an agency or program and members actually vie with one another to find ways to add to the administration's budget request. Because a number of HHS programs deal with health issues and matters of life and death, those programs (especially the research efforts) are able to generate considerable support within the Congress.

The NIH budget process is unlike any other part of the appropriations process, both in the way that the agency makes its presentation to the subcommittees and—perhaps more importantly—in the way that members treat the agency. As John Trattner characterized it, "The Congress has been turned on by the NIH for years. Legislators of both parties . . . have since the 1960s been generous with NIH budgets, consistently giving the agency more than it requested even in times of severe federal deficit and fierce battles for available funds."[26] The reality of biomedical research means that NIH reports its work to the Congress not in terms of accomplishments during any one specific year or focused on a specific allocation, but in terms of efforts over many years and across subunits within the NIH. For the world of research, unanticipated results were often more useful than those contained in research protocols.

During much of the 1990s, members of Congress across both political parties were largely willing to provide NIH with funds with minimal earmarking for specific units or specific diseases, departing from the traditional way of adding funds to administration requests. A large percentage of the NIH budget (approximately 60 percent of the funds in FY 1995) was designated as basic research that frequently cut across subunits within the agency and contributed to the pursuit of understanding of a collection of diseases.[27] As the director of NIH put it, "The clinical triumphs that we enjoy this year were possible only because we had invested successfully in many fields of basic science—bacteriology, virology, enzymology, chemistry and others."[28] The arguments that were advanced during appropriations committee hearings emphasized the bipartisan support for these types of programs. The logic of this argument had little, if any, use for the kind of information that was developed by either GPRA or PART.

In other program areas, however, members of Congress used the appropriations process to target specific issues. During the late 1990s, members of the Congressional Black Caucus raised issues during the appropriations process about the level of funds that were being spent to deal with HIV and AIDS issues among African American citizens. According to the Centers for Disease Control, the rate of HIV infection among African American men is much higher than among white men.[29] In addition, the caucus also expressed concern about what they viewed as inadequate attention to the problems of African Americans within NIH and the Health Resources and Services Administration (HRSA). Efforts were also developed to encourage nonprofit and indigenous organizations serving African Americans to get involved in the provision of comprehensive outpatient HIV primary care services. When $50 million was earmarked in the FY 2000 and 2001 budgets for prevention and treatment of individuals with HIV/AIDS in minority communities, Congress required that the department submit an operating plan for the use of those funds to both the House and Senate Appropriations Committees. These concerns were not reflected in either the GPRA or PART submissions. (See chapter 5 for a discussion of the relationship between equity concerns and performance measurement.)

Some years earlier, advocates of women's issues had also put pressure within the appropriations process on NIH to pay more attention to diseases of women as well as focusing on differences between men and women during clinical trials. Both of these concerns resulted in the creation of specialized offices within the office of the director of NIH to focus on these populations.

Congress has also used a variant on the legislative veto to limit the discretion of the HHS agencies. In the FY 2000 budget, HRSA was told that before it could issue regulations related to the organ transplant program it had to give the Congress forty-two days to review those regulations. The previous year, HRSA was told that its final regulations could not become effective for one year. Both of these actions provided the Congress with the ability to stop the agency from acting to change the program in a direction that some members of Congress opposed. Even though officials in HRSA and HHS believed that the proposed regulations would improve the performance of the organ transplant program, Congress determined that pressure from those who were opposed to those regulations was more important.

The appropriations process for some of the HHS programs can be characterized as highly volatile and conflict laden. Often these conflicts are embedded in very different partisan perspectives on programs, particularly in environments of divided government. During the mid-1990s, after the Republicans gained control of both the House and the Senate, the Republicans were able to use studies and reports issued by GAO during the appropriations hearings and afterwards to raise serious questions about programs. In the case of the Head Start program, for example, a series of GAO reports related to GPRA were cited by Republicans on the relevant appropriations subcommittee to question the effectiveness of the federal expenditures for that program. The GAO reports not only helped the majority side of the subcommittee staff draft questions to the Administration for Children and Families assistant secretary, but those reports also were used to generate follow-up questions to the agency. The answers to those questions were developed by the agency for the subcommittee.

Majority Leader Dick Armey actually formed a "Results Caucus" and published grades for departments and agencies in his congressional newsletter. He ranked the HHS strategic plan as 17th of 24 plans and its first performance plan as 14th of 24 plans.[30] During a joint hearing of the Senate Appropriations and Governmental Affairs Committee, an Assessment of Agency GPRA Strategic Plans based on House and Senate GPRA teams ranked HHS as "poor." Other analyses of the HHS submissions were conducted by GAO. In mid-July 1999, GAO issued a report titled "Observations on the Department of Health and Human Services' Performance Plan for Fiscal Year 2000." That report viewed the department-wide summary document and thirteen individual agency plans as a single entity and criticized the multiple documents for inconsistencies in their presentation of goals, data, and strategies.[31]

But for other programs, support for federal expenditures transcended partisan differences because the programs were important for constituents. Several programs within HRSA generated significant Republican support because they provide essential services to citizens in districts. Both the community health centers and the rural health programs were viewed as important by Republican members of Congress representing small towns or rural areas. If either of those programs evaporated or were significantly cut, there would be no health services at all in those districts. This support occurred despite some opposition to the programs within the Republican party leadership.

Since 1997, the Congress has had available to it the information developed by agencies under the requirements of GPRA. Although there may have been a few instances where congressional decisions regarding HHS budget allocations were affected by the GPRA submissions, for the most part the GPRA data were used by members of Congress only to support preexisting positions on specific programs. For example, members of Congress who were not supporters of the Head Start program did use performance information presented by GAO as evidence of problems with the program; that, however, was a rarity. It was rare for GPRA documents to be cited by members of Congress during the appropriations development process. While members may have given rhetorical attention to the GPRA documents, they continued to rely on more traditional sources of information to make budget and policy decisions.

When OMB placed its emphasis on the PART program, there were concerns in the Congress about the role of the legislative branch in that performance assessment process. For some observers, the assessment of program purpose and design that is a part of PART can be viewed as an attempt to preempt the role of the Congress. Legislation is often constructed for a range of political reasons that may not be clear or relevant to OMB budget examiners. Some critics believe that it is not appropriate for OMB to second-guess Congress in terms of assessment of program purpose and design. Some members of the House of Representatives proposed a piece of legislation that would require an assessment of the effectiveness of each federal program at least once every five years.

While this proposal was described as an amendment to GPRA, it deviated from GPRA. Instead of requiring *agencies* to set performance goals and evaluate the performance of their programs, the bill requires the *White House*, through the Office of Management and

Budget, to pick the criteria and evaluate performance. As one critic of the proposed legislation put it, "Congress expresses its priorities through statutes authorizing agency activities. But OMB doesn't implement those statutes. OMB implements the priorities of the White House. In fact, many agencies, and especially those charged with protecting public health, worker safety, and the environment, view OMB as hostile to the agencies' fundamental missions. This bill actually encourages OMB to infringe on Congress's prerogatives."[32] The contrast between the perspectives of OMB within the executive branch and the congressional institutions was clearly defined by GAO in its October 2003 report.[33]

Conclusion

This chapter has argued that the structure of the U.S. political system makes it difficult to meet the legitimate but multiple and diverse needs and perspectives of both the legislative and executive branches. These perspectives are found within OMB and the White House, in the Congress, and in federal agencies themselves. As a result, it is very difficult—if not impossible—to craft a single government-wide effort that measures performance of agencies and also holds a single set of actors accountable for that performance. The political process—not an analytical strategy—provides the mechanism for tradeoffs between these varied perspectives. While all of these actors are concerned about accountability and performance, their definitions are neither simple nor consistent.

While GPRA and PART have carved out somewhat different approaches to performance management, both of these efforts illustrate the problems that emerge from the attempt to superimpose a rational and consistent strategy on top of the American political structure. There are three main players in the process, each with different motivations, roles, and expectations: OMB, the Congress, and federal agencies.

The OMB Role

OMB's role is not that of a controller or commander of the executive branch. Not only does it have to share powers with Congress, but it also has to deal with quite different programs, agency cultures, and strategies within the federal government portfolio. It sees itself as the guardian of the performance management process but also serves as the overseer for a range of requirements and regulations that intersect with the performance role. At the same time, its role as the "keeper" of the president's budget makes it a force to be reckoned with.

The Role of Congress

The multiple voices within Congress play different roles and carry out varied functions. In addition, the nature of many policy issues means that policy problems cross over the jurisdictional lines within the Congress. On top of this fragmentation is the reality of partisan politics. Unless the partisan agenda supports it, few in Congress will defer to an analytical "fix."

The Agency Role

Administrative agencies charged with implementing programs also have to balance multiple roles, functions, and realities. They are charged with finding a way to carry out programs that may contain multiple and often conflicting goals. They have to deal with OMB, particularly through the budget process, as well as with the appropriate committees of the Congress. They are charged with planning, budgeting, and management responsibilities; each of these roles demands different performance measurement approaches.

The complexity and fragmentation within the U.S. political system makes it almost ludicrous to argue for an approach to performance measurement that is based on a one-size-fits-all strategy. There is not one size that is appropriate government-wide. There is not one single format that makes sense to be applied to diverse agencies. There is not one size that will meet the many actors in Congress. And there is not even one size that meets the needs of a diverse array of OMB budget examiners. As a result, the performance assessment process must be tailored to meet specific needs of specific programs, and the performance standards that are developed must be sensitive to the attributes of specific programs.

Enid Brown's dilemma is not uncommon. As a career civil servant who has reached the top ranks of the career bureaucracy, she is subject to all of the forces that have been discussed in this chapter. If she focuses on the needs of her staff, she is likely to incur the wrath of OMB officials. And if she focuses on the expectations of the OMB staff, she is likely to face quite different expectations from congressional actors, particularly those on the appropriations committees. She has to decide which actors and issues to take the most seriously and which to deal with in a narrow compliance mode.

Notes

1. Much of this discussion is drawn from Beryl A. Radin, "The Government Performance and Results Act (GPRA) and the Tradition of Federal Management Reform: Square Pegs in Round Holes?" *Journal of Public Administration Research and Theory* 10, no. 1 (January 2000).

2. General Accounting Office, *Performance Budgeting: Past Initiatives Offer Insights for GPRA Implementation*, GAO/AIMD-97-46, March 1997, p. 7.

3. Senate Committee on Governmental Affairs, *Report to Provide for the Establishment, Testing, and Evaluation of Strategic Planning and Performance Measurement in the Federal Government, and for Other Purposes*, http://server. conginst.org/canginst/results/gprapt.html.

4. Ibid.

5. Ibid.

6. See Office of Management and Budget, "Performance and Management Assessments," *Budget of the United States Government*, Fiscal Year 2004, December 2004.

7. Ibid.

8. "PART Frequently Asked Questions," Question 27, Office of Management and Budget, http://www.whitehouse.gov/omb/part/2004_faq. html (accessed December 2004).

9. Congressional Record: "The Introduction of the Program Assessment and Results Act," January 4, 2005 (Extensions)] [Page E15] [DOCID:cr04ja05-55]. From the Congressional Record Online via GPO Access, wais.gpo-access.gov/crecord/ (or see http://www.ombwatch.org/regs/2005/para/ PlattsIntroduction.pdf) (accessed December 2004.).

10. U.S. Congress, House of Representatives Committee Report, *Departments of Transportation, Treasury, and Housing and Urban Development, the Judi-*

ciary, District of Columbia, and Independent Agencies Appropriations Bill, 2006.
HRPT 109-153, June 24, 2005. http://frwebgate.access.gpo.gov/cgi-bin/
getdoc.cgi?dbname=109_cong_reports&docid=f:hr153.109   (accessed
December 2004).

11. OMB Watch, *The OMB Watcher*, February 22, 2005, Volume 6, Nov. 4.

12. See David H. Rosenbloom, "The Government Performance and Results
    Act and the Constitutional Separation of Powers" (paper delivered at the
    Association for Public Policy Analysis and Management, Washington, D.C.,
    October 29–31, 1998).

13. See, for example, Robert Nakamura and Frank Smallwood, *The Politics of
    Policy Implementation* (New York: St. Martins Press, 1980).

14. Rosenbloom argues that the legislative involvement in agency strategic
    planning does "fit the institutional role Congress designed for itself in
    1946." Rosenbloom, "The Government Performance and Results Act."

15. This was anticipated by Judith Gruber, *Controlling Bureaucracies: Dilemmas
    in Democratic Governance* (Berkeley: University of California Press, 1987).

16. Quoted in Stephen Barr, "OPM's Budget Justifications Displease House
    Appropriations Committee," *Washington Post*, July 30, 2004, p. B 2.

17. GAO, "Performance Budgeting: PART Focuses Attention on Program
    Performance, but More Can Be Done to Engage Congress," Report to
    the chairman, Subcommittee on Government Management, Finance, and
    Accountability, Committee on Government Reform, House of Repre-
    sentatives, GAO-06-28, October 2005.

18. This is still true, even though the Republican majority in the Congress is
    more disciplined than had been the case in the past.

19. Letter to Jacob J. Lew, Director, Office of Management and Budget, from
    Dan Burton, House Committee on Government Reform; John R. Kasich,
    House Committee on the Budget; Dick Armey, House Majority Leader; and
    Fred Thompson, Senate Governmental Affairs Committee, July 1, 1999.

20. See Beryl A. Radin, *The Accountable Juggler: The Art of Leadership in a Federal
    Agency* (Washington, D.C.: CQ Press, 2002) for a discussion of the HHS
    administrative world.

21. This is drawn from Beryl A. Radin, "The Challenge of Managing Across
    Boundaries: The Case of the Office of the Secretary in the U.S. Depart-
    ment of Health and Human Services," *PWC Endowment for the Business of
    Government* (November 2000).

22. Quoted in Beryl A. Radin, "The Government Performance and Results
    Act (GPRA): Hydra-Headed Monster or Effective Policy Tool?" *Public
    Administration Review* 58, no. 4 (July/August 1998).

23. GAO, *Performance Budgeting: Observations on the Use of OMB's Program Assessment
    Rating Tool for the Fiscal Year 2004 Budget*, GAO-04-174, January 2004, p. 34.

24. This discussion draws on Radin, *The Accountable Juggler*, ch. 5.

25. Drawn from listing of testimony for calendar year 2004, Assistant Secretary for Legislation, ASL, HHS. http://www.hhs.gov/asl/testimony.html.

26. John H. Trattner, *The 2000 Prune Book: How to Succeed in Washington's Top Jobs* (Washington, D.C.: Council for Excellence in Government and Brookings Institution Press, 2000), 230.

27. Comments of NIH Director Harold Varmus to the Committee on Appropriations, U.S. House of Representatives, Subcommittee on the Departments of Labor, Health and Human Services, Education, and Related Agencies, Hearings on the National Institutes of Health, 1994 (Washington, D.C.: U.S. Government Printing Office, April 19, 1994), 18.

28. Ibid., 3.

29. Robert Herbert, "The Quiet Scourge," *New York Times*, January 11, 2001, p. A 25.

30. Majority Leader Dick Armey, "Towards a Smaller, Smarter, Common Sense Government: Results Act: It's the Law," November 1997.

31. GAO, *HHS's Fiscal Year 2000 Performance Plan*, GAO/HEHS-99-149R, July 20, 1999.

32. Statement of Rep. Henry Waxman, House Committee on Government Reform, on the Waxman Amendment regarding who performs the assessments under HR 3826, the Program Assessment and Results Act, June 3, 2004.

33. See GAO-06-28.

intergovernmental relationships: power and authority in the u.s. political system

7

          Karen O'Grady is the director of Medicaid for the state of New Jersey. She is a career official within the state and has been working in health policy areas for more than fifteen years. During that time she has been able to work with the diverse constituencies surrounding health services for the poor. That has required her to develop good working relationships with the medical community, the diverse array of providers, insurance companies, advocacy groups for citizens who would receive services and, of course, both federal and state appointed and elected officials.

When she took over as the director of the Medicaid program she realized that she was confronting two very different sets of performance expectations. Half of the funding for the program came from the state through the state appropriations process. Thus she worried about the support for the program from the state legislature, the governor's office, and the state budget office. In the past few years the state's budget has been overwhelmed by Medicaid expenditures, and current fiscal problems make both the legislature and the governor's office worry about costs attached to requirements of this federal program. Although the state political leaders would like to cover more people and services through Medicaid, the budget problems make that extremely difficult to accomplish. In addition, the decisions that were made about eligibility and the array of services within the state had to be acceptable to the provider community. Without their support, there would not be doctors, hospitals, and others who would agree to provide services for the Medicaid population. And these groups have the organizations available to put pressure on state actors.

But the other half of the funding for the program comes from the federal government. The program had been devised with some general federal guidelines that set the framework for state discretion. Over the years states varied quite significantly in the way that they constructed their Medicaid programs. And over the years states also were given opportunities to waive specific federal requirements as long as the changed processes did not have a negative impact on the budget—that is, they did not increase the budget for the program.

Recently, however, federal policies on performance outcomes have required states to report their performance under the program within the framework of specific federally defined goals and measures. While Ms. O'Grady believes that her office should be accountable for the expenditure of the funds, the federally defined requirements do not reflect the expectations of the state officials who appropriate half of the funding for the program. Although she has raised this issue with the congressional delegation from her state, it appears that it involves a level of administrative detail that makes it difficult to get their attention. In addition, the federal requirements would not allow New Jersey to use its existing data system because it differs from the federal data requirements.

She is concerned that attention given to the federal requirements will lead to dissatisfaction within the state, with the possible result that the state half of the Medicaid budget will be decreased. Since the federal contribution is designed to match the state contribution, that could lead to a significant decrease in the total budget for her department.

In addition to the horizontal separation of powers defined by the separate branches of government, the U.S. system is designed to minimize the power that is lodged in the national government. Debate over the appropriate role of the federal government has been a constant element for policy and administrative players since the beginning of the nation. While often this discussion takes place in the context of specific policies and programs, it is also a part of the overall rhetoric about the role of government in this country. During the past several decades, there has been increasing attention to the devolution of responsibilities for the implementation of programs that are partially or mainly funded with federal dollars. There are fewer and fewer federal domestic programs that are entirely implemented by federal staff. Instead, responsibility for making allocation decisions and actually delivering services has been delegated to state and local governments or to other third parties (often nonprofit organizations).[1]

Because so many of the federal programs involve intricate intergovernmental relationships, federal agencies have struggled with ways to structure these relationships. Federal agencies are balancing two competing imperatives. On one hand, they are attempting to hold third parties accountable for the use of the federal monies but, on the other hand, they are constrained by the political and legal realities that provide significant discretion and leeway to the third parties for the use of these federal dollars.

The federal efforts dealing with performance—both GPRA and PART—move against the devolution tide. Efforts to hold federal government agencies accountable for the way that programs are implemented actually assumes that these agencies have legitimate authority to enforce the requirements that are included in performance measures. In some cases, the federal agencies have worked closely with these other partners to devise a set of performance measures that are mutually agreed upon. The relationship around these efforts must be collaborative and not merely depend on federal officials telling states or localities what to do. More often, however, these other partners—especially states—have worked to protect their discretion in programs that are politically sensitive, such as Medicaid and TANF. In addition, states have taken action to ignore provisions of the No Child Left Behind Act, arguing that the federal requirements conflict with state goals, are intrusive, and require state expenditure of funds. For example, the Utah legislature passed such a bill; the Attorney General of Connecticut announced he would sue the Department of Education; and Texas openly defied an expansion of standardized tests for disabled children.[2]

The criticism of the No Child Left Behind testing requirements led to the federal government backing away from standardized tests that would be given across the country and, instead, allowing states to use their own tests to meet the law's requirements. This has resulted in a disparity between results from the National Assessment of Educational Progress test (a federal test mandated by No Child Left Behind) and state tests. Some educators have argued that a number of states have created easy exams to avoid the sanctions that NCLB imposes on low-scoring schools.[3]

There are a number of issues that deal with the impact of performance activity on intergovernmental relationships in the United States. They include dimensions of third-party government, the impact of both GPRA and PART on intergovernmental relationships, and reviews other approaches, including performance partnerships, incentives, negotiated performance measures, performance goals in legislation, development of standards, and waiver processes.

Third-Party Government and Performance

Paul Posner has written about the accountability challenges posed by what has been termed "third-party" government. Third-party government refers to collaborative actions of governments and private institutions at multiple levels. He notes that the major challenge stems from diffuse political authority embedded in third-party relationships. These players have independent bases of political power and often have conflicting goals and interests. Posner suggests that these third-party partners often have the upper hand in both policy formulation and implementation and thus require the federal role to be that of a partner involved in bargaining relationships.[4]

Posner argues that there are a number of features in third-party relationships that have implications for accountability. First, these providers (including states, nonprofits, universities, or defense contractors) influence both the setting of goals and the implementation of these goals. Second, the participation of these parties is voluntary. Third, these providers often have monopolies over the means of program production. Fourth, these players often have inside knowledge, creating information asymmetries that tilt in their favor. Fifth, these providers are involved in efforts that Posner terms "complex implementation chains," in which the federal activity is only one of a number of actions.[5]

Many third-party arrangements are crafted to minimize the federal role; despite the transfer of federal funds to these parties, there is often significant political conflict over the appropriate role of the federal government. Even though it may pay (at least partially) for programs, the extent of its role is disputed by both the third parties and their political supporters.

Third-party perspectives thus create a major problem in the performance context determining which party defines the outcomes that are expected. States that already have performance measurement systems in place also do not want to shift to a national system if their current activities provide them with the information that is useful to them. In this sense, if performance measurement is taken very seriously, it can lead to centralization—an increase in the federal role.

One of the expectations of the performance movement has focused on the realities of the intergovernmental system, particularly the tension between those who both devise programs and fund them (at least in part) and those who actually implement them. For some, performance measurement is viewed as the bridge between the goals of the federal government for accountability and the demands of state or local government for discretion and flexibility. In this sense, the performance movement and performance measurement are seen as a way to avoid the traditional command and control perspective of the federal government and to substitute performance outcome requirements for input and process requirements.[6] According to some proponents of the performance movement, the traditional forms of accountability that are seen to evoke a compliance mentality will be replaced by performance measures that emphasize results.

The concern about performance is closely linked to the reinvention movement popularized by Osborne and Gaebler and others who

have emphasized reinvention of government at the state and local government levels. The reinvention movement accentuates the
importance of measuring results. According to Osborne and Gaebler, "Because they don't measure results, bureaucratic governments
rarely achieve them. . . . With so little information about results,
bureaucratic governments reward their employees based on other
things."[7]

Two of the most popular approaches to performance at these
levels have been report cards[8] and efforts attached to contracting
out and privatization.[9] Report cards have frequently been used in
the education sector, where schools, classrooms, and often teachers are evaluated based on the test scores of the students. And the
increased use of contracting out and other forms of involvement
by the private sector have led to performance contracting, where
contractees are held accountable for specific outcomes written into
contract language. These and other performance efforts have been
focused largely on the service delivery level, where government
agencies either deliver the services themselves or establish relationships with others for the specific delivery of services.

While some of these state and local efforts do raise interesting
and important intergovernmental issues, the concern about performance at the federal government level is much more complex and
difficult than efforts at the state and local levels. In many ways, the
performance movement at the federal level collides with strategies
of devolution and a diminished federal role, because it puts the focus for change on federal agencies and assumes that they have the
ability to require the states and localities to follow their lead. What
is most interesting about this situation is that few of the individuals
within the policymaking world (particularly in the Congress) are
aware that they are setting up incompatible strategies. Those who
argue for more compliance-oriented federal government accountability are often those who also argue for a decreased federal role
and increased autonomy for states in the way that they expend the
federal dollars.

While this collision seems obvious from the vantage point of
hindsight, it is clear that neither the designers of GPRA nor those
of PART focused on the difficulties that federal agencies had in establishing measures of performance for programs designed as block

grants or with high levels of discretion provided for third-party implementers, particularly state agencies.

In fact, when one examines the development of both of the main federal performance activities, there is little in that background that provides real guidance regarding federal agency dependence on other levels of government. The only specification of consultation with "external" parties is found in fairly vague language regarding the development of the agency strategic plans. Agencies are not required to deal with these external parties as they devise their annual performance plans; state and local governments who act as agents for the federal government are relegated to the category of external parties even though the implementation of programs depends on their activity. Similarly, in the development of GPRA there was little attention to the form that the program takes (e.g., whether it is a competitive grant program, a block grant, or some other form of formula funding).

Over the past several years, at least some federal agencies have been pressured to take direct responsibility for the performance outcomes achieved through federal programs, whether or not the federal agency actually delivers the services provided through federal funding. In some instances, this has moved the agency away from a focus on performance that values state flexibility and discretion and back to a more traditional compliance-oriented posture. Both GPRA and PART have tended to highlight the federal role of defining goals at a national level rather than leaving it to states (those Laboratories of Democracy) to bargain about specific goals and outcomes for their jurisdictions.[10]

GPRA and Intergovernmental Relations

Although there was minimal attention to third-party grants in the design of the GPRA legislation, at least one arm of the Congress did acknowledge the special problems involving the balance between flexibility and accountability in the performance activities. Two reports of the GAO from the Advanced Studies and Evaluation Methodology General Government Division did warn about these problems.[11] However, it does not appear that these warnings had much of an impact either on other GAO reports or on comments from Republican congressional leaders. These GAO reports are discussed because they provide a perspective that seeks to recognize the special problems experienced in the implementation of performance measurement in programs with limited federal authority. GAO emphasized the special problems involved in block (or what they call flexible) grants, issues related to availability of performance data, and suggested some strategies that could be used to address these problems.

The February 1998 testimony by GAO official Susan Westin drew on a GAO study that focused on what were called "flexible grant programs"—programs in transportation, health, social services, education, criminal justice, and employment. It outlined conceptual problems that were likely to be faced in the GPRA performance planning process in terms of both existing grant programs and proposals for additional block grants. Westin testified that

> [f]lexible grants are an adaptable policy tool and are used in fields from urban transit to community mental health. They are alike in that each addresses a national purpose but gives state or local grantees the flexibility to adapt funded activities to fit the state or local context. However, there are vast differences among them as well. Some offer flexibility within a narrow range, as do many so-called "categorical" programs, while others offer choice so broad that they come close to resembling revenue sharing.[12]

The testimony emphasized three federal program design features. First, it noted that objectives of grant programs can be characterized as either primarily performance related or primary fiscal. Performance-related objectives, according to the GAO study, focus on services, but fiscal or financial assistance objectives focus on providing dollars (such as support for goods or services) and targeting funding to needed jurisdictions. The second critical feature focuses on the nature of the operations: should national objectives be achieved through a grant-specific operating program or simply through adding to the stream of funds supporting ongoing state or local programs? The report noted that "[g]rants that operate as a funding stream are not federal 'programs' in this sense. Here, the federal agency provides funds that are merged with funds from state or local sources (and sometimes from other federal sources as well) to support state or local activities allowable under the flexible grant." The third feature deals with the activities; some flexible grants focus on a single major activity or a limited set of activities, while others allow unrestricted choice among a wide variety of allowable activities.[13]

Westin pointed to limitations of performance data in the flexible grant context. She noted that "few grant programs are able to obtain these data program-wide"; that descriptive information is useful to convey the variety of conditions under which programs operate; and that formal evaluation studies—if available—can be helpful. She noted that whatever sources are used, they are likely to be more helpful "when backed by statutory authorization and budget resources than when [they] are not."[14]

Several months later, following the review of the first annual performance plans for FY 1999, the same office in GAO released a report based on six case studies of how agencies were able to address the challenge of developing performance measures for outcome goals that are influenced by external factors. The report noted that "many, if not most, federal programs aim to improve some aspects of complex systems, such as the economy or the environment, or share responsibilities with other agencies for achieving their objectives, and thus face the challenge of setting goals that both are far-reaching and can be realistically affected by the programs."[15]

The report noted that earlier reviews of agencies' first performance plans indicated that few performance goals were outcome oriented, largely because these outcomes "are the result of complex systems or phenomena outside of government control." As a result, it was difficult for agencies to "confidently attribute a causal connection between the program and its desired outcomes. . . . In cases where external factors influence the program's outcomes, an examination of performance measures alone will not accurately reflect a program's performance or effectiveness."[16] The report commented that "agencies were faced with the dilemma of whether to select (1) annual performance goals that represent the ultimate benefits of their activities to the taxpayer or (2) goals that they could reasonably expect to achieve directly and for which they could be held accountable."[17]

As a result of the analysis of six agencies, the report outlined a range of strategies that could address a number of challenges. These included limited control over intended outcomes, multiple goals, end outcomes taking years to develop, variability in local program activities, variability and incompatibility of data, and potential data collection burden.[18] According to GAO, the strategies that were used by the six agencies studied, "appeared to have benefited from considerable and perhaps unusual access to analytical resources and from previous experience in measuring their results."[19] This comment suggested that most agencies would not be able to employ these strategies.

In a report issued more than five years later, GAO acknowledged that one of the persistent challenges in setting outcome-oriented goals, measuring performance, and collecting useful data circled is the difficulties encountered in meeting GPRA reporting requirements for intergovernmental grant programs.[20] Unlike the general tone of the report, this commentary was hardly optimistic.

> Programs that do not deliver a readily measurable product or service are likely to have difficulty meeting GPRA performance measurement and reporting requirements. Intergovernmental grant programs, particularly those with the flexibility inherent in classic block grant design, may be more likely to have difficulty producing performance measures at the national level and raise delicate issues of accountability. Although most flexible grant programs we reviewed reported simple activity or client counts, relatively few of them collected uniform data on the outcomes of state or local service activities. Collecting such data requires conditions (such as uniformity of activities, objectives, and measures) that do not exist under many flexible program designs, and even where overall performance of a state or local program can be measured, the amount attributable to federal funding often cannot be separated out.[21]

Further, the 2004 GAO report cited findings from focus groups as well as surveys of federal agency staff to suggest that performance data from relevant partner organizations and timely and consistent national data were both difficult to obtain. One respondent was quoted as saying: "Defining meaningful measures for the work we do is extremely difficult; and even if they could be defined, performance and accomplishment is [*sic*] dependent on so many factors outside our control that it is difficult, if not impossible, to make valid conclusions."[22]

PART and Intergovernmental Relations

When the Bush White House developed its own performance measurement system after assuming office, the initial design of the system acknowledged that there were special attributes for different types of programs (see discussion in chapter 3).[23] A range of program approaches were defined; among them were block/formula grant programs. In the initial instructions for agencies, OMB noted:

> Some block grant programs provide resources to non-Federal levels of government to focus on specific program areas, such as education, job training, or violence prevention. While the funds can often be used for a variety of activities, they are for a specific purpose. In these cases, national goals can be articulated that focus on outcomes to highlight for grantees the ultimate purpose of program funds. Targets for these measures may be set by surveying grantees to gauge the expected scale of their work or by looking at historical trend data. A system could be developed that uses performance measures and national standards to promote "joint" accountability for results. With this approach, after agreeing on an appropriate set of performance measures, program targets can be set at the local level and aggregated up to national targets. . . .
>
> Some Federal programs are both large and diverse. They may be designed to address multiple objectives or support a broad range of activities or both. Block grant programs often have these characteristics, with the added feature of allowing grantees the flexibility to set priorities and make spending choices. Increased flexibility at the local

level can limit efforts to set national goals and standards or create obstacles for ensuring accountability. In other cases, the program may focus on a limited set of activities which in turn are used for multiple purposes by many distinct stakeholders. Establishing performance measures for these types of programs can be challenging.[24]

Each program type received specific questions that, theoretically, would be sensitive to the construct and demands of that type. Yet the questions developed for the intergovernmental programs did not reflect the challenges that had been raised both by GAO and by OMB itself. Among the questions devised for the block/formula grant programs were the following:

- Does the program have a limited number of specific, ambitious long-term performance goals that focus on outcomes and meaningfully reflect the purpose of the program?
- Does the program have a limited number of annual performance goals that demonstrate progress toward achieving the long-term goals?
- Do all program partners (grantees, subgrantees, contractors, etc.) commit to and report on performance that relates to and supports the output and outcome goals of the program?
- Is the program budget aligned with the program goals in such a way that the impact of funding, policy, and legislative changes on performance is readily known?
- Does the agency regularly collect timely and credible performance information and use it to manage the program?
- Are performance measurements used to increase accountability?
- Are all funds (federal and partners) spent for the intended purpose?
- Does the agency have sufficient knowledge about grantee activities?
- Does the program collect performance data on an annual basis and is it public and transparent in a meaningful manner?
- Has the program demonstrated adequate progress in achieving its long-term outcome goal(s)?

- Does the program (including program partners) achieve its annual performance goals?
- Were program goals achieved within budgeted costs and established schedules?
- Does the performance of this program compare favorably to that of other programs with similar purpose and goals?[25]

If a program had fiscal objectives, was designed to operate within a broader funding stream, and supported diverse activities, it would be difficult for it to come out very well in the PART evaluation process, since it would not be able to respond to a number of these questions.

In fact, this was the case for the block/formula grant programs that were included in the PART analysis for the FY 2005 budget. The PART effort during that budget year included 399 programs; 70 of those programs were designed as block/formula grant programs and 7 of them were designated specifically as block grant programs. Table 7.1 compares the distribution of ratings for the block/formula grant programs with the broader pattern for the 399 program efforts.

Fewer programs in the block/formula grant category were rated as effective and twice as many programs were rated as ineffective as in all programs. This is true even though there are different types of grants; some have a history of more active federal presence while others have a clear agenda for more autonomy for the grantees. When one looks only at the seven block grants, the pattern is even

Table 7.1 Block/Formula Grant Program Ratings, FY 2005

Rating	All 399 programs	Block/formula grant programs	Block grant programs only
Effective	11%	less than 3%	0%
Moderately effective	26%	27%	14%
Adequate	21%	20%	14%
Ineffective	5%	10%	43%
Results not demonstrated	37%	40%	28%

more divergent. No program was rated effective and three of them were rated ineffective. The block grant program that was rated as adequate was the Community Mental Health Services Block Grant. Yet its sister block grant, the Substance Abuse Block Grant, was rated as ineffective. Both of the programs could be viewed as efforts that were designed with fiscal objectives that sought to operate within a broader funding stream and supported diverse activities. But the PART framework did not provide a way to acknowledge those realities, and observers believed that the differences in rating were attributable to differences between OMB budget examiners.[26]

It is important to remember that many of the grant programs involved policy areas that have been criticized by the Bush administration. But these grantees are faced with performance review efforts that highlight the federal government's oversight role, while the premise of block grants is that funds are sent to the states with freedom from complex federal oversight requirements. Many state and local governments have their own performance and accountability review processes; overlaying federal PART reviews has the effect of overriding state and local government self-management, contrary to the intent of block grant projects. This set of problems is likely to continue unless OMB acknowledges that the federal role is passive not active in some program areas.

Other Approaches to Performance in an Intergovernmental Context
Although the implementation of GPRA and PART has provided the framework and a point of focus for federal performance efforts, other efforts have been undertaken within federal agencies to balance the two often conflicting imperatives: to provide states with flexibility and yet maintain a commitment to performance outcomes that acknowledges the expectations of those who fund and authorize programs.

The analysis that follows is an effort to explore some techniques that have been used by the federal government as it has attempted to bridge the goals of funders with the demands of those who carry out programs. It suggests that the initial expectations of those who believed performance measures would be a relatively easy way to address intergovernmental tensions were naïve and quite unrealistic. Such research would also build on the extant literature that deals with the more technical questions focusing on development of performance outcomes, particularly the techniques that have been devised to deal with multiple stakeholders and situations where competing values are at play.

The discussion highlights six different approaches that have been taken recently within federal agencies to deal with issues of performance. Some of these efforts predated both the GPRA and PART initiatives, some are distinct from them, and others have been melded into the GPRA and PART framework. Some have been devised as a result of legislation and others through administrative action. All are struggling with the tension between federal agency accountability and devolution and discretion provided to state and local agencies. These include: performance partnerships; incentives; negotiated measures; building performance goals into legislation; establishment of standards; and waivers.

Performance Partnerships

Over the past decade, a number of federal agencies have adopted or at least explored the possibility of moving categorical programs into performance partnerships. These partnerships have become increasingly popular as agencies realize the limitations of their ability to achieve desired changes in complex settings. While partnerships between various agencies and government have been around in some form for some years, the performance orientation of the contemporary effort is new. However, these efforts do build on the concept of grantors and grantees as coequal, not as a relationship between a principal and agents. The image of the partnership is one in which partners discuss how to combine resources from both players to achieve a prespecified end state. This end state is expected to be measurable in order for a partnership to be successful.

The design of a performance partnership addresses what some have viewed as one of the most troubling problems faced by federal managers: lack of control over outcomes. While the managers may have control over inputs, processes, and outputs, they cannot specify end outcomes. Performance partnerships may involve agreements between federal officials and state or local agencies; they may be ad hoc or permanent.

The performance partnerships entered into by the Environmental Protection Agency (EPA) and states have been among the most visible of these arrangements. However, there have been proposals for the development of performance partnerships involving health programs, programs for children, and the Office of National Drug Control Policy.

The National Environmental Performance Partnership System began in FY 1996 with six pilot states; by the end of FY 1998, forty-five states had entered into these arrangements along with a number of Indian tribes.[27] According to EPA,

> Performance Partnerships establish a new working relationship whereby the States and EPA determine on an annual basis what and how work will be performed. Traditionally, the process for funding and addressing environmental and public health priorities has been conducted with a single media focus. States have submitted up to 16 annual workplans and received multiple grants to support air, drinking water, hazardous waste, and other pollution control programs. . . . [T]his approach has fueled administrative management and oversight activity, diverting resources from on-the-ground improvement efforts. . . . Performance Partnerships are designed to place much greater emphasis on environmental results and to achieve better coordination between Federal and State environmental programs.[28]

Further, according to GAO, "the two-way negotiation process inherent in the program has fostered more frequent and effective communication between regional and state participants and improved their overall working relationship."[29] At the same time, however, GAO noted that the process is not without problems. It highlighted a number of "technical challenges":

- An absence of baseline data to use as the basis for measuring improvements

- The difficulty of quantifying certain results
- The difficulty of linking program activities to environmental results
- The level of resources needed to develop a high quality performance measurement system.[30]

GAO also noted that states and EPA disagreed over the degree to which states would be permitted to vary from the national core measures and the composition of the measures. Because each of the EPA regional offices enters into the arrangements with the states in their region, there is some variation between agreements across the country. This was of concern to the GAO analysts.

EPA's experience with performance partnerships illustrates some of the problems that are intrinsic to this performance strategy and agreement form. The individual negotiation between the federal agency and (in this case) states is likely to result in variability of agreements across the country. To some, in fact, the individual tailoring of agreements is the strength of the mechanism. However, others are concerned that this variation results from differential treatment of jurisdictions.

The problems with data that were identified by GAO are also a predictable problem with any performance partnership agreement. The strategy is often attractive to federal agencies charged with the implementation of programs involving policy sectors that do not have well-established data systems or even data definitions. In such settings, it is difficult to establish and to garner data for the performance measures required to achieve the expectations of the approach.

Incentives

Over the past several decades, as the economics paradigm has increasingly influenced policy, some policy analysts have focused on the use of incentives as a way to change behavior. Incentives seek to induce behavior rather than command it. According to Weimer and Vining, bureaucrats and politicians have tended to be less enthusiastic about this approach than are those trained in economics.[31] This has occurred, they argue, because bureaucrats and politicians tend to be attracted to direct regulation, since they believe that incentives also require governmental intervention and therefore involve regulation.

To some degree, however, incentives have been at play in the past in a number of federal programs through matching fund requirements. When the federal government offers funds as an incentive to induce states to provide their own funds, the matching requirements do serve an incentive function. In many cases, however, performance expectations are not usually made explicit, particularly in programs carried over from the past.

Probably the most dramatic recent example of performance incentives in the contemporary American scene is found in the High Performance Bonus program attached to the Temporary Assistance for Needy Families (TANF) welfare program. That 1996 legislation called on the secretary of the Department of Health and Human Services, in consultation with the National Governors' Association and the American Public Welfare Association, to develop a formula measuring state performance relative to block grant goals. Bonuses to an individual state cannot exceed 5 percent of the family assistance grant. In addition, the law established a bonus for states that demonstrate that the number of out-of-wedlock births and abortions that occurred in the state in the most recent two-year period decreased compared to the number of such births in the previous period. The top five states will receive a bonus of up to $20 million each, and if less than five states qualify, the grant will be increased to $25 million each.

The first high-performance bonus awards were made in December 1999. These awards were made in four categories: job placement, job success (measured by retention and earnings), biggest improvement in job placement, and biggest improvement in job success. The awards, $200 million in total, were made to twenty-seven states; states were chosen on the basis of their ranking in each of the four categories. The states ranked the highest in each category were Indiana for job placement; Minnesota for job retention and earnings; Washington for the biggest improvement in job placement; and Florida for the biggest improvement in job retention and earnings. Eleven states received bonuses in two categories and one (Minnesota) was successful in three.

HHS proposed that additional criteria be added during the following year to the existing four measures; these are family formation measures, enrollment in Medicaid and the Children's Health Insurance Program, and enrollment in the Food Stamps program.

The bonus effort within TANF has been a subject of some controversy both during the period when the criteria were established for awarding the funds and following the first awards. At one point, a proposal was made to simply divide the $200 million available annually for these awards equally among the fifty states and others eligible for the funds. Some critics of the bonus requirement argue that the categories established for the allocations are not directly related to the behavior of the state welfare agencies charged with implementing the TANF program. Economic conditions within the state are thought to be more responsible for the increases or decreases than the action of the state agency. Others have argued that the established criteria do not measure the real goal of TANF—the well-being of children. They call for the establishment of performance measures that highlight child welfare, child care, and Head Start and other noncash programs, rather than focusing only on the employment behavior of adults. The availability of data, however, has been viewed as one of the reasons why other criteria have not been used to date.

The TANF experience illustrates the dilemma involved in using an incentive strategy. It is difficult to ascertain the direct relationship between the behavior of the state or local government and specific outcomes. In addition, complex programs such as TANF have an array of program goals and expectations, and it is not easy to achieve agreement on performance standards. Some critics of the incentive strategy argue that state or local jurisdictions will attempt to game the system and develop policies that may meet the performance measures rather than achieve the basic expectations of the legislation. Others argue that this already occurs and so the situation is not much different than it had been in the past. Similar problems were experienced in the Job Training and Partnership Act (JTPA). Burt Barnow and Jeffrey Smith have noted how difficult it is to apply the principal-agent framework to that program because of difficulty the federal government had in defining goals.[32]

Negotiated Performance Measures

One of the most common complaints by state and local governments is that the federal government imposes a set of requirements to its funds that do not meet the needs of the nonfederal jurisdiction. Indeed, this is one of the arguments that has been used to justify the transformation of categorical program grants into block grant efforts. Block grants have proven to be one of the most difficult grant forms on which to impose the GPRA requirements. It has been problematic for federal officials to balance the flexibility of the block grant (allowing states and localities to meet their own particular needs) with a desire for greater accountability for the use of those funds.

The Maternal and Child Health (MCH) Services, Title V Block Grant to States has operated as a federal–state partnership for most of its sixty-year history. Even when the program was converted to a block grant in 1981, the professional relationship between the federal agency charged with implementing the program and the state MCH agencies continued to be relatively close. The Omnibus Budget Reconciliation Act of 1989 did require states to report on progress on key maternal and child health indicators and other program information.

In 1996, the MCH bureau in the Health Resources and Services Administration of HHS began a process with states that would establish a set of mutually agreed upon measures with data sources that would be used in the program. In the development phase of this process, the MCH bureau created an external committee of thirty experts representing various interests in the maternal and child health field that would help set overall direction for the process, provide technical expertise, and endorse the final results. Participants from associations and advocacy groups were expected to engage their own constituencies to ensure accurate representation. Review and comment from the state agency officials was solicited at various points during the process.

In March 1997, draft performance measures and guidance revision principles were presented at the annual meeting of the Association of Maternal and Child Health Programs; this meeting was attended by virtually all the relevant directors in the country. Eight representative states, chosen from seventeen volunteers, were selected to pilot test the measures for practicality and data collection issues. The consultation process that was used was approximately two years in duration; one year was spent on the development of the measures and one on pilot testing the process.

By the end of 1997, the MCH bureau established eighteen national performance measures, which were incorporated into the application and reporting guidance for the Title V block grant funds. These measures were drawn from goals related to Healthy People 2000 objectives, over which grantees exercised substantial control. The measures were categorized as capacity measures (ability to affect the delivery of services), process measures (related to service delivery), and risk factors (involving health problems). Each individual state also was required to establish and report on between seven and ten of its own supplemental performance measures to provide a more complete picture of the program within that state. In addition, the MCH bureau set six national outcome measures— ultimate goals toward which the performance measures are directed and for which ultimate achievement depends on external factors beyond the control of the state grantee.

As a result of this process, MCH block grant applications and annual reports contain a wealth of information concerning state initiatives, state-supported programs, and other state-based responses designed to address their MCH needs. The electronic information system that has been developed in this program, based on the applications and reports, collects both qualitative and quantitative data that are useful to a number of audiences.

The MCH experience indicates that it is possible to achieve agreement on performance measures when certain conditions are met. Programs that are not politically volatile or that do not have a widely disparate set of expert opinions are appropriate for this process. In addition, prior work and data systems (in this case involving Healthy People 2000) laid the foundation for consensus on many outcome and process objectives. The measures recognized and separated objectives over which grantees exercise influence and control from those that depend on external factors beyond their control. But even when these conditions are present, the negotiation process is time consuming and requires an investment of staff and resources by federal agencies.

Building Performance Goals into Legislation

Over the past few years various pieces of legislation have been crafted with attention to performance goals. This approach emphasizes the authorizing role in Congress, while the GPRA approach focuses on the appropriations process. Two pieces of legislation illustrate this strategy: the modifications to the Vocational Education program and the creation of the Workforce Investment Act as a replacement for the Job Training Partnership Act. In both cases, the legislation represented a move from an emphasis on input or process requirements to a focus on performance outcomes.

The Workforce Investment Act, signed into law in August 1998, reforms the federal job training programs and creates a new comprehensive workforce investment system. It was constructed on top of the JTPA experience. The reformed system is intended to be customer focused, to help Americans access the tools they need to manage their careers through information and high-quality services, and to help U.S. companies find skilled workers. Increased accountability is one of the principles embodied in the legislation. The Act specifies core indicators of performance that become the structure for states and local reporting. These core indicators include measures of entry into unsubsidized employment, earnings received, and attainment of a credential involving educational skills. Indicators were also specified in the legislation for eligible youth and customer satisfaction measures. States are expected to submit expected levels of performance for these indicators in their state plans. Similar indicators of performance were also established in the Carl D. Perkins Vocational and Applied Technology Education Amendments of 1998. The modifications to the existing program emphasized the importance of establishing a state performance accountability system. The legislation requires states to identify core indicators in their state plans involving student skill achievement, attainment of educational credentials, and placement in education, employment, or military service.

Further refinement of these requirements was established by both federal departments through the regulations development process. In drafting both of these pieces of legislation, Congress assumed that the core indicators reflect common practices across the country and that data systems are available to report on achievement of the goals. These assumptions have not been supported in practice.

Establishment of Standards

In some cases, the role of the federal government has been to establish performance standards that are meant to guide the behavior of state and local governments. At least theoretically these standards are to be voluntary, and the ability of a state or locality to conform to them is not tied to eligibility for specific federal dollars. The federal role in this strategy may involve the development of the standards and the provision of technical assistance and at times could include payment for meeting these norms and guidelines.

The Clinton administration's proposal for the development of voluntary national tests in reading and mathematics served as an example of this approach. In contrast to the No Child Left Behind legislation developed by the Bush administration, the Clinton standards were voluntary and did not have sanctions attached to them that could be imposed on states and localities. But the response to the limited Clinton proposal, particularly by some governors and educational leaders, illustrates the types of problems that may emerge from this strategy.

According to then–Secretary of Education Richard W. Riley, "[T]hese proposed voluntary tests are about high standards, improving expectations, and giving our young people the basic skills they need that will prepare them for our knowledge-driven economy in the twenty-first century."[33] The proposal would build on existing educational assessment surveys (the National Assessment of Educational Progress and the Third International Math and Science Study). The new tests that would be given in English at grade 4 and mathematics at grade 8 would be based on content criteria established through national consensus processes. The information that would be available through these tests would be at the individual student level, providing information on how an individual student stacks up against others in the classroom, the school, and the country.

Although several governors were supporters of this administration proposal in 1997, others expressed concern about the initiative.[34] A number of states already had test systems in place and did not want to replace their existing performance accountability systems with the national approach. Still others were uncomfortable with the content of the tests, particularly their accuracy and validity in measuring achievement and their substantive scope.

The proposal for voluntary tests in mathematics and English also uncovered another problem that is likely to be confronted whenever the standards strategy is employed: fear that the information gathered through these assessments has a life of its own and will be used inappropriately. This is particularly problematic because the information that is collected was meant to illustrate achievement at the individual level. Questions of privacy and information security have been raised and were not answered to the satisfaction of critics.

Waivers

Authority to grant waivers to state or local governments for specific programs has been in place for many years. While the waiver authority has been viewed as a way to meet the unique needs of individual states, it has also been closely tied to a research and development strategy, providing latitude to nonfederal jurisdictions to experiment with new innovations and new ways to deliver services. For example, the secretary of HHS had the authority under Section 115 of the Social Security Act to waive specified provisions of the act in the case of demonstration projects that were likely to promote the objectives of the act. These waivers were expected to be rigorously evaluated. The waiver authorization has usually been defined in the context of specific programs and the criteria for granting the waivers are established within the authorizing legislation or implementing regulations. Certain requirements (such as civil rights requirements or filing performance information) cannot be waived.

This authority has been employed extensively in the past in several program areas, particularly involving welfare, Medicaid, and the Job Training Partnership Act. Waivers have been used to allow states to establish their own approach and to eliminate or modify input or process requirements. Many of the waivers require the proposed modification to be budget neutral—that is, it does not incur new costs for either the waiving jurisdiction or the federal government. For some, the waiver process is a mechanism that can be used to make a case for policy change. The experience with waivers in the AFDC program and in the JTPA program became an important part of the justification for major changes in each of the programs, leading to the TANF program and the Workforce Investment Act.

In November 1999, the House Government Management, Information and Technology Subcommittee marked up a bill that addresses waivers of regulatory and statutory requirements. This legislation has three main requirements:

- Agencies would have to establish a streamlined 120-day review process to respond to states that request waivers of regulatory or statutory requirements of federal grant programs. (While this is similar to an August 1999 Executive Order, the legislation would be judicially reviewable).
- Agencies would have to develop an expedited review process to waive a state's statutory or regulatory requirements if a similar waiver has already been approved for another state.
- OMB, HHS, and USDA would have to develop common approaches and requirements related to budget neutrality in consultation with the National Governors' Association and the National Conference of State Legislatures.

The hearings that were held on this proposed legislation elicited both support and questions by those who testified. The Executive Director of the National Governors' Association, Ray Scheppach, testified in favor of the legislation, expressing concern about the current process. He called the current efforts "a redundant process" whereby states must produce and defend waiver requests even if other states had already received approval to implement similar waivers.[35] Administration witnesses, however, emphasized the importance of dealing with each waiver on its own. Then HHS Assistant Secretary for Management and Budget John Callahan likened the process to contract negotiations where both parties need to attain a mutual goal of creating program innovation and flexibility. Other administration witnesses reminded the members of Congress that some of what they viewed as denials of waivers actually came about because the agency had no authority to waive a particular requirement.

At least one House member, Congressman Major Owens (D–NY), expressed concern about the process. He queried: "In this process of rushing to grant waivers and place our faith in the State governments, do we have some safeguards? And can we have more safeguards and some stringent penalties for people who violate the law because the waivers give them a situation where nobody will be watching, monitoring, holding them accountable?"[36]

As Owens suggested, the proposed legislation did not focus on questions of performance. Although some of the existing waiver authorities did highlight performance issues when they required evaluation as a condition of the waiver, the proposed legislation accentuated the streamlining of the process, not the results that emerged from the changes.

Conclusion

The appropriate role of the federal government in the intergovernmental system has been debated for many years. Despite the rhetoric that is used to describe one perspective or another (e.g., a strong federal government, or a federal presence that defers to other levels of government), most of the shifts that have occurred over the years have taken place as specific legislation is crafted. The pendulum swings in terms of both the rhetoric used and specific policy design; over the past few decades, however, there has been emphasis on the devolution of responsibilities to states and localities for the implementation of programs that are partially or mainly funded with federal dollars. There are fewer and fewer federal domestic programs that are entirely implemented by federal staff.

Because so many of the federal programs involve intricate intergovernmental relationships, federal agencies have struggled with ways to structure these relationships while balancing accountability for the use of federal dollars with discretion to the third parties in terms of their use of federal monies.

As has been discussed in this chapter, efforts to hold federal government agencies accountable for the way that programs are implemented assume that these agencies have legitimate authority to enforce the requirements that are included in performance measures. Despite the ubiquitous nature of the performance rhetoric, the examples that have been discussed suggest that there are many pathways that can be taken to join the federal-level concern about performance with sensitivity to the needs of the governmental third parties involved in implementing the programs. In some cases, the two goals are not compatible; in others it is possible to work out a mutually agreeable scenario. In this age of fiscal scarcity, both the federal government and the states are extremely conscious of requirements that actually increase their costs for program implementation.

It is not easy to craft a strategy for performance measurement activity that addresses the tensions surrounding the intergovernmental system. The approach that is taken must be sensitive to differences among policies and programs, differences among the players involved, the complexity of the worlds of both the federal and nonfederal agencies involved, and the level of goal agreement or conflict. One of the most vexing problems in the performance area involves the availability of "good" data—data that have been verified and can be believed to be valid by all parties to the relationship. (See chapter 8 for a detailed discussion of these problems.) The data problem cuts across all of the strategies. Few policy sectors have the tradition or past investment in the creation of good data systems that would allow one to know whether performance has actually been achieved. In addition, the experience with all of these efforts indicates how difficult is to achieve a performance measurement system that focuses on outcomes. Part of the problem relates to the lack of control many agencies have over the achievement of program goals and the difficulty of linking program activities to results, even when those results can be measured.

This repertoire of performance efforts also indicates that government-wide policies such as GPRA and PART are not particularly effective because they do not respond flexibly to the differences in programs with third-party and intergovernmental dimensions. Without acknowledging these differences, the performance agenda leads to increased centralization and definition of outcomes by the federal government. It collides with strategies of devolution and a diminished federal role. The process of defining performance measures seems to work when it is devised in the context of specific programs, modest in its reach, and sensitive to the unique qualities surrounding those initiatives. If performance requirements are not sensitive to the differences in program and policy design, they are likely to fan increased conflict between levels of government. That is likely to lead to behaviors that diminish the possibility of emphasizing outcomes and performance, because the actors in the system do not trust one another enough to develop appropriate measures.

Karen O'Grady's situation is one of the most difficult intergovernmental situations to face because it involves funding not simply program requirements. The expectations of the New Jersey legislature don't mesh at all with those of the federal Medicaid program. As a state employee, she has limited authority or even influence over the federal officials. Her best strategy would be to have both the health community (doctors, hospitals, and others) and state elected officials make the case for increased discretion for the state. She could use either a waiver process or some form of negotiated performance requirements to substitute for federally defined requirements. She could also work with the New Jersey congressional delegation to push for more modest requirements from OMB and others calling for compliance with federal stipulations.

Notes

1. This chapter draws on Beryl A. Radin, "Intergovernmental Relationships and the Federal Performance Movement," *Publius: The Journal of Federalism* 30, no. 1–2 (Winter–Spring 2000).
2. See Sam Dillon, "Utah Vote Rejects Parts of Education Law," *New York Times,* April 20, 2005, p. A 14.
3. Sam Dillon, "Students Ace State Tests, but Earn D's from US," *New York Times,* Nov. 26, 2005, p. A 1.
4. Paul L. Posner, "Accountability Challenges of Third-Party Government," in Lester M. Salamon, ed., *The Tools of Government: A Guide to the New Governance* (Oxford: Oxford University Press, 2002), 525.
5. Ibid., 525–28.

6. See, for example, discussion in Deil S. Wright, *Understanding Intergovern-mental Relations*, 3rd ed. (Pacific Grove, Calif.: Brooks/Cole Publishing, 1988), 244–48.

7. David Osborne and Ted Gaebler, *Reinventing Government: How the Entre-preneurial Spirit Is Transforming the Public Sector* (Reading, Mass: Addison Wesley, 1992), 139.

8. See William T. Gormley Jr. and David L. Weimer, *Organizational Report Cards* (Cambridge, Mass.: Harvard University Press, 1999).

9. See Stephen Rathgeb Smith and Michael Lipsky, *Nonprofits for Hire: The Welfare State in the Age of Contracting* (Cambridge, Mass: Harvard University Press, 1993).

10. See, for example, Helen Ingram, "Policy Implementation through Bar-gaining: The Case of Federal Grants-in-Aid," *Public Policy* 25 (Fall 1977): 499–526.

11. Susan S. Westin, Associate Director Advanced Studies and Evaluation Methodology, General Government Division, USGAO, *Balancing Flexibil-ity and Accountability: Grant Program Design in Education and Other Areas* (testimony before the Education Task Force, Committee on the Budget, U.S. Senate, February 11, 1998, GAO/T-GGD/HEHS-98-94), 1. (referred to as GAO, *Measuring Program Results*). See chapter 3.

12. Ibid., 1.

13. Ibid., 3–4.

14. Ibid., 13.

15. Ibid., 1.

16. Ibid., 4.

17. Ibid., 8.

18. Ibid., 10.

19. Ibid., 2.

20. GAO, *Results-Oriented Government: GPRA Has Established a Solid Founda-tion for Achieving Greater Results, Report to Congressional Requesters*, GAO-04-38, March 2004.

21. Ibid., 90–91.

22. Ibid., 91.

23. See chapter 6 for a detailed discussion of PART.

24. OMB Circular Performance Measurement Challenges and Strategies (June 18, 2003), p. 11–12.

25. OMB, Draft FY 2002 Spring Review, OMB Program Assessment Rating Tool (PART), Block/Formula Grant Programs.

26. A similar argument was made in a January 2004 GAO report. See GAO, *Performance Budgeting: Observations on the Use of OMB's Program Assessment Rating Tool for the Fiscal Year 2004 Budget*, GAO-04-174, January 2004.

27. See GAO, *Environmental Protection: Collaborative EPA-State Effort Needed to Improve New Performance Partnership System*, GAO/RED-99-171, June 1999, p. 3. See also Michael E. Kraft and Denise Scheberle, "Environmental Federalism at Decade's End: New Approaches and Strategies," *Publius: The Journal of Federalism* 28, no. 1, (Winter 1998).

28. EPA, *New Directions: A Report on Regulatory Reinvention*, 1977, http://www.epa.gov/reinvent/new#Performance (accessed April 2005).

29. GAO, *Environmental Protection*, p. 8.

30. Ibid., 3–4.

31. See discussion in David L. Weimer and Aidan R. Vining, *Policy Analysis: Concepts and Practice*, 2nd ed. (Englewood Cliffs, N.J.: Prentice Hall, 1992), 152–53.

32. Burt S. Barnow and Jeffrey A. Smith, "Performance Management of U.S. Job Training Programs: Lessons from the Job Training Partnership Act," *Public Finance and Management* 4, no. 3 (2004): 247–87.

33. U.S. Secretary of Education Richard W. Riley, Statement before the House Subcommittee on Early Childhood, Youth and Families, Committee on Education and the Workforce, April 29, 1997.

34. Rene Sanchez, "Education Initiatives Off to a Slow Start," *Washington Post*, July 11, 1998, p. 18.

35. National Governors' Association, Ray Sheppach, Testimony on the Federal Grant Waiver Process for States before the House Government Reform Committee, Subcommittee on National Economic Growth, Natural Resources, and Regulatory Affairs, and Subcommittee on Government Management, Information and Technology, September 30, 1999.

36. Ibid.

8

inᚻormaᚌion, inᚎerests, anᗞ iᗞEOLOGY

Elaine Waters lives in a suburb of Boston and has been an active member of the parent-teachers organization for more than ten years. She has been concerned about the quality of education received by her three children in the local public school during that time. Her collaborative activity with several other parents resulted in a number of innovations that have taken place in that local school system. The elementary school that her children attended has gone through quite dramatic changes over this decade. The changes began with the departure of the former principal and the hiring of a new principal who has worked closely with the parents to assure that the school responded to the diverse learning needs of the students. In addition to the new principal, a number of new teachers have also been hired for the school.

For the past several years, Ms. Waters and the other parents have been very pleased with the results of these changes. The faculty is composed of teachers with different approaches to teaching and learning; this range enables the parents to be sure that a particular teacher is able to respond to the learning needs of individual students. Ms. Waters's three children illustrate those differences. One of them is interested in science and does well in highly structured classrooms. Another is a talented creative writer who responds to teachers who appreciate a more flexible learning environment. And the third is an individual who learns through highly experiential approaches.

However, during the past two years, as a result of both federal and state policies, the local school district has determined that the performance of schools and teachers will be assessed based on the performance of children on standardized educational achievement tests. This has resulted in a change in the curriculum in the school and student and faculty perceptions that there is only one way to teach and learn. While this approach works for one of Ms. Waters's children, the other two have not performed well on these tests. She is concerned about the impact of their performance on these tests on their views of self-worth; she doesn't know how to deal with the school system changes.

Much of the literature about performance hovers around arguments based on rhetoric rather than reality. Given the intent of the performance movement, this is somewhat ironic. Information about performance is the crux of performance measurement, yet the rhetoric of the performance movement rarely talks about the availability of information or the difficulties of obtaining it. Performance assessment of all types makes a number of assumptions about the kind of information that will serve as the foundation for the movement in all its various permutations.

In a sense, one could argue that the performance movement is constructed on false or, at least, unrealistic assumptions. These assumptions make up what I call the "unreal or naïve approach." They are:

- Information is already available. It is like gold that simply needs to be mined. It is found in existing information systems. While it may have been designed to meet other needs, it can easily be converted to performance measurement strategies.
- Information is neutral. One can separate fact and value and determine what is true and what is false. This assumption is embedded in the positivist intellectual tradition in which one believes that knowledge can be acquired through direct observation and experimentation rather than through some other means.

- We know what we are measuring. Programs of all sorts (whether governmental or professionally defined) have clear and simple goals. One can thus determine whether an effort has been successful based on the definition of those goals. We emphasize clarity rather than the complexity that comes from multiple and conflicting goals.
- We can define cause-effect relationships in programs. We know what will cause a particular type of intervention to occur. We assume that modifying those elements will provide the basis for achieving more effective or efficient performance.
- Baseline information is available. One assumes not only that new information is available but that the system is already churning out information that provides a standard to which similar things can be compared. This information will allow one to determine whether improvement has been made in a particular program area.
- Almost all activities can be measured and quantified. The information that can be used to determine whether an activity has "succeeded" or not can be produced in the form of metrics and quantification. As the dictionary puts it, a metric is "a mathematical function defined for a coordinates system that associates properties to each pair of elements that are analogous to distance between points on a line." This assumption relies on the collection of quantitative data and tends to avoid any qualitative data.

While these assumptions are built into most of the performance measurement efforts, they are rarely articulated. In part this is because the advocates of the performance movement are so committed to the process that they have tended to minimize the obstacles to attaining them. Indeed, when they are listed as discussed above, the assumptions seem blatant and unreasonable. Yet they are implicit in the wide range of activities that are found in the performance movement. They lurk in the background of the Governmental Performance and Results Act, in the Program Assessment Rating Tool, in standardized education tests, and in measurement of leverage potential of foundation grants. For example, during the early days of the implementation of the GPRA, Joseph Wholey wrote that "[p]erformance measurement systems should not be too costly in terms of the management and staff time required to collect, analyze, and use performance information; the costs of any contracts for data collection and analysis; the burden imposed on reporting entities; political and bureaucratic costs; and other important negative consequences of performance measurements. Managers might be able to use existing records or sampling to limit the costs of performance measurement."[1]

There are a number of issues that are important to examine as one thinks about the role of information in the performance movement. It is relevant to examine who wants the information, particularly the agendas of those who advocate its use. It is also germane to focus on the kind of information that is appropriate in terms of the type of agency involved, the stage of the policy process, and the level of analysis. Information is attached to diverse functions within that process—program management, planning, the budget process, control by funders, and data that would satisfy a political agenda. The discussion that follows deals with a number of issues that are related to the production, use, and functions of performance information. It provides contemporary examples of problems involved in measuring performance to illustrate the difficulty of following the "unreal or naïve" approach. One result of this path is to generate responses from organizational staff that at best are narrow and literal responses to requirements (supporting a compliance mindset) and at worst are examples of "gaming" the system in ways that avoid any real change.

What Do We Expect from Information?

The assumptions of those who are strong advocates for government-wide approaches to performance measurement move one toward a mechanistic approach, in which information is produced in a machine-like process. They assume that politics, interests, and other human issues can be removed from the equation. In short, they move toward management and decision making by measurement. One of the clearest examples of this approach is found in the State of Texas *Guide to Performance Measure Management, 2000 Edition*.[2] This document lays out a model of performance measurement that resembles an electrical circuit board rather than a complex political and human set of demands.

There are a few observers who have focused on the unintended and undesirable impact of these changes. Schwartz and Mayne have written:

> There is a desire to supply managers, policymakers, legislators and the general public with evaluative information that is perceived to be reliable, valid and credible. Yet, mechanisms for assessing the quality of evaluative information conjure up perverse images of what has been termed an audit ... characterized by increasing layers of inspection, audit, evaluation and assessment.[3]

To some extent, one should not be surprised about the presence of these assumptions related to information that are a part of the performance movement. As Carol Weiss has noted, "Few ideological commitments in modern Western societies are stronger than the ideas of rationality and intelligent choice, and no institutions are more normatively committed to the application of information to decisions than bureaucratic organizations." She further quotes Feldman and March: "Command of information and information sources enhances perceived competence and inspires confidence. . . . A good decision maker is one who makes decisions in the way a good decision maker does, and decision makers and organizations establish their legitimacy by their use of information."[4]

While the concern about and reliance on information may have strong symbolic impact, taking the "rational" approach embedded in the assumptions discussed above actually creates its own negative dynamic. As many have argued over the years, information is not a value-free, neutral enterprise. Max Weber noted that information is an instrument of power, an important resource to be guarded and held closely.[5] Robert Merton reminded us that there are real limits to what information can actually be found and used. "The importance of ignorance as a factor is enhanced by the fact that the exigencies of practical life frequently compel us to act with some confidence even though it is manifest that the information on which we base our action is not complete. We usually act . . . not on the basis of scientific knowledge, but opinion and estimate."[6] Others have focused on the various aspects of information that make its production, use, and functions much more complex than is assumed by the classic performance measurement approach. Still others have defined situations in which information that is produced for one use is applied inappropriately to other settings.

Carol Weiss has created a framework that helps one understand this complexity. She has argued that policies are the product of an interplay among three elements: ideology, interests, and information. Consequently, information must be viewed not as a standalone enterprise but rather as a resource that is intertwined with a range of ideological approaches (philosophy, principles, values, and political orientation) as well as interests expressed as power, reputation, and financial rewards. She notes that "information is only one basis upon which policy actors take their positions."[7]

This alternative approach to the function of information in the performance movement provides the basis for a very different perspective on this topic. It suggests that the search for "perfect" information is a Sisyphus-like enterprise. Sisyphus was a king of Corinth who was condemned for eternity to roll a boulder up a hill, only to have it roll down again just before it reached the top. But unlike the labor of Sisyphus, the search for value-free and neutral performance information never comes close to the top.

These dilemmas have effectively been glossed over in the performance literature and in practice. While various writers about performance issues have noted that the production and use of information is much more complex and difficult than they expected, few have acknowledged that the assumptions they have made about information are far from attainment. For example, *Paths to Performance in State and Local Government*, the final assessment of the Government Performance Project of the Maxwell School of Citizenship and Public Affairs, focuses on the management subsystem of information technology as the key to providing "timely decision-making support by critical information . . . [that] creates a system in which key decision-makers have the information they need when they need it."[8] Focusing only on the systems design, the study does not examine the budget allocation within agencies for information collection and analysis.[9] While participants in the project have acknowledged that measurement is a problem, they have argued that "[w]ith the performance equation more fully specified, however, the potential for linking specific organizational characteristics with specific outputs or outcomes is greatly improved. Performance linkages become clearer."[10] GAO, in a report titled *Program Evaluation, Agencies Challenged by New Demand for Information on Program Results*, highlights the costs of obtaining program results information. However, it does not deal with basic and structural problems involved in obtaining information.[11]

Who Wants the Information?

The multiple agendas at play in the performance measurement world help one understand the motivations behind the urge for a focus on performance and define very different approaches to performance information. Indeed, acknowledging these different agendas allows one to understand the misfit between the assumptions embedded in the classic performance movement and the reality of its use for information collection.

A Negative Agenda: This agenda seeks to eliminate programs and tends to blame those running the programs for problems. Given this motivation, the kind of information that is useful to those who approach the performance activities with this agenda is clearly defined by ideology and by specific interests. Information that is useful to these advocates provides evidence that programs do not work and also highlights the limitations of those who are charged with the implementation of the programs.

A Neutral Agenda: This focuses on a concern about change. Individuals who work from this agenda argue that what worked in past does not always make sense in the current or future environment. Thus the information that is useful to those operating from this agenda does not begin with a clear vision of the future, because it assumes that agendas of organizations are constantly shifting. This mindset is likely to lead to more complexity and uncertainty, making it difficult to determine baseline information that is useful for the future as well as to define information around unclear goals.

A Positive Agenda: Advocates of this approach want to get value for taxes and expenditures and emphasize efforts to ensure accountability. The information that is useful to those operating from this agenda emphasizes the concerns of the various interests involved in a program area. And in a pluralistic society such as the United States, the focus on accountability leads one to a multiplicity of expectations and interests.[12]

Each of these three agendas illustrates the limits of the naïve approach. The negative agenda directly collides with the assumptions that information is neutral and that we can define cause–effect relationships without limiting alternative methods of proceeding. The neutral agenda illustrates the difficulties of defining goals and determining what should be measured, because the context for an organization is constantly changing. And the positive agenda indicates the difficulty of separating fact and value when multiple interests are involved and it is difficult to quantify those different values. As the examples that are included in this chapter indicate, these structural limitations make it extremely difficult to devise performance measures and performance information that are neutral and noncontroversial. In addition, differences between organization types, policy or program variation, and functions suggest how naïve it is to think about the development of performance information as a relatively simple activity. And placed on top of these structural constraints are responses to information collection. There are times when the attempt to collect information provokes responses that are best described as gaming the system.

Information Needs Vary by Stage and Level of Analysis

With very few exceptions, those who write and advocate for performance measures focus only on the outcome stage of the policy or programmatic process. This process, largely drawn from the systems analysis field, is defined as beginning with inputs, moving to processes, then to outputs, and finally to outcomes. As has been discussed earlier, the widespread dissatisfaction with the way that policies and programs are carried out has led to the performance movement; as Harry Hatry has written, "[P]erformance measurement enables managers to define and use specific indicators to measure the outcomes and efficiency of their services or programs on a regular basis."[13] Hatry is one of the few advocates and writers in the field who has defined performance information in a broad and inclusive fashion. He has developed categories of performance information that acknowledge the wide variety of information types that can be useful to those concerned about performance. His definition, largely summarized below, sets the foundation for an acknowledgement of a variety of players with different expectations about performance.[14]

Inputs: Information in this category deals with the amount of resources actually used in the operation of a policy or program. It may include the amount of funds expended or the number of employees used to carry out the program. Hatry notes that this category produces indicators of efficiency or productivity. Others have noted that inputs may include equipment, supplies, and other elements along with funds and personnel. This information is the easiest to measure and most likely type of information to be available.

Process: Information in this category includes the amount of work that comes into a program. It could include the number of customers who come in for services or the internal organizational processes undertaken to carry out the work. Workload information is important to program managers and can set the context for an analysis of service outcomes. This information is not always easy to develop. Processes are often counted in varying or inconsistent ways; as a result, aggregated statistics about processes can be misleading. Perrin has commented on "senior management who apparently are unaware that these 'straightforward' terms are anything but!"[15]

Outputs: This category measures the amount of products and services completed during the reporting period. That might include the number of people served, the number of reports issued, or the products produced. Hatry defines outputs as things that the program's personnel have done themselves. Others have defined outputs as tabulations, calculations, or recordings of activity or effort that can be expressed in a quantitative or qualitative manner. In some cases, process measures are subsumed within this category.[16]

Outcomes: Outcome information defines the events, activities, or changes that indicate progress toward achievement of the mission and objectives of the program. Hatry notes that outcomes are not what the program itself did but the consequences of what the program did. Outcomes can be financial, direct effects, or side effects; they can also include measures of service quality. Hatry argues that it is important to differentiate intermediate outcomes from end outcomes. Intermediate outcomes are activities that are expected to lead to a desired end but not ends in themselves. End outcomes focus on the end results that are sought.

While these definitions suggest some level of clarity, others have noted that it is often difficult to sort them out. Brown has described this dilemma:

> As an example of the use of these terms, consider a government program such as Head Start, which attempts to give disadvantaged children a boost through early education. Inputs here would be dollars into the program and outputs would be the number of children that pass through the program; the program's efficiency would be the number of children handled by the program per dollar. None of these things are really indicative of the degree of success or failure of the program. Rather, we are more interested in such outcomes as the increase in standardized test scores such as the SATs when the children become older, as well as their admission rates to colleges. And we are even more concerned with the program's impacts, which might be the overall decrease in the community's unemployment rate, the improvement in the local economy, and perhaps a decrease in the crime rate. The program's effectiveness is the degree to which these outcomes and impacts are realized. It should be apparent that the quantification of outcomes, impacts, and effectiveness, and especially placing a dollar value on these so that a 'return on investment' may be calculated, is much harder than quantifying inputs, outputs, and efficiency.[17]

Information and Diverse Functions

The breadth of Hatry's definitions of performance information lays the framework for an approach that acknowledges the variety of functions that can be included in a concern about performance.

There are at least seven different functions that are potentially involved in defining information needs.[18] They are:

- Program management
- Planning
- Service delivery
- Policy development
- Budget process
- Control by funders
- Political agenda

Program Management

The focus of much of the performance literature has been the way that individuals who serve as managers of programs are able to use information to develop more effective management practices. Managers are the individuals who are responsible for the operation of a program or policy. They are often responsible for decisions around allocation of resources, staffing, structuring, and a range of other traditional administrative services. They seek information that will allow them to monitor the detailed operation of the program and make appropriate changes to their requirements. Most managers want information that will acknowledge the constraints that they face and the limited authority they have over the macro system. Rarely do the concerns of managers move to a political agenda or even to budget decision making. Behn has identified eight purposes that public managers have for measuring performance: evaluate, control, budget, motivate, promote, celebrate, learn, and improve.[19]

One example of information used in management comes from airport performance measurement. According to Humphreys et al., airport managers and governments measure airport performance for three main purposes: to measure financial and operational efficiency, to evaluate alternative investment strategies, and to allow governments to regulate airport activity. All of these functions stay at a technical management level and do not move up the decision-making process. They note that "[a]irport managers need to have information to enable them to monitor performance and to identify areas that are performing well and those that are not. Once performance is known, management can examine the underlying processes taking place so that appropriate corrective action can be proposed."[20]

Another example of management-focused performance information comes from the police department in Falls Church, Virginia. That department requires each patrol officer to write an average of three tickets, or make three arrests, every twelve-hour shift, and to accumulate a minimum total of four hundred tickets and arrests per year. Writing a ticket for a broken taillight carries the same weight as an arrest for armed robbery. Failure to meet the quotas results in an automatic ninety-day probationary period with no pay raise and a possible demotion or dismissal if the individual does not meet acceptable levels. Patrol officers are required to meet these levels whether or not they are on vacation time, extended leave, or military duty. Thus they must write more tickets when they return to the streets to compensate for their time away.[21]

Planning

This function includes a variety of approaches to the definition of goals, explication of needs, determination of resources, and establishment of priorities and objectives. There are a number of different planning functions, but many of the performance activities focus on one of the types—strategic planning efforts. This is an attempt to match organizational competencies with threats and opportunities from the environment.[22] This approach calls for information with a longer time frame and a broader perspective on future activities. The information that is developed to meet this function tends to focus on unmet needs rather than on evaluating existing programs.

A classic example of information developed for planning purposes is the publication of the series of reports titled *Healthy People*, by the U.S. Department of Health and Human Services. The series began in 1990 with the publication of *Healthy People 2000*, a document that took a comprehensive approach to health issues in the United States. Its goals were to increase years of healthy life, reduce disparities in health among different population groups, and achieve access to preventive health services. A second report, *Healthy*

People 2010, followed. Both documents sought to offer "a simple but powerful idea: provide the information and knowledge about how to improve health in a format that enables diverse groups to combine their efforts and work as a team. It is a roadmap to better health for all that can be utilized by many different people, by States and communities, professional organizations, groups concerned with a particular threat to health or a particular population group."[23]

Another example of data used for planning purposes comes through the Boston Indicators Project. This is a comprehensive framework of goals and measures in ten sectors to stimulate informed public discourse and civic action. Organized as a partnership among the city of Boston, the Boston Foundation, the Metropolitan Area Planning Council, and local institutions, public agencies, organizations, and universities, it has involved thousands of Bostonians and data from more than 150 partners. It is designed to improve the city's capacity to make informed choices about the future.[24] Again, this information does not evaluate existing programs but rather sets out a picture of future needs.

Service Delivery

This function narrows in on the actual point of service delivery, where the program official interacts with the individual receiving the service. Some may call that individual (or organization) the customer of the service; others prefer defining that person as a citizen or client of the agency or organization. Information that is useful here may be developed from the perspective of the individual or group receiving the service and is likely to highlight questions related to service quality. Information that meets these needs should be disaggregated and categories established that break out particular population groups.

The information that is produced to satisfy this function can be used as both an allocative and a quality function. For example, the Compstat program that was introduced in the New York City Police Department during the tenure of policy commissioner William Bratton provides information that can be used by precinct commanders. They are viewed as the locus for operational authority and accountability as well as community-oriented problem solving.

While the information was devised by central management and by centrally deployed supplemental resources, precinct commanders were given tools to analyze up-to-date statistics, find patterns of crime and police activity, and devise solutions to problems. What is interesting about this information is that it is available to both the precinct leadership and central administration.[25] A variation on this process was put in place in New York City in the Department of Human Resources Administration as it developed data and performance tracking systems to monitor work and welfare reform.[26] A similar effort was undertaken in the city of Baltimore, where performance information was used to establish direct communication between the mayor and key officials in the city government.[27]

Service delivery information can be obtained both from participants inside the organization and from those outside. Surveys of citizen satisfaction can be used along with information from managers and service deliverers. Data have been devised to analyze performance in prisons. Camp et al. have studied public and private prisons and have sought to provide information from inmates about prison conditions that can be aggregated into institutional-level performance measures. Where possible, those responses were compared to staff responses.[28]

Performance information from citizens has not been as widely used as internally devised data. As Kelly and Swindell note, there has not been a wide consensus on the utility of citizen satisfaction surveys as a reliable indicator of government performance. They note that there are two general types of errors that citizens are likely to make in evaluating local services. The first is what they call errors of attribution: a citizen may believe government is providing a service that it is not providing, or the reverse, that governments are not providing services when they are. The second error occurs when the citizen evaluation of quality of services is not consistent with internally defined performance measures.[29]

Policy Development

Information that is useful for policy development seeks to indicate broad patterns of behavior and practice. It moves to the macro level and, unlike the service delivery information, looks for aggregate patterns. Because there are many different types of actors involved in the policy development process, the information that is collected to meet this perspective needs to be constructed around the authority base of the group or individual involved. It also must be sensitive to the assumptions that the policy actor brings to the table. For example, when a congressional committee commissioned a study of the compensatory education programs (Title I of the Elementary and Secondary Education Act), it was clear that the committee did not want summative evaluation information. That is, it did not want the study to determine whether the program should be continued or should be eliminated. Rather, the committee wanted information that would allow it to make modifications in the program through the reauthorization process. Thus the information collected focused on areas in which changes might be made to make the program more effective.

Policy sectors vary tremendously in the availability and acceptance of basic information systems. Gormley's work on organizational report cards notes that health data are often available and provide the basis for hospital report cards that can be used for policy development.[30] In addition, the policy pronouncements around information collection can collide with other policy demands. This is most dramatically illustrated by the conflict between the requirement of information for implementation of GPRA and the requirements of the Paperwork Reduction Act. At the same time that agencies have been told to develop new information systems, they are also required to minimize the paperwork burden they impose.[31]

Budget Process

There are at least two distinct stages in the budget process: budget execution and budget creation. Information that is appropriate for the budget execution stage is usually defined by accountants and auditors; it indicates patterns of expenditure and detailed allocation within broader budget categories. Information for the budget creation stage is closely linked to political needs; it focuses on estimates that indicate the level of resources required to attain program or policy objectives and seeks to determine whether expectations of past budget decisions have been obtained. Unlike the information describing substantive program management and implementation issues (which is frequently qualitative and complex), budget information is defined around budget numbers. As a result, it appears to be clear and straightforward. Specific amounts of money are allocated and expended for what are viewed as specific activities.

One of the assumptions contained within the performance movement involves a belief that there can be a direct relationship between performance information and budget decision making. Underlying this belief is an assumption that it is possible to make budget decisions based on technical assessments and not on political grounds. There is little evidence that this is possible, not only because budget decisions involve value determinations but because there is not really agreement on what actually constitutes performance-based budgeting.

Several authors have attempted to define performance-based budgeting. Joyce and Tompkins have noted that there at least four prerequisites to successful use of performance information at any stage of the budget process. They are:

- Public entities need to know what they are supposed to accomplish.
- Valid measures of performance need to exist.
- Accurate measures of cost need to be developed.
- Cost and performance information need to be brought together for budgeting decisions.[32]

Pollitt warns that "[t]here are dangers in speaking of 'financial management' and 'performance management' as though they were homogeneous activities. In reality they are broad labels, each covering a wide range of decisions and activities made and carried out at different levels and for different purposes." He defines five categories as levels of decision making:

- Agreeing on the global totals for public expenditure
- Dividing the total between major sectors
- Allocating resources to particular programs within a sector

- Allocating resources to particular activities or institutions within a program
- Allocating resources within a particular institution or activity.[33]

In the past, the State of California's Legislative Analyst's Office was required to develop a cost-benefit analysis for each new piece of legislation. However, it has not continued this practice.[34] And the Program Planning Budgeting process that was undertaken in the United States during the 1960s provides another example of information that was expected to be used in the budget process. Over the years, the experience of linking performance information with budget decisions has elicited both positive and negative views. There are times when the organization of the budget information skews the linkage. For example, recently the U.S. Department of Interior has argued that the budget for the National Park Service is the highest ever. According to the department, the budget has more funds per employee, per acre, and per visitor than at any previous time. Others, however, have argued that the department has faced budget shortfalls.[35]

All of these sources make it evident that a clear relationship between performance information and budget decision making is extremely difficult to accomplish. Despite this, there continues to be a strong desire to move in that direction. In addition, there are times when performance requirements and budget allocations appear to be on separate tracks. Federal budget decisions for the 2005–2006 school year will mean that more than two-thirds of the districts will not receive as much financing as before. The Center on Education Policy reported that the reduced funding will make it more difficult for states and school districts to reach all schools in need of improvement as a result of the requirements in the No Child Left Behind legislation.[36]

Control by Funders

While most of the language around performance downplays this function, it is clear that a concern about control is a subtext in the performance movement. Usually this motivation follows existing funding decisions. It can come from various funders—

governments, foundations, school districts, health maintenance organizations. Information that meets the needs of this function is often cloaked in the vocabulary of accountability but the unspoken motivation deals with the funders' attempt to make sure that those they are funding are implementing the program following the funders' agenda. In such a case, this definition of accountability does not deal with concern about the impact of a program or policy.

In his writing on performance management in employment and training programs, Barnow has commented that "performance management systems generally seek answers to simpler outcome and process questions that are associated with the goals of the program; the issue is more one of accountability than impact." He contrasts performance management information with evaluations and argues that "evaluations of human service programs are generally costly and require the use of comparison or control groups to identify what would have occurred in the absence of the program. Performance management systems are generally less intrusive, but they then must sacrifice including impact measures."[37]

Recently, some foundations have used quantitative metrics to carry out what they argue are fiduciary and programmatic responsibilities. For example, the John Templeton Foundation has established guidelines for applicants that clearly communicate a control agenda. They describe their requirements as a form of performance measure and ask potential grantees to stipulate their goals and measures of those goals when they propose specific activities. The foundation notes, "We are using a variety of mathematical metrics as a heuristic to promote more ambitious and entrepreneurial implementation of projects. Unlike the 'bottom-line' in the for-profit sector, in educational and intellectual work there is no single metric for success and many non-quantifiable intangibles."[38]

Similarly, the William and Flora Hewlett Foundation asks applicants to submit a proposal that follows a causal model outlining a path from inputs to activities to outputs to outcomes. Each element of the model must be followed, specifying indicators, baselines, and numerical targets.[39]

Political Agenda

It is not surprising that performance information is sometimes desired to meet political agendas of particular players. If a funder (such as a member of a legislative body) is attempting to either kill, modify, or begin a particular policy or program, that perspective defines the kind of information that is desired. When this becomes public, it appears that the actor is behaving in an inappropriate manner. Yet one could interpret this behavior as intrinsic and predictable. Given the dynamics of decision making in a complex representative democratic system, where ideology and political agendas are not always made public, one should not be surprised when that occurs. Whether or not political actors are consciously skewing information sources, when that information is used in a volatile political environment there will always be suspicion about its veracity.

A number of recent examples of this problem illustrate this behavior.

Medicare Estimates. In June 2003, both the Senate and the House approved bills that created a Medicare prescription drug program. Members of both bodies were assured that the cost of the program would not exceed $400 billion over ten years. Two weeks before this occurred, Richard Foster, chief actuary of the Medicare program, had estimated that drug benefits would be in the range of $500 billion to $600 billion. He was told by Thomas Scully, administrator of the Centers for Medicare and Medicaid Services, that he was not allowed to disclose these estimates to Congress. The alternative estimate became public within the year but after the legislation had already been enacted and signed. Democrats called for an investigation of charges that the Bush administration threatened to fire Foster if he gave the data to Congress. Even an internal investigation by the Department of Health and Human Services acknowledged the situation.[40] The experience with the Medicare estimates indicates how difficult it is to collect neutral data within a highly politicized environment. Information like this would be the basis for performance measurement in the Medicare program and make it difficult to have confidence in the information that is produced.

Mercury Emissions Rule. Political appointees in the Environmental Protection Agency bypassed agency professional staff and a federal advisory panel in 2003 to craft a rule on mercury emissions preferred by the industry and the White House. EPA staffers said they were told not to undertake the normal scientific and economic studies called for under a standing executive order. According to a Republican environmental regulator from Ohio who cochaired the EPA appointed advisory panel, the administration chose a process "that would support the conclusion they wanted to reach."[41]

Racial Disparities. In January 2004, it was disclosed that a federal report on racial disparities in health was revised at the direction of top administration officials in the Department of Health and Human Services. The early draft of the report that was issued by the Institute of Medicine, a branch of the National Academy of Sciences, showed stronger imbalances and emphasized the lack of equality. That report suggested that widespread racial differences in health care were rooted in historic and contemporary inequities. According to a member of the IOM committee, the final version "does not really help people focus on the major problem areas."[42]

Report on World Terrorism. In June 2004, the U.S. State Department issued a report on the incidence of terrorism around the world. Citing a reduction of acts of terrorism between 2002 and 2003, the deputy secretary of state commented that "you will find in these pages clear evidence that we are prevailing in the fight."[43] After expressions of concern by members of Congress, the State Department revised its data. Issuing the revised report, John Brennan, the Director of the Terrorist Threat Integration Center (TTIC), commented:

> Numerous factors contributed to the inaccurate information contained in the 2003 Patterns of Global Terrorism publication. TTIC provided incomplete statistics to CIA, which incorporated those statistics into material passed to the Department of State. . . . There was insufficient review and quality control throughout the entire data compilation, drafting and publication process, including the inaccurate and incomplete database numbers provided by TTIC.[44]

There are also times when political actors want to avoid defining performance measures that will hold them accountable for action. One example of this involves attempts to avoid developing a set of specific benchmarks for measuring progress toward military and political stability in Iraq. The defense spending bill that was passed by Congress in May 2005 required the Defense Department to devise a comprehensive set of performance indicators and measures of stability and security. These included measures of the number of engagements per day, the number of trained Iraqi forces, the strength of the Iraqi insurgency, as well as indicators of economic activity in Iraq. According to some observers, the White House has been resisting the development of such data.[45]

Performance Information and Multiple Types of Agencies

As has been discussed earlier, it is difficult to establish a single standard for performance measurement activities that is appropriate in all situations. Attempts to create one-size-fits-all requirements frequently include assumptions that there are universal information approaches to meet these requirements. It is important to acknowledge that organizations differ from one another in terms of their work and activities, their interests and perspectives, and the type of policy involved. As a result, we should assume that performance information also varies in terms of the types of agencies that are involved. Agencies vary in a number of ways. Several authors provide typologies about organizational types that are relevant to this issue.

James Q. Wilson has argued that agencies differ from one another in two main respects. (See discussion in chapter 3.) He writes: "Can the activities of their operators be observed? Can the results of those activities be observed? The first factor involves *outputs*—what the teachers, doctors, lawyers, engineers, police officers, and grant-givers do on a day-to-day basis. . . . The second factor involves *outcomes*—how, if at all, the world changes because of the outputs."[46] Wilson notes that observing outputs and outcomes produces four kinds of agencies. They are:

Production organizations, where both outputs and outcomes can be observed. Information within these organizations is relatively straightforward and clear; both outputs and outcomes can be counted.

Procedural organizations, where outputs but not outcomes can be observed. Information within these organizations may describe what is done within the organization (often in process terms) but cannot provide a sense of the outcomes of those activities.

Craft organizations, where outcomes but not outputs can be observed. Information within these organizations is not able to describe what is done but can document the effects of that activity.

Coping organizations, where neither outputs nor outcomes can be observed. This is the most problematic type of organization for information collection. It is difficult to collect information about what is done or the impact of that activity. In these organizations, Wilson notes that there is likely to be a high degree of conflict between managers and operators, particularly in those organizations that must cope with clients not of their own choosing.[47]

It is not always easy to determine whether outputs or outcomes can be observed or agreed upon. Dall Forsythe has commented,

> Debate over whether to use output or outcome data may reflect differences in interests as well as perspectives. In monitoring activities of the U.S. Forest Service, for example, the lumber industry and its allies focus on traditional output measures such as board feet of timber harvested and associated revenue. Environmentalists, in contrast, downplay timber-cutting goals and are trying to develop broader indicators of ecosystem health to assess the agency's success or failure."[48]

Other types of organizations with responsibilities for implementing different types of policies also create particular issues for performance information collection. The Lowi typology that differentiates between redistributive, regulatory, and distributive or developmental policies is one frequently used framework.[49] These three types create different demands on performance information.

Redistributive policies have been defined in several ways. In one definition, these are simply the policies that derive from zero-sum politics: some groups win and some lose in the pushing and pulling of the political system. Policies in this area might take the form of targeting specific population groups that are viewed as particularly needy, or the establishment of rights for groups that require protection. Methods of redistribution may focus on individuals (e.g., income transfer programs or vouchers) or focus on groups. Within this latter category, programs may emphasize the territorial discrepancies within the country (e.g., disparities between regions) or particular groups within a geographic area. In these instances, redistribution occurs between levels of government rather than between government and an individual. Redistributive policies do create tensions in performance information collection as groups that "win" want to show that the policy is effective while groups that have "lost" want to show that the policy decision has not been effective in achieving its ends.

Regulatory policies focus on the imposition of limitations or control of behavior of certain individuals or groups for the benefit of the broader society. These limitations can be imposed on individuals, on private groups, or on other governments. These limitations are often referred to as *mandates*, whereby grantees are provided funds conditioned by their agreement to accept certain requirements or standards. Regulatory policies set up expectations in terms of both those regulated and those who regulate. As a result, the performance information that is devised in those settings attempts to show formal compliance with the policies but also to minimize the disruption that would come from such compliance.

Distributive or *developmental policies* are considered to be policies for which the benefits or results are concentrated or clearly focused; they have been defined with the following characteristics: they provide subsidies to encourage private activities; they convey tangible governmental benefits to individuals, groups, or firms; they appear to produce only winners, not losers; they are typically based on decisions guided by short-run consequences; they involve a high degree of cooperation and mutually rewarding logrolling; they are marked by low visibility; and they are fairly stable over time.[50] Performance information desired from these policy settings can be expected to indicate that recipients of program funds should continue to receive funds in the future.

While the Lowi typology is useful, often programs and policies are constructed around multiple approaches. Contained within a single program or piece of legislation may be more than one type of approach. This makes it difficult to sort out the type of information that would be useful. Agencies may find themselves implementing multiple programs that have very different approaches to information.

Networks, Partnerships, and Intergovernmental Policies

If this variety of organizations and policies were not complicated enough, in recent years there has been a dramatic increase in programs and policies that cross traditional organizational and sectoral lines. The growth of networks and partnerships has meant that the boundaries between organizations and policy arenas are less distinct than they were in the past. This has occurred because changes within the society and limited resources have required the involvement of a range of actors to assure program effectiveness. For example, over the past two decades, those who are concerned about rural development have acknowledged that changes for the rural population require involvement not only of traditional agricultural organizations and players but also of education, health, housing, economic development, and environmental actors.[51] Some policymakers, such as those in health, have thought about devising partnerships that would require information networks.[52] Situations in which there is increased interdependency between players clearly complexifies the performance information collection task. Organizations are likely to vary considerably in the data systems that they have put in place; even if the system is considered to be effective when viewed within the organization's boundaries, most of the systems that have been devised are not easily converted to integrated data systems.

In addition, there has been a growing perception that many policy areas cross jurisdictional lines. Thus interdependencies between federal, state, and local levels of government have become much more common than they were in the past (see chapter 7). And in some cases, the growth of globalization means that programs and policies require involvement of actors beyond national boundaries. Heinrich has commented that although one of the goals of the Workforce Investment Act was to standardize the types of performance data collected and to compel states to develop capacity to produce more accurate and comparable measures of program performance, the flexibility and discretion of states built into the program made this very difficult.[53] Agencies that implement more than one program may be faced with very different relationships between federal and nonfederal actors. David Frederickson's analysis of the performance management activities for Medicare and Medicaid contrasts the two efforts. He quotes an official involved in the implementation of the program: "There is really only one Medicare program, but there are essentially 56 separate Medicaid programs."[54]

Conclusion

As this discussion suggests, the assumptions about information that are integral to the performance movement do not "fit" the variegated world of program design, demands, and forms that makes up the U.S. policy and program system. It is probably helpful to summarize the argument by comparing the six assumptions that make up what I called the "unreal or naïve approach" with the reality.

Information is already available. Organizations have found that the information that may already be available is not appropriate for the functions that are expected from various actors involved in the performance movement. The existing information may focus on other aspects of the decision process (inputs, processes, or outputs) but do not emphasize program outcomes. They have also learned that data systems vary in terms of the design of the program.

Information is neutral. This assumption is particularly difficult to support in programs within the public sector. Multiple players in a democracy have very different expectations about what they believe is true and what is false. One actor's "fact" is another actor's "value." This has a direct effect on what is measured and how. When one scratches the surface, one is likely to find biases of various sorts within data systems. Some sources are more value laden than others. The complexity of the policy and program world means that we cannot acquire information in the way that traditional social scientists suggest. Because various players are likely to use the information to meet their varied agendas, it is rational for those who are the subject of the data to find ways to game the system.[55]

We know what we are measuring. Many programs—particularly those with large expenditures attached to them—have multiple and often conflicting goals. The policymaking process very rarely produces programs with clear and easily defined goals. Multiple goals make it extremely difficult to determine whether a program is successful or not. In addition, programs that involve multiple actors (particularly intergovernmental programs with high degrees of discretion to state or local agencies) are designed to minimize the federal role. If the federal government requires specific forms of information from these third parties, they view this as a somewhat indirect way of establishing federal control. In addition, information that seeks to measure program quality often requires qualitative data that are difficult to aggregate.

We can define cause-effect relationships in programs. While this is true for some programs, many programs are based on incomplete understanding of cause-effect relationships. Indeed, often programs are designed as natural experiments, providing various intervention strategies because it is not clear what causes something to occur. In addition, the impact of many programs and policies is so closely related to broader environmental and contextual changes that it is difficult to attribute causation to the intervention.

Baseline information is available. Very few public organizations have had the kind of baseline information available that would allow someone to determine whether there has been an improvement or not in program performance. One can attribute this to a number of causes. First, those who determine budget allocations have been reluctant to appropriate funds for such information. Second, it is not clear to program administrators that such an investment of resources will make any difference, because decisions about the program are political rather than technical in nature. And third, the external environment changes so rapidly that what is measured at one point in time is not relevant at a future date.

Almost all activities can be measured and quantified. This assumption collides with several realities. It ignores the importance of assessing qualitative attributes of programs; program service deliverers are often most concerned about quality issues, and many of these are not appropriate for quantification. It also leads to behaviors in which officials are attracted to the development of data systems that measure what is easy to measure. In addition, individuals inside the organization skew their production to meet the requirements, whether or not these requirements actually lead to achievement of an effort's goals. And, as the familiar maxim puts it, "garbage in, garbage out."

Elaine Waters faces a situation in which she has significant questions about the kinds of information that are being collected in the school that her children attends. She knows that the information is useful to at least one of her children's teachers but that it is misleading and hardly neutral for the other two. She does not believe that the tests that are given to the students really measure learning and problem solving skills. And she doesn't think that the teachers really know what causes some children to do well on the tests and others not. She is afraid that the two children who learn in a different way will be labelled as nonachievers by the school, which may limit their future educational opportunities. Because she knows that many teachers agree with her and share her concerns, her strategy is to develop allies among them and organize other parents who are worried about the same issues.

Notes

1. Joseph S. Wholey, "Performance-Based Management: Responding to the Challenges," *Public Productivity & Management Review* 22, no. 3 (March 1999): 291.

2. John Keel, Albert Hawkins, Lawrence F. Alwin, Legislative Budget Board, *Guide to Performance Measure Management: 2000 Edition*, SAO, No. 00-318, Austin, Texas December 1999. Available at www.sao.state.tx.us/resources/manuals/prfmguide/guide2000.pdf.

3. John Mayne and Robert Schwartz, "Assuring the Quality of Evaluative Information," in Robert Schwartz and John Mayne, eds., *Quality Matters: Seeking Confidence in Evaluation, Auditing and Performance Reporting* (New Brunswick, N.J.: Transaction, 2005).

4. Carol H. Weiss, "Ideology, Interests and Information: The Basis of Policy Positions," in Daniel Callahan and Bruce Jennings, eds., *Ethics, The Social Sciences, and Policy Analysis* (New York: Plenum Press, 1983), 233–34.

5. H. H. Gerth and C. Wright Mills, *From Max Weber: Essays in Sociology* (New York: Oxford University Press, 1946), 233.

6. Robert K. Merton, "The Unanticipated Consequences of Purposive Social Action," *American Sociological Review* 1, no. 6 (December 1936): 900.

7. Weiss, "Ideology, Interests and Information," 220.

8. Government Performance Project of the Maxwell School of Citizenship and Public Affairs, *Paths to Performance in State and Local Government* (2003), 29.

9. See Anne Laurent, "Stacking Up: The Government Performance Project Rates Management at 15 Federal Agencies," *Government Executive* (February 1999): 13–18.

10. Yilin Hou, Donald P. Moynihan, and Patricia Wallace Ingraham, "Capacity, Management and Performance: Exploring the Links," *American Review of Public Administration* 33, no. 3 (September 2003): 296.

11. GAO, *Program Evaluation: Agencies Challenged by New Demand for Information on Program Results*, GAO/GGD-98-53, April 1998.

12. See Barbara S. Romzek and Melvin J. Dubnick, "Accountability in the Public Sector: Lessons from the Challenger Tragedy," *Public Administration Review* (May–June 1987), and Beryl A. Radin, *The Accountable Juggler: The Art of Leadership in a Federal Agency* (Washington, D.C.: CQ Press, 2002).

13. Harry P. Hatry, *Performance Measurement: Getting Results*, (Washington, D.C.: The Urban Institute Press, 1999). See also Roger P. Straw, "Evaluation of Public Health Service Programs under the Government Performance and Results Act," *Evaluation and the Health Professions* 19, no. 3 (September 1996): 394–404.

14. Hatry, *Performance Measurement*, 12–18.

15. Burt Perrin, "Effective Use and Misuse of Performance Measurement," *American Journal of Evaluation* 19, no. 3 (1998): 370.

16. Straw, *Evaluation*, 398.

17. E. A. Brown, "Conforming the Government R&D Function with the Requirements of the Government Performance and Results Act: Planning the Unplannable? Measuring the Unmeasureable," *Scientometrics* 36, no. 3 (1996): 447.

18. Many of the issues that are discussed in this chapter are similar to the problems that are experienced by those who engage in policy and program evaluation activities. But the performance measurement efforts have higher visibility and are expected to lead directly to policy and program changes and involve political actors. By contrast, evaluation activities are more likely to focus on issues of concern to program managers and professionals involved in program implementation.

19. Robert D. Behn, "Why Measure Performance? Different Purposes Require Different Measures," *Public Administration Review* 63, no. 5 (September/October 2003).

20. Ian Humphreys, Graham Francis, and Jackie Fry, "Performance Measurement in Airports: A Critical International Comparison," *Public Works Management and Policy* 6, no. 4 (April 2002): 265.

21. Tom Jackman, "Falls Church Police Must Meet Quota for Tickets," *Washington Post*, August 8, 2004, p. C 1.

22. See Radin, "The Government Performance and Results Act and the Tradition of Federal Management Reform: Square Pegs in Round Holes," *Journal of Public Administration Research and Theory* 10, no. 1 (January 2000): 127.

23. U.S. Department of Health and Human Services, HHS Working Group on Sentinel Objectives, *Leading Indicators for Healthy People 2010*, Washington, D.C., March 1998, p. 1.

24. See The Boston Indicators Project, http://www.tbf.org/indicatorsProject/ (accessed July 23, 2005).

25. For an analysis of the Compstat effort see Dennis C. Smith with William J. Bratton, "Performance Management in New York City: Compstat and the Revolution in Police Management," in Dall W. Forsythe, ed., *Quicker, Better, Cheaper: Managing Performance in American Government* (Albany, N.Y.: The Rockefeller Institute Press, 2001), 453–82.

26. Demetra Smith Nightingale et al., "Work and Welfare Reform in New York City During the Giuliani Administration: A Study of Program Implementation," The Urban Institute, Washington, D.C., July 2002.

27. Lenneal J. Henderson, "The Baltimore CitiStat Program: Performance and Accountability," in John M. Kemensky and Albert Morales, eds., *Managing for Results 2005* (Lanham, Md.: Rowman and Littlefield, 2005), 465–98.

28. Scott D. Camp, Gerald G. Gaes, Jody Klein-Saffran, Dawn M. Daggett, and William G. Saylor, "Using Inmate Survey Data in Assessing Prison Performance: A Case Study Comparing Private and Public Prisons," *Criminal Justice Review* 27, no. 1 (Spring 2002): 26–51.

29. Janet M. Kelly and David Swindell, "A Multiple-Indicator Approach to Municipal Service Evaluation: Correlating Performance Measurement and Citizen Satisfaction across Jurisdictions," *Public Administration Review* 62, no. 5 (September/October 2002): 534. See also Jack Molnar and Brenda Stup, "Using Clients to Monitor Performance," *Evaluation Practice* 15, no. 1 (1994): 29–35.

30. William T. Gormley Jr., "Using Organizational Report Cards" (paper presented at the National Public Management Research Conference, Georgetown University, Washington, D.C., October 11, 2003).

31. Victor S. Rezendes, GAO, *Paperwork Reduction Act: Burden Increases and Violations Persist* (testimony before the Subcommittee on Energy, Policy, Natural Resources, and Regulatory Affairs, Committee on Government Reform, House of Representatives), GAO-02-598T, April 11, 2002.

32. Philip G. Joyce and Susan Sieg Tompkins, "Using Performance Information for Budgeting: Clarifying the Framework and Investigating Recent State Experience," in Kathryn Newcomer et al., ed., *Meeting the Challenges of Performance-Oriented Government* (Washington, D.C.: American Society for Public Administration, 2002), 69.

33. Christopher Pollitt, *Integrating Financial Management and Performance Management*, Public Management Service, Public Management Committee, OECD, PUMA/SBO(99)4/FINAL1999, Paris: Organization for Economic Cooperation and Development (1999), 7.

34. See Elizabeth Hill, "The California Legislative Analyst's Office," in *Organizations for Policy Analysis: Helping Government Think*, Carol H. Weiss, ed. (Newbury Park, Calif.: Sage Publications, 1992), 256–73.

35. Mary Fitzgerald, "Norton: Park Service Funding Highest Ever," *Washington Post*, July 9, 2004, p. A10.

36. The Center on Education Policy, "School Officials Say Student Achievement Is Improving, But That They Lack the Capacity to Research All Schools in Need of Support Under No Child Left Behind" (press release, March 23, 2005).

37. Burt S. Barnow, "The Effects of Performance Standards on State and Local Programs," in Charles F. Manski and Irwin Garfinkel, eds., *Evaluating Welfare and Training Programs* (Cambridge, Mass: Harvard University Press, 1992), 279.

38. See http://templeton.org/whitepaper.asp.

39. The William and Flora Hewlett Foundation, Guidelines for Grant Proposals (online).

40. Robert Pear, "Inquiry Confirms Top Medicare Official Threatened Actuary over Cost of Drug Benefits," *New York Times*, July 7, 2004, p. A 12. See also Amy Goldstein, "Official Says He Was Told to Withhold Medicare Data," *Washington Post*, March 13, 2004, p. A 1.

41. Tom Hamburger and Alan C. Miller, "Mercury Emissions Rule Geared to Benefit Industry, Staffers Say," http://www.latimes.com/news/nationworld/nation/la-na-mercury16mar16.1.5139740.story?coll=la-home-headlines. (accessed March 2005).

42. Shankar Vedantam, "Racial Disparities Played Down at Request of Top Officials, Report on Health Care Differs from Draft," *Washington Post*, January 14, 2004, p. A 17.

43. Associated Press, "U.S. Wrongly Reported Drop in World Terrorism in 2003," *New York Times*, June 11, 2004, p. A 8.

44. John Brennan, "Remarks on the Release of the Revised Patterns of Global Terrorism 2003 Annual Report," June 22, 2004, U.S. Department of State, http://www.state.gov/ct/rls/rm/2004/33801.htm (accessed March 2005).

45. See David S. Broder, "The Metrics of Success in Iraq," *Washington Post*, July 3, 2005, B 07.

46. James Q. Wilson, *Bureaucracy: What Government Agencies Do and Why They Do It* (New York: Basic Books, 1989), 158.

47. Ibid., 159–71.

48. Dall W. Forsythe, "Pitfalls in Designing and Implementing Performance Management Systems," in Forsythe, ed., *Quicker, Better, Cheaper* (Albany, N.Y.: The Rockefeller Institute Press, 2001), 524.

49. See Theodore J. Lowi, "Four Systems of Policy, Politics and Choice," *Public Administration Review* 32 (July/August 1972): 298–310, and Theodore J. Lowi, *The End of Liberalism* (New York: Norton, 1969).

50. Ibid., 339.

51. See Beryl A. Radin et al., *New Governance for Rural America* (Lawrence, Kans: University Press of Kansas, 1996).

52. See, for example, Edward B. Perrin, Jane S. Durch, and Susan Skillman, *Health Performance Measurement in the Public Sector* (Washington D.C.: National Academy Press, 1999), and Stephen Page, "Measuring Accountability for Results in Interagency Collaboratives," *Public Administration Review* 64, no. 5 (September 2004).

53. Carolyn J. Heinrich, "Improving Public-Sector Performance Management: One Step Forward, Two Steps Back?" http://www.pmranet.org/conferences/georgetownpapers/Heinrich.pdf.

54. David G. Frederickson, "Differently Hollowed-Out: The Implementation of the Government Performance and Results Act in the Medicare and Medicaid Programs" (paper presented to the 7th National Public Management Research Conference, Georgetown University, Washington, D.C., October 2003), 30.

55. See Peter Smith, "On the Unintended Consequences of Publishing Performance Data in the Public Sector," *International Journal of Public Administration* 18, nos. 2 & 3 (1995): 277–310.

COMPETING VALUES IN A GLOBAL CONTEXT: PERFORMANCE ACTIVITIES IN THE WORLD BANK

9

Brian Segretti is a staff member at the World Bank who has been given the task of devising a social accountability agenda for three countries in South America. He has been at the Bank for more than a decade and has been frustrated in his attempts to develop projects that meet the Bank's "efficiency" agenda but are at the same time responsive to the concerns of nongovernmental organizations (NGOs) within countries. He has experienced a range of projects that do not avoid corrupt practices within the countries and often seem to do more to reinforce centralized power within those countries than to meet citizen needs. He is hard pressed to define accountability relationships within these projects.

Segretti has been intrigued by the development of strategies that seek to improve the performance of programs supported by the World Bank and by other international bodies. It seems that every day he reads about efforts to improve public sector management around the world by adopting private sector practices (such as decentralization and using market-based concepts such as consumer satisfaction). These efforts have been called the New Public Management.

While he finds these public management reform approaches quite convincing, he believes that projects will not be effective until they find ways to engage the citizens who are supposed to be the beneficiaries of these project services. He has seen too many projects that were designed, managed, and evaluated without input from these citizens. Given that, one should not be surprised that programs are not seen to be effective. Over the past fifteen years or so, he has learned that NGO groups that represent citizens provide a vehicle for input at all stages of the project cycle. They can help to formulate project design elements and can be involved in a range of performance monitoring activities. These activities are often called initiatives that foster social accountability. But these groups often have an agenda that is at odds with the stance of government officials within their country.

Segretti hasn't figured out a way to balance these two approaches. He finds it interesting that both the public sector management advocates and those who accentuate the role of NGOs are attracted to some of the same techniques (such as budget analysis and report cards). But he knows that these two groups approach these techniques with different values and agendas. It is a challenge to figure out a way to deal with these two approaches within the confines of the World Bank.

Although much of this book deals with performance issues within the United States, concern about performance and accountability is found across the globe. Indeed, the initial activity within the United States was modeled on past experience in New Zealand (and to a lesser extent Australia and Britain).[1]

The New Zealand activity took place in a centralized and small country where it was relatively easy to focus on outcomes. In addition to the scale and simplicity of the New Zealand governmental structure, the performance activity took place during a period of major change, when private sector and public choice theories drove the reform process.

As the concept is applied to developing countries, there is a clear challenge: how can one link the concerns of public sector management reforms with the values of NGOs and civil society advocates? There is increasing attention to the role of these latter two groups in addressing development needs. This was the challenge faced by the World Bank as it attempted to support performance activities within the context of its relationships with developing countries. The Bank actually supported two types of activities related to performance. One, called "civic engagement," focused on a bottom-up process by which NGOs defined performance outcomes and were involved in assessing the achievement of those outcomes. The other drew from the New Zealand experience and was a top-down effort that emphasized efficiency outcomes and market-based solutions.

This discussion illustrates two faces of the performance movement and uses examples of activities within the World Bank (or recommended by the Bank) that are viewed as a part of that movement. The two approaches within the Bank rarely interact with one another. At the same time, the Bank has adopted techniques such as report cards and budget analysis without acknowledging that there are different values that undergird use of these techniques. For example, when a government agency devises report cards to compare different program settings with one another, that agency focuses on program implementation within the government structure. By contrast, when a civil society group advocates use of report cards, it is often attempting to show how the government does not serve a particular citizen or client group.

The two strategies undertaken in the World Bank illustrate the impact of different value sets in approaching performance activities. The examples that are included in this discussion emerge from the Public Sector Management Group of the Bank (a group that emphasizes administrative reform, decentralization, and anticorruption activities) and from the Social Development Group (which emphasizes civil society activity and uses the term "social accountability" to describe its approach).

The Social Development Group

This World Bank group seeks to find a way to determine how what they call "civic engagement" fits into a macro system that includes the policy framework, the regulatory environment, resources (information), and capacities. Civic engagement, or social accountability, according to this approach, includes the following:

- Budget formulation
- Budget analysis
- Budget tracking
- Performance monitoring:
  - Report card surveys
  - Community scorecards

The Backdrop to the Term "Social Accountability"

According to Sasha Courville, many of the issues related to social accountability are associated with an array of initiatives and coalitions of actors subsumed in the expression "corporate social responsibility." According to Courville, "These actors are mainly private, nonstate bodies working to address social justice and social accountability issues—issues that are generally seen to be in the public good—within the context of the private sector."[2]

The effort began with concern about the lack of government enforcement of requirements involving environmental issues. It soon was expanded to include social justice issues involving labor practices; trade unions, businesses, and NGOs were committed to voluntary standards for workplaces based on International Labour Organization and other human rights conventions. An organization called Social Accountability International works to improve workplaces and combat sweatshops through the expansion and further development of the international workplace standard. This standard, called SA8000, was devised in 1996 through an international multi-stakeholder advisory board.

About the same time, similar issues were surfacing within the World Bank. The Bank's Independent Inspection Panel recommended that the Bank's Board of Executive Directors authorize a full investigation of the Yacyreta Hydroelectric Dam, located on the border between Argentina and Paraguay. A claim had been filed in September 1996 that asserted that the project had "serious impacts on [local people's] standards of living, their economic well-being and their health."[3] The Bank Information Center also noted that during the 1980s and 1990s there was increased pressure to adopt policies that were sensitive to environmental and social impacts of Multilateral Development Bank projects.[4] These activities resulted in a commitment within the Bank to attempt to assess the impact of their projects on grassroots populations. It assumed that it was not possible to get such information only from governments; thus the bottom–up approach to performance became a point of emphasis.

NGO Activity: Budget Analysis

As an increasing number of critics pointed to the lack of effectiveness of top–down, global approaches to change, a number of activities were undertaken during this period by NGOs committed to social change and empowerment of otherwise powerless groups within a particular country. The International Budget Project (IBP) of the U.S. Center on Budget and Policy Priorities was created in the 1990s to assist NGOs and researchers in their efforts both to analyze budget policies and to improve budget processes and institutions. It became a model for similar activities supported or encouraged by the World Bank.

The project is especially interested in assisting with applied research that is of use in ongoing policy debates and with research on the effects of budget policies on the poor. This is a form of performance assessment that is not often used in the United States. The overarching goal of the project is to make budget systems more responsive to the needs of society and, accordingly, to make these systems more transparent and accountable to the public. The project works primarily with researchers and NGOs in developing countries or new democracies.

The project organized or helped pull together an assortment of conferences and meetings. Most notably, in December 1997 the Center hosted a skill-building conference for researchers and NGO personnel working on budget issues. All regions of the world were represented, with attendees coming from Argentina, Brazil, Chile, Egypt, Germany, India, Israel, Lebanon, Mexico, Namibia, Pakistan, Peru, the Philippines, Poland, Russia, South Africa, the United States, and the West Bank.

The fourth international conference organized by the IBP took place in Mexico City March 9–13, 2000. It brought together 140 delegates from forty countries with an interest in applied budget work to share the diverse experiences, accomplishments, and challenges of this work by civil society advocates around the world. It was cohosted by several Mexican NGOs.

Other current activities of the project include joint research projects. One example is the Budget Transparency and Participation Scorecard for South Africa. Another is an examination of the feasibility of the creation of a government budget analysis institution in Israel that would be independent of the executive branch. This work is being undertaken with the Israeli group Adva. Besides informing the specific budget debates in those countries, the goals of these projects include the possibility that they can serve as model analyses that could be used in other countries.

According to the International Budget organization, its niche

reflects, in part, the dramatic transformations in systems of governments over the past decade. Dozens of countries have shifted from being closed to open societies and are constructing more participatory decision-making processes. The goals of this ongoing process extend beyond the establishment of free elections. Open and democratic societies require an informed citizenry, public participation, and governing processes that are transparent. Establishing open institutions and participatory decision-making processes is a daunting challenge, particularly in countries that have for their entire history been ruled by non-democratic regimes.

The nature of a country's budget process and the actual decisions on government budgets will play large roles in determining whether a country can meet the above challenges. The budget is perhaps the most important policy document, and the decisions made on the budget have profound effects on a nation's citizens. There is also a growing consensus that budget decisions need to be subjected to public scrutiny and debate.

As evidence of this growing consensus, there has been increased support given to non-governmental researchers undertaking independent and applied budget analysis. For instance, the Ford Foundation funds non-governmental policy organizations with a focus on analyzing budget and tax decisions in countries around the world.[5]

The Brazilian Forum on the Budget is another example of a bottom-up approach. It was formed by a coalition of over twenty Brazilian civil society organizations to promote socioeconomic development without environmental destruction, while also seeking the redistribution of income and wealth. It operates by monitoring and analyzing the federal public budget and creating mechanisms to broaden public participation in the budget process. It has no legal status, political allegiance, or religious affiliation. While advocacy for effective public policies involves initiatives that go beyond the budget, the budget is critical to the definition of public policies. Thus the forum intends to propose measures to democratize the budget process, particularly throughout the design of the Pluriannual Plan Act, Budget Guidelines Act, and Annual Budget Act, as well as the rendering of accounts by the executive branch of government.

Still another budget effort is found in Pathey, the Center for Budget Analysis and Policy Priorities, located in Ahmedabad, India, in the state of Gujarat. It analyzes budgets of all departments of the state as well as the federal government of India, especially in terms of provisions and commitments made towards the poor and powerless by the policy priorities of the government. Its analyses are confrontational in nature to create a demand for the ruling government to explain its positions during the budget debate. It does applied budget analysis for advocacy and lobbying activities with elected representatives to both the state assembly and national parliament to address how poor people are left out of budget policies and priorities. It examines budget spending trends and the impact of budget policies on the poor. The organization regularly provides training programs to build other NGOs, social activities, and researchers' capacity in budget analysis and good governance.

Much of the activity related to budget analysis has focused on the distribution of resources to previously ignored populations, including women. Advocates for gender equity have sought to examine the budget as it reflects priorities, values, and social norms.[6]

These analyses have often been linked to direct advocacy with policy makers and have also sought to bring more women into the budgetary process. The earliest example of gendered budget analysis was done in Australia in the mid-1980s with the creation of a women's budget—an assessment of public sector spending for gender impact. Changes in the Australian government, however, contributed to a decline of interest in gender budgets, but other countries adopted the process. It is difficult to determine the exact impact of budget analyses, but they are viewed as efforts that contribute to the public dialogue about programs and policies.

NGO Activity: Report Cards

Unlike the budget analysis, which tends to focus on the various stages of the budget process (budget formulation, budget analysis, and expenditure monitoring), another technique that was devised by NGOs in the 1990s focused on performance monitoring through report cards. The report card potential received significant attention from the World Bank and was highlighted by the Participation and Civic Engagement Group of the Social Development Department. Often the use of the report card was not linked to the agenda of particular NGO groups but, rather, was used as a mechanism to compare performance of government agencies.

According to one of its major proponents, Samuel Paul of the Public Affairs Center in Bangalore, India, this intervention was devised to assure that citizens who are also consumers of public services are watchful and able to assert their rights. Paul has written:

> By withholding information, public service agencies tend to weaken the bargaining power of their customers or the public they are meant to serve. The deadlines for providing a service or solving a problem, the standards pertaining to the quality of services and the rights of the customers with respect to service provisions are seldom disclosed to the people. Some observers believe that a weak civil society has encouraged those in authority to "highjack" the government and its agencies to serve their narrow and sectarian interests rather than public well being in the true sense.

The only time citizens are active is during elections. They may occasionally use the vote to throw out some political parties and leaders who exceed the limits. But between elections, people behave as if they are helpless spectators.[7]

Although report cards and customer service have been used in developed countries for some years (particularly in the private sector and in the public sector to compare performance of public organizations involved in delivering the same service),[8] Samuel Paul was able to adapt the technique to the values of NGO agendas. He focused on citizen (not organizational) report cards and has argued that it is a "cost-effective way for a government to find out whether its services are reaching the people, especially the poor. Users of a public service can tell the government a lot about the quality and value of a service."[9] Paul has noted that this form of information feedback is a way to minimize the "take it or leave it" attitude due to the reality that the government is the sole supplier of most essential services.

The first report card done by the Public Affairs Center was issued in 1994 on Bangalore's municipal services, water supply, electricity, telecom, and transport. The report card was based on random sample surveys of users of services and involved public ratings on different aspects of service quality (such as availability of services, usage, satisfaction, service standards, and perceived level of corruption). The ratings were issued publicly and received significant media publicity. Public discussions that followed brought the issues into the open and civil society groups began to organize themselves to voice their demands for better performance.

The report cards approach is constructed on the assumption that citizens have access to information they need to assess their satisfaction with services or government. It provides a means for accountability in contexts where people do not want to or cannot commit themselves to other forms of participation.

The first Bangalore citizen report cards were followed up with a second rating in 1999, and improvements were reflected in somewhat better ratings than the agencies received the first time around. At the same time, some agencies remained indifferent, and corruption levels continued to be high. A third survey was done in 2003, resulting in what Samuel Paul called "a surprising turnaround" in the city's services. It noted a remarkable rise in the citizen ratings of almost all of the agencies. Not only did public satisfaction improve across the board, but problem incidence and corruption seem to have declined perceptibly in the routine transactions between the public and the agencies.

Another citizen report card was undertaken by the Public Affairs Center in the Mumbai, India, slums. It was designed to determine information on the state of key public services in this area, to enable a coalition of NGOs to press for improved service delivery, and to generate inputs for greater citizen participation in policy formulation and program design. This study had two parts: one was for benchmarking (the assessment of overall availability, usage, and satisfaction and reasons for dissatisfaction with public services). The second was diagnostic (assessment of services where high levels of dissatisfaction were experienced, to identify the nature of stress, hidden costs, and initiatives for citizen participation). The response by the slum dwellers indicated that most preferred not to complain, that complaints fell on deaf ears, that problems never got solved, that bribery was not a way to solve problems, that there were not enough NGO efforts, and that they were ready to pay more for better service.

A similar effort was undertaken within the Philippines. The Philippine process involves multiple data collection methods to assess awareness of service, availability of service, use/non-use of service, satisfaction with service, comparisons of service, costs of service (actual and hidden), and recommendations for improvement. It involves the following methods:

> Reviews of official records
> Field visits
> Community interviews
> Key informant interviews
> Participant observation
> Focus group interviews
> Direct observation
> Questionnaires
> One-time survey

Panel surveys

The census

Issues for the survey were identified through focus group discussion. Dissemination included consultation with public service providers, consultations with Parliament, and public advocacy.[10]

Other NGO Activity: Anticorruption Efforts

Over the years, a number of NGOs across the globe have become increasingly concerned about citizens' ability to access information about their governments. They believe this information should be transparent and available to all citizens. As one of the groups involved in what they call the "global integrity approach" has noted, "Corruption erodes public trust in government, undermines the rule of law, weakens the state, and hinders economic growth by discouraging investment. Corruption has an extremely negative impact on social and civil society maturation and the establishment of effective and responsive democratic government."[11] Both the Center for Public Integrity and Transparency International have released indices that rate the existence and effectiveness of mechanisms that prevent abuse of power and promote public integrity.

The Public Integrity Index, a compilation of detailed data and comparative country perspectives of mechanisms in place to prevent abuses of power and promote public integrity, was released by the Center for Public Integrity in May 2004. Using a blend of social science and journalism, in-country teams of independent social scientists and investigative journalists report on the reality of corruption and anticorruption mechanisms in twenty-five countries. The Public Integrity Index measures three things: (1) the existence of public integrity mechanisms, including laws and institutions that promote public accountability and limit corruption; (2) the effectiveness of these mechanisms; and (3) the access that citizens have to public information to hold their government accountable. Indicators of existence assess the laws, regulations, and agencies or equivalently functioning mechanisms that are in place in a particular country. Indicators of effectiveness assess such aspects of public integrity as protection from political interference, appointments that support the independence of an agency; professional, full-time staff and funding; regular reports to the legislature; independently initiated investigation; and imposition of penalties. Indicators of citizen access assess the ready availability of public reports within a reasonable time period and at a reasonable cost.

The information that is developed by all of these activities has a life of its own. It can be used by the press, it may be used to organize and focus demonstrations and other forms of social protest, and it may also be used as a part of a legal strategy. In countries such as India and the United States, citizens and their associations have used litigation as a way of bringing themselves directly into the judicial accountability process. Using tools available through litigation, these groups have become part of an official fact-finding process. Courts in many countries are being reformed to increase the direct participation of poor people, enabling organizations to prosecute abuses of the rights of socially excluded groups and to hold power-holders more directly accountable to the poor.

According to Anne Marie Goetz and Rob Jenkins, many of the NGO efforts involving accountability have come from dissatisfaction with state-led experiments, which, they note, often seem driven by public relations concerns. They argue that "the suggestion that those worst afflicted by abuses of power ought to be directly involved in checking those abuses is hugely unfair." Further, they write:

> It is, moreover, unrealistic to expect relentlessly valiant behavior of ordinary people, who often lack the voice resources of other social groups—elite connections, education, media savvy. In many cases, voice initiatives—for instance, certain democratic decentralization programs and right to information laws—have resulted neither from pressure by the poor, nor from pure altruism. . . .
>
> Citizens' accountability initiatives, particularly those that end up establishing scrutiny processes parallel to, rather than in partnership with, official horizontal accountability institutions, have their own problems. The substitution of citizens' informal institutions for state accountability in-

stitutions inevitably runs into problems of legitimate authority, controls on power, and at the same time, limited impact.[12]

The Public Sector Management Group

Still another stream of change that is related to performance activity in the World Bank stems from the field that has come to be known as the New Public Management. This international movement has focused on such interventions as institutional rules and organizational routines affecting expenditure planning and financial management; civil service and labor relations; procurement; organization and methods; and audit and evaluation.[13] For the most part, despite its advocacy of decentralization and the market model, this activity focuses on a top-down approach inside of government. Its approach rests on government-wide strategies and central management agencies. While the best-known examples of its approach have been found in the UK, New Zealand, and Australia (largely in the 1980s), it has also reached into the management reform efforts in the United States (the National Performance Review during the Clinton administration) and structured the program of the Organisation for Economic Cooperation and Development (OECD)'s public management activities (known as PUMA).

The New Zealand activity received significant attention within this movement because its agenda took place across a wide range of areas (expenditure planning, financial management, organization, civil service, and labor relations) within a three-year period and because its arguments were developed in terms of economic theories of organization and government.[14] As one analyst noted, the public choice theory that underpinned the effort attempted to "institutionalize a clear distinction between 'outputs' and 'outcomes'"; he described the reliance on policy markets as "usually imagined rather than real."[15] Contracts would replace traditional public service, and these contracts would be developed around specific resources provided by one side and performance with those resources by the other. Most of the activity occurred inside of government with minimal consultative effort.

The small scale and simplicity of the New Zealand governmental structure minimized the problems associated with focusing on outcomes in other political systems. In many public programs, outcomes cannot be measured or determined in the short run; it requires decades to determine whether the programs actually accomplish their goals. As a result, many systems tend to focus on what they call intermediate outcomes or outputs (such as measures of numbers of individuals served by a program).

At the same time that this was taking place, a dramatic change was made in the country's electoral system. In 1996, a system of proportional representation was introduced that replaced the single-member constituency. About half of the members of Parliament would be elected in the traditional manner, with the other half elected from nationwide party lists. This change moved the country from running a two-party system to producing multi-party parliaments. This meant that single-party majority governments were replaced by coalitions and/or minority governments.

In 2001, a Labour-led coalition government came into power as a result of the new electoral system. That government commissioned a review of the public management activities and concluded that the existing system did not make interaction with government easy for citizens; it lacked a systematic approach to setting and achieving outcomes; and it did not understand and meet the needs of the Maori Pacific Island population.[16]

Despite these changes within New Zealand itself, for more than a decade the New Zealand experience became the model for management reform activity in the Bank and other international bodies without attention to a number of attributes in these activities that limit the ability of other countries to follow the New Zealand model:

- The structure, scale, and context of New Zealand. It is a relatively homogeneous, small, monocameral parliamentary system.
- The value framework that underpinned the reform agenda. No attention was given to distributional consequences of the activity. The efforts emphasized central control agencies and did not focus on those in the society who were poor or powerless.

- The contract process tended to support managers who would take a checklist approach to accountability—if it's not specified, it's not my responsibility.
- The unanticipated consequences of the reliance on the market for much of the change. The most frequently cited problem was the proliferation of agencies and fragmentation.

The attempt to use the New Zealand experience as a model for change in developing countries was roundly criticized by Allen Schick, a noted financial management academic and a consultant to the Public Sector Group of the World Bank. In a seminar in 1998, Schick's remarks, "Why Most Developing Countries Should Not Try New Zealand Reforms," noted that the Bank and other international organizations had showcased New Zealand's reforms and "some of the architects of the reforms have crisscrossed the globe extolling the virtues and portability of their country's version of results-oriented public management." Schick argued that "there are important preconditions for successfully implementing the New Public Management (NPM) approach; these should not be ignored by countries striving to uplift themselves after decades of mismanagement." Further, he noted, "can a country which gets things done by relying on informal practices that violate prescribed management rules sensibly broaden the discretion of managers while resorting to contractual formalities to safeguard public values and interests?"[17]

Despite Schick's warnings, both developed and developing countries were attracted to strategies that involved both an increase in managerial discretion and a reliance on performance contracting.[18] OECD noted that "devolving responsibilities and providing flexibility are corner-stones of reforms aimed at improving performance. Managers and organizations are given more freedom in operational decisions and unnecessary constraints are removed. In exchange, managers can be held accountable for results. Detailed control of input and processes is replaced by new incentives and focus on performance."[19]

Many of the proponents of this approach are trained or are at least comfortable with an economic perspective on performance and change. For this reason, they are able to influence the country-assigned staff within the Bank who have responsibility for the loans and projects supported by the international organization. In many instances they have more weight within the power structure of the Bank than do the proponents of the social accountability approach.

Government-Based Accountability Programs

While concern about accountability has become a global agenda item, it is not always easy to determine the motivation for this agenda. For some, the agenda is related to a concern about improving the effectiveness and efficiency of existing programs. For others, the private sector rhetoric about customer satisfaction pushes a government to devise methods of delivering services in a way that meets "customer" or citizen needs. For still others, accountability is related to anticorruption concerns. In some cases, the accountability agenda is tied to political relationships inside a government or to an attempt to control the way that programs are being administered by others (such as regional or local governments or third-party providers). In still other cases, these efforts are tied to the requirements of external funders (such as the Bank or other donors). The techniques that were developed by NGO groups often were adopted by governments that sought to increase their ability to target programs to particular client groups. These include community scorecards, citizen report card surveys, and training and decision-making efforts to involve a broader range of participants in the planning and allocation processes.

Because these activities are government-driven, they can reflect the political situation within a country. For example, following the political change in Peru, the new leaders found that there was a misuse of public institutions and social programs. The new government sought to develop collective action towards democracy between social organizations and political parties, to develop dialogue and negotiation mechanisms within an institutional and democratic framework, and to form a government with a national consensus. Three national processes were stressed: a concerted process for a fight against poverty, the elaboration of national development objectives, and decentralization reform. A national agreement was defined around thirty state policies by seven national parties, the church, industry, business, labor unions, and others. A regional level of authority was developed with requirements that participatory budgeting and concerted planning mechanisms be used at local and regional levels.

The Peru effort was viewed as an initiative incorporating transparency and participation as key components. The approach that was taken was possible because of the political change that took place within the country and included the following actions to promote social accountability:

- Participatory budgeting in municipalities and regions
- Report cards of protected programs
- Independent budget analysis conducted by civil society organizations
- Monitoring system of protected programs led by an ombudsman and involving others outside of government.[20]

The World Bank's "Take" on Social Accountability

As was noted at the beginning of this discussion, the World Bank's concern about issues related to social accountability stems from two very different parts of the Bank's structure. The Public Sector Management Group is in tune with the New Public Management agenda, highlighting administrative reform, decentralization, and anticorruption. This part of the Bank does not use the term social accountability and is focused on government-wide activities. In contrast, the Social Development Group emphasizes NGO and civil society activity and uses the term social accountability.

While committed to stakeholder involvement, it does not seem as if the Bank's analyses have moved beyond a rhetorical posture. What happens in a society when the various stakeholders are not willing to cooperate with government officials or with other groups within the society? In some cases, the social accountability activities have been related to policies of decentralization, privatization, or other shifts in the structure of government. In other cases, the activities do not seem to be related to one another.

Conclusion

The discussion of the two strategies related to performance within the World Bank illustrates several issues. First, the value orientation of the advocates for change makes a real difference in terms of the players in the process as well as the strategy for change. A top-down, government-focused approach is likely to define outcomes in aggregate efficiency terms unless the relevant government's political agenda emphasizes equity or redistributional values. In contrast, a bottom-up approach that is constructed around nongovernmental organizations committed to change is likely to focus on impacts of programs and policies on specific population groups. Second, the predominant professional orientation of the organization makes it difficult for individuals from other orientations to have an impact on decision making. The community organization constituency that advocates the social accountability approach does not speak the same language or conceptualize issues in a way that convinces economists.

While this chapter discusses the experience of the World Bank, the competing values that are found in that organization are not unique and are often present in other international organizations as well. The discussion in this chapter has focused on the difficulties experienced and the obstacles to finding a way to build bridges between the two elements within the current structure of the Bank. The variability of national structures and political cultures makes it difficult to devise any single strategy that would work in all countries. While there are examples of useful efforts around the globe, these efforts are usually modest in scale and designed to meet the unique elements within a particular country. They are developed as problem-solving approaches that have been created as targets of opportunity.

Brian Segretti believes that the social accountability approach is more likely to sustain lasting change in the three countries in South America in his portfolio than the New Public Management strategy. But the latter group is dominated by economists and individuals who have more influence on the distribution of resources within the Bank than those who advocate an NGO approach. As he develops his own work plan, he will try to find a way to bring representatives of both groups to the table and push both of them to deal with the specifics and needs of the particular country for which he is responsible. He thinks that focusing on budget analysis may be the best way to bridge the two perspectives.

Notes

This chapter is based on a paper that was commissioned and financed by the World Bank. The contents and opinions expressed therein are those of the author and not of the World Bank.

1. See Beryl A. Radin, "A Comparative Approach to Performance Management: Contrasting the Experience of Australia, New Zealand, and the United States," *International Journal of Public Administration* 26, no. 12 (2003).

2. Sasha Courville, "Social Accountability Audits: Challenging or Defending Democratic Governance," *Law and Policy* (July 2003), 271.

3. Kay Treackle, "Accountability at the World Bank: Introduction," Bank Information Center, September 1998, www.bicusa.org/bicusa/issues/misc_resources/374.php (accessed July 23, 2005).

4. Bank Information Center, "Environmental and Social Policies," http://www.bicusa.org/bicusa/issues/environmental_and_social_policies/index.php (accessed July 2004).

5. See The International Budget Project, http://www.internationalbudget.org/about/staff.htm (accessed July 23, 2005).

6. See Natasha Borges Sugiyama, "Gendered Budget Work in the Americas: Selected Country Experiences," October 2002, p. 2.

7. Samuel Paul, "Public services in a weak civil society," *India Together*, http://www.indiatogether.org/2003/gov-pubsvs04.htm (accessed July 2004).

8. See William T. Gormley Jr. and David L. Weimer, *Organizational Report Cards* (Cambridge, Mass.: Harvard University Press, 1999).

9. Samuel Paul, "Citizen Report Cards: An Accountability Tool," The World Bank Group, *Development Outreach*, http://www.worldbank.org/devoutreach/article.asp?id=235 (accessed July 2004).

10. www.worldbank.org/participation/events/workshops/gambia0303/clientreportcard.pdf.

11. The Center for Public Integrity, "Global Integrity: Methodology," http://www.publicintegrity.org/ga/default.aspx?act=methodology (accessed July 23, 2005).

12. Anne Marie Goetz and Rob Jenkins, "Voice Accountability in Service Delivery," Development Outreach: World Bank Institute, March 2004, http://www1.worldbank.org/deboutreach/march04/article.asp?id=234.

13. See Michael Barzelay, *The New Public Management* (Berkeley: University of California Press, 2001), 156.

14. Ibid., 159–60.

15. Robert Gregory, "All the King's Horses and All the King's Men: Putting New Zealand's Public Sector Back Together Again," *International Public Management Review* 4, no. 3 (2001): 43.

16. State Services Commission (New Zealand), "Current Problems in Public Management," http://www.ssc.govt.nz/display/document.asp?NavID=177&DocID=2757 (accessed July 23, 2005).

17. Allen Schick, "Why Most Developing Countries Should Not Try New Zealand Reforms," PREM Seminar Series, Public Sector Group (March 10, 1998), 1–2.

18. See, for example, OECD, *Performance Contracting: Lessons from Performance Contracting Case Studies: A Framework for Public Sector Performance Contracting*, PUMA/PAC, November 16, 1999.

19. OECD, "Devolution and Autonomy," http://www.oecd.org/puma/mgmtres/pac/devoluauton.htm (accessed June 2004).

20. The World Bank Group, *Participation and Civic Engagement*, "ESDD Week 2003, Social Accountability Session," http://www.worldbank.org/participation/events/essdwk03/essdwkppt.htm (accessed July 23, 2005).

10

CONFLICTING PATTERNS OF ASSUMPTIONS: WHERE DO WE GO FROM HERE?

Performance measurement activities turn out to be much more complex than is suggested by their advocates. The experience with a range of performance activities over the past decade illustrates a series of paradoxes. This volume has emphasized three such paradoxes: ambiguous rhetoric turned into formal processes, an emphasis on unmeasurable outcomes, and a critical stance on officials and professionals but ultimately relying on them. It has also discussed the conflict between analytical and political approaches as well as the tension between a one-size-fits-all strategy and a strategy that rests on individualized responses to specific programs and policies. These conflicts make the achievement of performance measurement much more difficult than is communicated by the language surrounding the field. While the motivation for the activities is usually legitimate, the arguments for change tend to set up expectations that performance measurement can be a panacea solution to thorny problems. But this solution at times generates consequences that actually inhibit or interfere with the achievement of performance goals.

The book has underscored several themes. It emphasized both the content and the context of the performance activity, particularly the variety of program and policy structures that face performance demands and the multiple values and expectations that are built into program goals. The variable context makes it difficult to develop information sources and to focus on program outcomes.

While the book has highlighted the problems with performance activities, at the same time it is relevant to acknowledge that the goals of performance measurement are commendable. There are examples of specific performance measurement activities that seem to be effective, particularly at state or local levels. But too frequently the efforts are difficult to absorb in a system characterized by complexity, multiple values, and pragmatism. This work has sought to emphasize the conceptual limitations of what I have described as the "classic" performance movement.

Alternative Assumptions

This volume has been attentive to the assumptions that surround the performance measurement movement. While these assumptions are built into most of the performance measurement efforts, they are rarely articulated. In part this is because the advocates of the performance movement are so committed to the process that they have tended to minimize the obstacles to attaining them. Performance measurement sometimes takes on the dimension of a religion—and its advocates put more emphasis on belief and faith in the process than on the political and organizational realities that surround the enterprise.

As the previous chapters indicate, these assumptions are implicit in the wide range of activities that are found in the performance movement. They lurk in the background of the Governmental Performance and Results Act, in the Program Assessment Rating Tool, in standardized education tests, in requirements for the delivery of health services, and in measurement of the leverage potential of foundation grants. Parents dealing with the education sector, doctors, teachers, and public sector officials, all are currently facing the consequences of the performance movement that flow from these faulty assumptions. Despite the attractive quality of the rhetoric of the performance movement, one should not be surprised that its clarity and siren call mask a much more complex reality. One is reminded of the quip by the iconoclastic writer, H. L. Mencken: "Explanations exist: they have existed for all times, for there is always an easy solution to every problem—neat, plausible and wrong."[1]

A Range of Assumptions

This conclusion summarizes the argument that is made in the volume by detailing the assumptions that are found in the performance movement and suggesting alternative assumptions to deal with these issues. It returns to the vignettes that have been used in the earlier chapters to suggest alternative approaches to the dilemmas that these fictional individuals face.

Intelligence

The classic assumptions: Like many planners and technocrats, the performance measurement community has been dominated by individuals who seek clarity and universal principles as they work through an issue. They approach problems looking for clear information and emphasize the linear approach to collecting information and taking action. They tend to focus on literal meanings of words and information. They assume that others approach problems as they do and do not acknowledge that there are other kinds of intelligence that may be useful to this process.

Alternative approaches: There are many different types of intelligence that can be used to approach the performance task. Gardner recommends that individuals cast the net widely as they move toward tasks like this one. It is particularly important to recognize that problem solving calls on individuals to devise information sources and open themselves up to empathy that allows them to see issues as others may see them. As Murray Edelman reminds us, organizations operate in both rational and symbolic modes. It is important that individuals involved with performance measurement think about the symbolic meanings that are attached to programs and policies.

The Nature of the World

The classic assumptions: Much of the activity in the performance measurement movement emphasizes linear patterns of cause and effect. We believe that we can attribute specific effects to specific identifiable causes. And while there is some rhetorical attention to relationships between system elements and complexity, the organization of performance activity approaches the components of systems as individual and discrete activities. In addition, there is a tendency in the classic approach to define future activities as extrapolations from the current situation. The planning process that is assumed in the movement is constructed on a belief that one can define goals and objectives and move forward, locking in those goals and objectives for the future.

Alternative approaches: If one assumes that issues are complex, constantly changing, and interdependent, then it seems important to be very modest about what you expect to accomplish. Believing that goals are very difficult to pin down—and many programs and policies are faced with multiple and often conflicting goals—it does not make sense to lock in a process that is constructed on the specification of such goals. One assumes that the analysis that is done through planning has to be viewed as limited, qualified, and often mercurial in nature. One needs to take care and avoid ascribing events to a single cause. We should also assume that we are prone to error because of the flux in the world and constantly changing dynamics.

Organizational Theory

The classic assumptions: The performance measurement effort, like many of the management reform efforts that preceded it, has adopted a set of assumptions about organizations that minimizes attention to the variety of forms and roles of these entities. These activities have emphasized generic approaches to organizations, spanning both public and private sector concerns. These methods support a search for principles of administration. They tend to focus on a series of decision and control processes that seem relevant to both types of organizations and often ignore the external elements that surround the organization. This set of assumptions leads to a national, aggregate approach to public management reform and a one-size-fits-all strategy for change. This approach also fosters a strategy that seeks to ignore politics and the relationship between politics and administration.

Alternative approaches: An alternative strategy would begin with an acknowledgement of the special attributes of public programs and organizations. It would not attempt to model change efforts on the experience of the private sector but would seek ways to sort out differences between agencies and programs (such as that devised by James Q. Wilson). Highlighting the differences among programs would lead one to acknowledge that it may be extremely difficult to measure outcomes in some instances, because of the nature of the work that an organization does or because of the volatility of the environment in which it operates.

Professionals

The classic assumptions: There appears to be a tendency within the performance measurement movement to establish processes and requirements that impose bureaucratic control over hitherto autonomous professionals. This is done for several reasons. First, it has been put in place because of dissatisfaction with the way that professionals operate, and second, it is a way to impose fiscal control over the expenditure of funds for the work performed by the professionals. In the latter situation, there is sometimes a conflict between quality norms defined by the professional group and the fiscal agenda of the organization.

Alternative approaches: An alternative approach to professionalism would begin with the assumption that most organizations require the skill and knowledge that professionals bring to the table. These individuals are trained to deal with complexity and understand the conflict between quality and efficiency standards. The professionals cannot be viewed as cogs in a machine without the ability to exercise discretion and judgment. It is important to devise situations in which professionals have the space to try new things, to adapt, and to be creative.

Values

The classic assumptions: The performance measurement movement is largely organized around the achievement of efficiency values, the values that have motivated management reformers for many years. Linking performance measurement to budgeting has been a way to accentuate the importance of efficiency and to find ways to ignore the political decisions made by the institutions of a democracy. Despite the reality that many government programs are designed to increase equity and establish processes that meet a sense of fairness, performance measurement rarely provides an opportunity to focus on those values.

Alternative approaches: Unlike the classic approach, an alternative way of dealing with values would begin with the assumption that most programs contain multiple goals that require opportunities to trade off multiple values. Balancing multiple values is not an easy task, but it is essential in many instances. Organizations are frequently faced with both efficiency and equity values and also, in some cases, effectiveness values. Efforts to quantify equity values are sometimes problematic because the society does not agree on definitions of equity or fairness. Data must be collected on a disaggregated basis that allows for the determination of how various population groups are affected (often disproportionately) by policies.

The American Political System

The classic assumptions: Neither of the two main performance measurement activities within the federal government—GPRA and PART—has been constructed on assumptions that rest on a realistic view of the institutional structures, functions, and political realities of the American system. That system is devised to fragment power and authority between executive, legislative, and judicial functions and, as well, to establish processes within each of these functions that create separate forces capable of generating conflict and multiple voices on most issues. Yet both of the federal performance management activities assume that it is possible to craft a government-wide effort that measures performance of agencies and that actors share strategies and defined needs. In addition, the reality of federalism in the United States (particularly drives to increase devolution to state, local, and third parties) does not mesh with a set of assumptions that it is possible to hold the federal government accountable for the achievement of program purposes. This approach assumes that if the federal government pays even a part of the bill, it legitimately can define performance expectations.

Alternative approaches: The construct of the American political system calls for an assumption that the multiple actors within the system have different agendas and hence different strategies for change. Performance measurement should thus begin with the assumption of these multiple expectations and look to the different perspectives found within the executive branch, the Congress and the agencies. And one should not be surprised when different congressional committees dealing with related issues have quite different perspectives on those issues. It is the political process that provides the mechanism for trade-offs between varied perspectives. In addition, federalism calls for performance measurement activities that are substantively sensitive to policies that have third-party and intergovernmental dimensions. One cannot assume that the performance agenda should lead to increased centralization of authority without political agreement by the Congress.

Assumptions about Numbers and Information

   The classic assumptions: There is a series of assumptions about information that characterize the classic approach to performance measurement. It begins with the belief that information is already available to measure performance, that the information is neutral, that we know what we are measuring, and that it is possible to define cause-effect relationships in programs. Further, the classic approach begins with the assumption that all activities can be measured and quantified. This leads to a reliance on numbers and quantitative presentation of accomplishments whether or not those numbers actually describe the reality of a program or policy.

   Alternative approaches: Performance measurement activities could begin with the acknowledgement that this "classic" approach should be turned on its head. Thus one would assume that available information is likely to be inappropriate for the performance measurement function and is variable in terms of the design of the program; also that information is likely to contain different values, reflecting the multiple agendas of the players in the system. Further, programs with multiple goals and multiple actors are likely to require qualitative, not quantitative, data that is difficult to aggregate.

   See Table 10.1 for a summary comparison of classic assumptions and alternative approaches.

Table 10.1 Comparing Classic Assumptions and Alternative Approaches in Performance Measurement

Issue	Classic Assumptions	Alternative Approaches
Intelligence	Clarity	Multiple sources
	Universal principles	Empathy
	Literal meanings	Combination of rational and symbolic modes
The Nature of the World	Linearity	Multiple and conflicting goals
	Discrete activities	
	Built on the past	Prone to error
	Clarify goals	Qualified action
Organizational Theory	Generic approaches	Differences public and private
	Principles of organizations	Differences among programs
	One size fits all	
	Internal focus	Focus on environment of organization
Approach to Professionals	Bureaucracy should control professionals	Essential to program operation
	Dissatisfaction with past operations	Training important
	Fiscal agenda predominant	Importance of exercising discretion
		Importance of quality issues
Values	Efficiency values predominant	Multiple values, multiple goals
	Depoliticize decisions	Difficult to quantify equity issues
		Collection of data on a disaggregated basis
The American Political System	Actors share strategies, values	Different actors have different strategies, values
	Executive and legislative branch on the same wave length	Conflict between legislative and executive branches
	Legislative committees have common approaches	Appropriation/ authorizing dif- ferences in Congress
	Federal government pays, thus can define performance	

Table 10.1 *Continued*

Issue	Classic Assumptions	Alternative Approaches
		Devolution of authority to states, localities, third parties
Numbers and Information	Information available	Not always available
	Information neutral	Costly
	Know what we are measuring	Value-laden
		Conflict over measures
	Can establish cause-effect relationships	Not clear about cause-effect relationships
	Better to use limited information than not	Concern about biases in the information sources

Faulty Assumptions that Lead to Problems: Drawing on the Vignettes

The eight vignettes that have been used to introduce the chapters in this book collectively illustrate the major issues that have been highlighted in the volume. These include the context in which the performance activity takes place, the predominant values in the situation, the experience of professionals, and issues related to information. The vignettes describe experiences within diverse contexts where the one-size-fits-all approach is inappropriate. They also illustrate the difficulties dealing with single measures of outcomes when multiple players are found inside the organization (such as the World Bank), related to governance structure (federalism and shared powers) or focused on issues related to service delivery effectiveness. The examples show how predominant values focus on efficiency and provide evidence of difficulty dealing with equity values. The preeminence of efficiency even minimizes attention to effectiveness. The vignettes also provide examples of situations in which professional norms are demeaned. And they show how reliance on single measures (such as standardized tests) creates inappropriate approaches to information.

Table 10.2 summarizes these experiences:

Table 10.2 The Vignette Experience

Example	The Context	Predominant Values	Professionals	Information
Robert Peacock	HMO. One size fits all not appropriate	Equity values avoided	Physician's norms demeaned	
George Hawthorne	School district. Local needs. One size fits all not appropriate	No equity values	Educator's norms demeaned	Relies on standardized tests
Elaine Waters	Citizen. One size fits all not appropriate	No role for citizens		Relies on standardized tests
Francine Fisher	Academic searching for foundation financial support	No effectiveness, just efficiency	Academic norms demeaned	Inappropriate measures, no way to present qualitative information
Raymond Wilson	Federal agency head. Conflict between executive and legislative, multiple "masters"	Efficiency values ignore politics		Grantee resistance to providing information
Karen O'Grady	State official, Fed vs. state decision making; doesn't deal with state needs and discretion	Efficiency values ignore federalism		Too rigid performance requirements
Enid Brown	Career public servant Conflict between executive and legislative "masters"	Balance effective service with fiscal responsibility	Managerial norms and research norms demeaned	Info requirements not useful to internal staff development
Brian Segretti	World Bank, balancing top-down and bottom-up strategy	Balance efficiency and equity	Dealing with economists	Dependent on countries to report

What to Do?

This book has emphasized the problems faced by those who are affected by the performance measurement movement. As I noted in the introduction, it is difficult to argue against a serious concern about performance, particularly in the public sector. Yet as we have seen, there are too many examples of perverse consequences of those performance measurement activities, many of which stem from faulty assumptions about the endeavor. The vignettes that have been used in the volume provide examples of situations in which efforts devised in the name of accountability actually interfere with the accomplishment of work that individuals have been asked to perform.

It is likely that this urge will continue in the future. One can only hope that the experience of the past decade is examined to provide a more realistic response to the problem. There are at least ten lessons that can be extrapolated from this past experience.

1. *Remember that performance measurement usually takes place in a society that is diverse, with multiple populations who have differing values.* There are public goods—not a single public good. A diverse society such as the United States experiences different perceptions and desires by region and by racial and ethnic group. Attempts to narrowly define a single set of values are not likely to be productive. Those who are engaged in performance management activities should reach out to a range of stakeholders and actors; a closed system of defining performance is not effective.

2. *It is useful to think about a repertoire of performance measures, not a narrow set of measures.* This reflects the diversity of the society with different expectations about programs and policies. Performance measures may focus not only on outcomes of programs but on inputs, processes, or outputs. There are times when programs are constructed and approved without a clear sense of outcomes expected. In those situations, accountability expectations may be developed around information dealing with resources available or methods of implementing a program, or by measuring specific outputs rather than focusing only on outcomes.

3. *Provide opportunities for trade-offs between multiple actors and conflicting values.* There is rarely one best way to accomplish goals because of these varied perspectives. Actors may include program managers, departmental figures responsible for policy and budget proposals, White House staff, and a range of congressional players. These players may be involved in detailed management, planning, budgeting, and oversight functions. In addition, these various actors are often balancing multiple values and attempting to accomplish several things at once; these expectations are not always consistent with one another.

4. *Don't forget that the political system provides the best approach in a democracy to achieve the trade-offs.* It is essential to find ways to balance analytical approaches with political strategies. The U.S. political structure is very different from a parliamentary system. The executive branch in the United States is not able to proceed on its own but must find ways to deal with the Congress. And Congress has yet to find ways to take its oversight role seriously. The congressional institutions can adopt the spirit of performance measurement and not the form. Both the authorizing and appropriations processes within the Congress offer venues for discussing these trade-offs. In addition, the Congress has the ability to draw on a range of perspectives through the Government Accountability Office, the Congressional Budget Office, the Congressional Research Service, and the inspectors general in the various departments.

5. *Modesty does become you.* Don't establish systems that are all or nothing. Find ways to examine your activity that allow you to revise your earlier approaches. Performance measurement activities usually have to deal with the reality of a constantly changing environment. Not only are the specific expectations of programs changing, but issues that seem to be separate and independent are often found to be interrelated to one another.

6. *Involve a range of actors in the definition of goals.* Your perception of those goals may be limited and not reflect the reality of all those in the policy system. The U.S. policy system is defined not only by shared powers but by fragmentation. This is true not only for the executive branch but also for Congress. Multiple com-

mittees and subcommittees are involved in the authorization, appropriations, and oversight decisions. It is also important to involve groups who represent a range of interests involved in a specific program. These might include representatives of both recipients of specific programs and those who are involved in providing that service.

7. *Try to predict negative responses to the requirements.* There are so many ways that individuals can game the system or turn the process into a compliance activity. Don't be surprised when that happens. It is not enough to rest with the good intentions of advocates of performance activity. One should anticipate different responses to these requirements, including gaming and even direct resistance. And what seems to you to be a negative response to performance requirements may actually be rational to those who appear to be gaming the system. Try to figure out why they are responding to you in that fashion.

8. *Be skeptical about data systems.* They are rarely what you would like them to be. Information does have a life of its own and cannot be separated from interests or ideology. And creation of data systems is costly and often difficult to put into place. There are many different types of information. What may seem to be innocuous and neutral information to one set of actors can be intimidating or inflammatory to others. In a changing society, the data that seem to be rigorous and helpful one day may be out of date the following day. Try to develop a range of sources for information so you are not dependent on a single source for your assessments of performance. Think about a combination of both quantitative and qualitative data sources.

9. *Be skeptical about panacea solutions.* The complexity of society and the multiple and legitimate perspectives on programs and policies rarely lead to accomplishment of promises. Programs are often crafted in broad strokes, devised to avoid conflict and maximize the base of support. This results in programs with multiple outcome expectations. Each of these decision processes produces a unique set of relationships and expectations. That makes the one-size-fits-all approach very unhelpful. Remember that the goals that are established in legislation and political speeches are not always designed to be turned into action. You may need

to discount that language and figure out what are realistic goals and objectives for programs and policies.

10. *Develop allies in your response to the performance measurement requirements.* You are likely to be more effective when you seek others who may share your perspective and concerns. This might involve those in your profession or groups that share your values. This suggests that organizations and staff facing difficult performance requirements might move outside their organization and involve various groups that represent clients, providers, or others with an interest in the program. When the performance requirements appear to attack the norms of a specific profession, it is useful to call on representatives of those professional organizations to emphasize the importance of those professional values.

I began this book noting that it was my hope that this volume will lead to a new discussion about performance measurement that integrates the issues of complexity into the consideration of these efforts. I have attempted to raise a series of concerns about this enterprise that suggests alternative approaches to achieve the quest for accountability and performance. I have called for the recognition and acknowledgement of various types of intelligence, of the complexity of the world we live in, of differences between organizational structures and contexts, of the importance of professionals, and of the realization that programs and policies contain multiple values. I have emphasized the components of the American political system that set the structural framework for decision making. And I have stressed the limitations and traps of information sources. My goal is not to trash the urge for performance. Rather, I have attempted to suggest ways to devise performance activities that are appropriate and effective. The task is commendable but difficult. It requires attention to individual settings and calls for creativity and commitment by those concerned about accountability.

Note
1. H. L. Mencken, *A Mencken Chrestomathy* (New York: Alfred A. Knopf, 1949), 443.

index